**MANAGE MORE
BY DOING LESS**

MANAGE MORE BY DOING LESS

RAYMOND O. LOEN

Management Consultant

McGRAW-HILL BOOK COMPANY

New York   St. Louis   San Francisco   Düsseldorf   Johannesburg
Kuala Lumpur   London   Mexico   Montreal   New Delhi
Panama   Rio de Janeiro   Singapore   Sydney   Toronto

Sponsoring Editors M. Joseph Dooher/Dale L. Dutton
Director of Production Stephen J. Boldish
Designer Naomi Auerbach
Editing Supervisor Carolyn Nagy
Editing and Production Staff Gretlyn Blau,
  Teresa F. Leaden, George E. Oechsner

MANAGE MORE BY DOING LESS

07-038370-7

567890 KPKP 79876543

To my wife, Lin
And to my children: Thatch, Jon, Pip, Pam, Brock

FOREWORD

Among the proponents of management by objectives, there exists a popular adage, "If you don't know where you're going, any road will take you there." Indeed, for many years most of a manager's time was spent reacting to outside stimuli—the fires and the crises—rather than effecting sound planning. Today, more time is given to planning just where the company is going, and to developing action plans which constitute the "roadmap" for getting there. Naturally, we will always have crises, and fires to put out; unforeseen deviations almost always occur. But competition is too keen, business too complex, and reaction time too slow to let the fate of a company drift along on the whims of circumstance, hunches, and chance. Thus, the decade of the 60's saw increasing emphasis on corporate planning.

The sophistication of corporate planning techniques continues, aided by computer analyses, market surveys, economic forecasts, etc. Unfortunately, executive echelons have been so occupied in their planning process, they too often have neglected to insure the installation of it in the middle and lower levels of management, where the application is just as valid.

Consequently, we still have too many managers who do not manage their jobs; their jobs manage them. The crises and fires dictate how they will spend their time and efforts. They are not planning their supplemental roadmaps to reinforce those of top management.

The situation has been magnified by the rapid rate at which we promoted men to managerships in the 60's, and by the increasing need for technical specialists due to the technological information explosion. The need for an increasing number of managers gave rise to the promotion of those who were good doers. Too often they continue to *do* rather than to manage. Frequently, it is upper management who emphasizes doing instead of managing, and who fails to provide opportunities for these lower levels to improve their managerial finesse.

Inherent in good planning, for example, are objectives which incorporate specific measurements and timing commitments. Such planning becomes, however, a paper exercise unless some degree of accuracy is involved. We must give our managers skills in participative management—methods by which they can utilize the input of subordinates who are technically more proficient than they, who are closer to the work, and who have a better feel for what is obtainable. Only thus, can accuracy be obtained.

Good decision-making-logic techniques and effective people-skills are not usually highly developed in good doers; they become critical in good managers. Managers soon sense which objectives—including management development objectives—of the executive level should be worked toward, and which ones may be regarded as simply "lip service." If we really value management development, we had better begin asking to review individual development plans. The responsibility for development of these managerial skills still rests largely on companies rather than the schools. It is we who must provide the emphasis, climate, opportunity, and *control* to ensure it.

Corporations tend to get the kind of management they ask for. It is the executive level which, by example, must emphasize good management and provide the lower levels with the opportunity to increase their managerial expertise. As the knowledge explosion grows, it becomes impossible for any manager to be as technically proficient as those specialists whom he manages. He no longer can be omnipotent, technically. He will have to be expert, managerially.

Inasmuch as effective management requires the development of certain skills in managers, most large firms utilize colleges, consultants, internal training departments, etc., to get the job done. General Mills is no exception. Among the consultants whose services we have utilized is Ray Loen.

For several years, Ray has worked with us, developing "objectives" training programs for our middle management levels. Indeed, much of what appears in this book has evolved from our mutual association. While much has been done, more remains ahead of us. This book will help managers assess their effectiveness. It is up to us, corporate management, to give them the development they need to increase that effectiveness.

JAMES P. MCFARLAND
Chairman of the Board
Chief Executive Officer
General Mills, Inc.
Minneapolis, Minnesota

CONTENTS

26. IMPROVING 234

Part 6. CONCLUSION

27. APPLYING WHAT'S IN THIS BOOK 243

WHAT THIS BOOK WILL DO FOR YOU

Chances are you can talk a pretty good game of managing; chances are you probably excel in certain phases of managing; and chances are you *cannot* distinguish clearly between what is managing and what is doing (nonmanaging) in your particular job!

Surprising as this may seem, I find that most managers have the same difficulty. That's the reason for this book. I feel so strongly about the potential good which managers everywhere can effect that I hate to see them water down their efforts unknowingly.

I realize that most managers have important *doing* responsibilities. I also realize that your organization probably cannot afford to have managers who just manage. However, if you have any responsibility for getting results through others, isn't it important that you be able to make a clear distinction between managing and doing?

When you manage, you multiply your efforts through others. You create a synergistic effect—where the whole is greater than the sum of the parts (as in a baseball team). This means that there is probably nothing you do *besides* managing that can make a greater contribution to your organization and to those your organization serves. That is why you should concentrate your efforts on managing rather than on doing. That is why you should manage more by *doing* less. This doesn't necessarily mean that you should work less; it means that you should perform fewer *doing* activities.

This book will help you make a clear distinction between managing and doing in your particular job. And it will provide you with a practical concept of managing that is applicable to managers at any level of responsibility.

The premises on which this book is based are:

1. Managing is a distinct and separate activity.

2. Managing cuts across all lines of endeavor, whether your job is within marketing, production, engineering, accounting, personnel, a profession, general management, or whatever.

3. Managing cuts across business, governmental, non-profit-making, religious, cooperative, and volunteer organizations.

In this book, I have tried to make the ideas simple and easy for you to apply. Each chapter has only one key point. In the last chapter, the book is summarized on one page of how to's: "Guide to Help You Manage More by Doing Less." As a matter of fact, the book can be summarized in six words: Accomplish *planned* results *through* your people. While these words may have meaning for you now, they will have much more meaning after you have read the book and applied some of the key ideas in your job.

Part **1**

INTRODUCTION

1

ARE YOU MANAGER OR DOER?

Do you know that the skills that helped you to *become* a manager may prevent you from being a *good* manager?

It is likely that you became a manager—with responsibility to get results through your people—because you excelled as an individual *doer*. You excelled as

Accountant	Operator
Analyst	Planner
Assistant	Programmer
Auditor	Researcher
Buyer	Salesman
Clerk	Specialist
Craftsman	Teacher
Doctor	Technician
Engineer	Worker
Lawyer	Writer

or in some other capacity as a doer. Yet, if you continue to excel in the same way when you are a manager, you concentrate your efforts on the tasks of a doer rather than on the tasks of the manager.

QUIZ: IS THIS MANAGING OR DOING?

If you want to concentrate your efforts on the tasks of a manager, you should be able to look at the tasks you perform and distinguish whether

3

they are managing or doing (nonmanaging). Take the twenty tasks shown in Figure 1-1. Which do you feel are managing tasks, and which do you feel are doing tasks?

FIGURE 1-1   Is This Managing or Doing?

Managing	*Doing*	
——	——	1. Making a call with one of your people to assist him in solving a technical problem
——	——	2. Signing a check to approve a routine expenditure
——	——	3. Conducting the initial screening interview of a job applicant
——	——	4. Giving one of your experienced people your solution to a new problem without first asking for his recommendation
——	——	5. Giving your solution to a recurring problem that one of your new people has just asked you about
——	——	6. Conducting a meeting to explain to your people a new procedure
——	——	7. Phoning a department to request help in solving a problem that one of your people is trying to solve
——	——	8. Filling out a form to give one of your people a pay increase
——	——	9. Explaining to one of your people why he is receiving a merit pay increase
——	——	10. Deciding whether to add a position
——	——	11. Asking one of your people what he thinks about an idea you have that will affect your people
——	——	12. Transferring a desirable assignment from Employee A to Employee B because Employee A did not devote the necessary effort
——	——	13. Reviewing regular written reports to determine your people's progress toward their objectives
——	——	14. Giving a regular progress report by phone to your superior
——	——	15. Giving a tour to an important visitor from outside of your organization
——	——	16. Drafting an improved layout of facilities
——	——	17. Discussing with your key people the extent to which they should use staff services during the next year
——	——	18. Deciding what your expense-budget request will be for your area of responsibility
——	——	19. Attending a professional or industrial meeting to learn detailed technical developments
——	——	20. Giving a talk on your work activities to a local community group

I'll give you my answers later in the chapter. But if you are like most managers who have taken this kind of a quiz, you were probably surprised to find that some of the tasks were difficult to make decisions about. As a matter of fact, I find that, at the outset, there is considerable disagreement among managers who take this kind of quiz in a group. How can this be? All managers have experience in managing; most managers have read articles and books on managing; many managers have taken courses or attended seminars on management subjects; and some managers even have one or more university degrees in the field of management. Yet these managers spend their time *doing* when they should be *managing*; they limit their effectiveness and potential in management.

How about you? Are you more of a doer than a manager?

WHY YOU MAY DO RATHER THAN MANAGE

There are at least five reasons why you may *do* rather than *manage*. These are also reasons why you may not distinguish clearly between managing tasks and doing tasks.

1. *You have excelled as a doer.* Most people like to feel secure in what they are doing. They generally feel most secure when they are performing those activities which they like and which they know how to do well. If you excelled as a doer, it is perfectly natural that you would want to continue performing those doing activities which you like and know how to do well—especially if you spent enough years as a doer to have engrained habits.

The fact that many salesmen continue to *do* after they become managers was brought out in a study conducted by Dr. Robert T. Davis. Among fifty-four industrial and service companies with large industrial sales forces, he found that

> . . . many field sales managers are more supersalesmen than they are administrators. They excel at personal selling, at trouble shooting (which is usually customer oriented), and at the mechanics of running the field office; they are weakest at developing and supervising salesmen and at analyzing and planning their operations.[1]

Look at your organization. Don't you find that many managers—regardless of their areas of responsibility—continue performing the same doing activities that they performed before they became managers? For example, don't many of your managers solve work problems *for* their people? Do you do the same thing—i.e., do you solve work problems *for* your people, or do you help them to *solve their own problems?*

You, like everyone else, are a product of your own background. Therefore, you are more likely to recognize those problems in the areas to which you have devoted the most time and effort. If, for example, you have devoted most of your career to the study and practice of engineering, you are more likely to recognize engineering problems than managing problems, even though you may now be a manager with responsibility to get results through your people. You are more likely to recognize and try to solve *technical* problems than you are to recognize and try to solve *managing* problems. Your excellence at engineering may actually hurt your performance as a manager unless you study and become proficient at managing.

2. *You see yourself more as a leader than as a manager.*   No doubt you've been exposed countless times to the idea that a manager should be a leader. But should you? It depends upon your concept of a leader.

Many managers see a leader as someone who leads and who has followers. They see him as someone who exudes wisdom, makes great decisions, solves his people's problems, outperforms his people, and does anything that he asks his people to do—like the second lieutenant who leads his men into battle. They see him as someone who is able to get his followers to have confidence in *him*.

Which is more important for a *manager:* that his people have confidence in *him* or that his people have confidence in *themselves?*

Most managers want both results; but between the two choices, I believe you'll agree that it's more important that a manager's people have confidence in themselves.

If you believe that it's more important that your people have confidence in themselves, then how important is it that you be able to lead your people—e.g., by outperforming them in the jobs they are responsible for doing? Isn't it more important that you be skilled in *managing?*

Of course you need leadership skills to plan, direct, and control the efforts of your people; but there is a danger if you lead to the point where your people rely more on you than on themselves.

3. *You have important doing responsibility.*   Every manager must perform some doing activities—generally because there is no one else to do them. But the manager gets in trouble when he neglects his managing responsibility. This is a special problem for the manager who has important doing responsibility. It is a special problem for *you* if you are responsible for getting results through your subordinates *and* if you are responsible for

    a. Personal production in sales, engineering, or some other area of responsibility

    b. Being the technical authority in your area of responsibility (The controller, for example, is often expected to be an authority on general accounting, cost accounting, taxes, insurance, budgets, systems and procedures, and electronic data processing in addition to being a manager.)

    c. Maintaining personal relationships with outside customers, suppliers, or others

These are doing responsibilities because they can be performed by an individual doer, and they may even be more important to your organization than your managing responsibility. Your effectiveness as a manager both now and *in the future* will suffer, however, if you slight whatever managing responsibility you have.

4. *Your previous training may be confusing.* Many of today's management courses and programs are more concerned with the functional technology of marketing, production, accounting, finance, research, engineering, personnel, labor relations, public relations, or law than they are with how a manager gets results through his people. Other management courses and programs center around management tools and techniques such as computers, operations research, value analysis, PERT (Program Evaluation and Review Technique), methods engineering, and programmed instruction. Is it any wonder that managers have difficulty in distinguishing what managing is?

Many management books also add to the confusion. In an article on management books, *Business Week* magazine made this observation:

> Even when they include the word "management," there's no guarantee that the authors are really concerned with managing, as distinguished from finance, accounting, marketing, or any other specialized essential function of business.[2]

In other words, designing the product is not managing; making the product is not managing; selling the product is not managing; financing the product is not managing; and doing accounting for the product is not managing. Managing *can* occur in connection with any of these activities, but it *does* occur only when a manager is trying to get results through his people.

5. *Your boss may be a doer.* If your boss spends most of his time on doing activities, you have a poor model to emulate—assuming you wish to be an effective manager. To make matters worse, he may expect you to approach your managing job the way he does his.

I recall a certain division manager in a medium-sized manufacturing company. He reported to a vice president who expected him to have detailed knowledge about all the activities for which he was responsible. The result was that the division manager had great difficulty in delegating work to his people, and he felt forced to duplicate many of his people's efforts.

Earlier in my career, I was with the management consulting firm of H. B. Maynard and Co., Inc. When I was there, the firm made a study of how fifty presidents of successful companies spent their time. Findings showed that there was a strong tendency for a president to concentrate his attention in the functional area where he had the most experience. But the worst example was the president who spent 57 percent of his time on clerical or routine work—clearly doing activities that could have been delegated. Apparently the president performed these activities because they made him feel productive.

If you report to a boss who is like either of the two persons I have described, you have the challenge of pleasing him while still practicing effective managing. As a foundation for meeting this kind of challenge, you need a clear perspective about what managing is.

WHAT, THEN, IS MANAGING?

Managing can be defined as planning, directing, and controlling the activities of subordinates* to achieve or exceed objectives. It occurs at any level of responsibility in any organization wherever a manager is trying to get results through his people.

Contrary to what many sales people think, managing differs markedly from selling even though a salesman is also supposed to get results through others, i.e., through customers and prospects. A manager not only has the responsibility to get results through his people but also has the *authority* to plan, direct, and control the activities of his people—assuming his people want to remain on the payroll. I doubt whether any salesman has this kind of authority with his customers and prospects.

From our definition, managing consists of three major activities:

1. Planning
2. Directing
3. Controlling

It may be helpful for you to think of planning as *developing your plan,* directing as *implementing your plan,* and controlling as *seeing that your plan was carried out*—in each instance through your people.

Planning can be divided into nine elements. A manager should plan or develop

---

* Persons in some organizations—especially volunteer organizations—often object to being identified as "subordinates" even though they are responsible to someone with managing responsibility as far as the organization's activities are concerned. Managers in these organizations may prefer to substitute in the managing definition the phrase "other people in the same organization" for the term "subordinates."

Objectives	Organization structure
Programs	Policies
Schedules	Procedures
Budgets	Standards
Forecasts	

Directing can be divided into seven elements:

Staffing	Motivating
Training	Counseling
Supervising	Coordinating
Delegating	

Controlling has three elements:

Measuring
Evaluating
Correcting

In addition, a manager should be skilled at

Deciding
Communicating
Improving

These three are integrative elements in that they are applicable to all the other elements of managing. A manager must *make decisions* as he plans, directs, and controls. A manager must *communicate* with his people, his superior, and others as he plans, directs, and controls. Furthermore, a manager should strive to *improve* the way he plans, directs, and controls.

Altogether, there are nineteen elements of managing under planning, directing, and controlling plus three integrative elements. Definitions are shown in Figure 1-2.

FIGURE 1-2 A Concept of Managing for Managers at Any Level

MANAGING   *Planning, directing, and controlling the activities of subordinates to achieve or exceed objectives*

PLANNING   *Determining what needs to be done, by whom and by when, to fulfill one's assigned responsibility*

Objective: A goal, target, or quota to be achieved by a certain time

Program: Strategy to be followed and major actions to be taken to achieve or exceed objectives

Schedule: A plan showing when individual or group activities or accomplishments will be started and/or completed

Budget: Planned expenditures required to achieve or exceed objectives

Forecast: A projection of what will happen by a certain time

Organization: Design of the number and kinds of positions, along with corresponding duties and responsibilities, required to achieve or exceed objectives

Policy: A general guide for decision making and individual actions

Procedure: A detailed method for carrying out a policy

Standard: A level of individual or group performance defined as adequate or acceptable

DIRECTING *Implementing and carrying out approved plans through subordinates to achieve or exceed objectives*

Staffing: Seeing that a qualified person is selected for each position

Training: Teaching individuals or groups how to fulfill their duties and responsibilities

Supervising: Giving subordinates day-to-day instruction, guidance, and discipline as required for them to fulfill their duties and responsibilities

Delegating: Assigning work, responsibility, and authority so subordinates can make maximum use of their abilities

Motivating: Encouraging subordinates to perform by fulfilling or appealing to their needs

Counseling: Holding private discussion with a subordinate about how he might do better work, solve a personal problem, or realize his ambitions

Coordinating: Seeing that activities are carried out in relation to their importance with a minimum of conflict

CONTROLLING *Measuring progress toward objectives, evaluating what needs to be done, and then taking corrective action to achieve or exceed objectives*

Measuring: Determining through formal and informal reports the degree to which progress toward objectives is being made

Evaluating: Determining causes of and possible ways to act upon significant deviations from planned performance

Correcting: Taking control action to correct an unfavorable trend or to take advantage of an unusually favorable trend

INTEGRATIVE ELEMENTS

Deciding: Making a judgment about a course of action to be taken

Communicating: Exchanging information with subordinates, associates, superiors, and others about plans, progress, and problems

Improving: Developing more effective and/or economical methods of managing

A manager performs the various managing elements for one purpose only: to get results through his people. However, a doer also performs many of the same elements—e.g., setting objectives, developing standards, staffing, correcting, and communicating—but he does so to get results as an *individual*. This is another reason managers confuse managing with doing: the same terms have different meanings.

Take staffing. A manager must have people before he can manage, so he must participate in staffing activities such as interviewing, selecting, and hiring. Yet staffing is also a personnel function. A doer (with no subordinates) can perform staffing activities such as recruiting, screening, interviewing, selecting, and possibly even hiring, but he does so as a specialist within the personnel function to get results as an individual.

Many organizations have specialists to plan and develop objectives, programs, schedules, budgets, forecasts, organization structures, policies, procedures, and standards; many organizations also have specialists to do staffing, training, motivating, coordinating, counseling, measuring, evaluating, correcting, and improving. Specialists even do supervising and delegating when they provide functional direction— e.g., when a budget specialist sees that proper budgeting procedures are followed throughout an entire organization. But such specialists are not managers (as we have been using the term) unless they have subordinates and unless they have the authority and responsibility to plan, direct, and control all the work activities of their subordinates.
In summary:

1. You are *managing* if you are trying to get results through (not with or for) your people.

2. You are *doing* if the activity could be performed by an individual doer or specialist—whether or not you actually have a subordinate to perform the activity.

Now perhaps you'd like to retake the quiz shown in Figure 1-1. When you want to see suggested answers, turn to Figure 1-3.

FIGURE 1-3 Suggested Answers to Quiz: Is This Managing or Doing?

1. *Doing.* The stated purpose of the call is to assist in solving a *technical* problem rather than to perform managing elements such as training or supervising.

2. *Doing*—for two reasons. Signing checks is a clerical or mechanical function; approving *routine* expenditures should generally be delegated with a defined procedure and with provision for an occasional compliance audit.

3. *Doing.* This is a personnel function. Deciding whether to hire someone *after* the recruiting, screening, and selecting have been done would be staffing, an element of managing.

4. *Doing.* This is *not* managing unless you at least ask your subordinate for his recommended solution.

5. *Managing.* This is supervising or training since a *new* employee is involved. A new employee would have little or no basis for suggesting a solution to any work problem — whether recurring or new.

6. *Managing.* This is training.

7. *Doing.* The purpose of your phone call is *not* to get results *through* your subordinate but rather *for* him.

8. *Doing.* Filling out the form is clerical. Instructing your secretary to complete the form would be managing in that it would be delegating.

9. *Managing.* This is motivating.

10. *Managing.* This is developing your organization structure.

11. *Managing.* This is communicating for purposes of planning a policy, procedure, program, or the like. It could also be a form of motivating if your purpose is to get participation now as a prelude to your getting acceptance later.

12. *Managing.* This is correcting — taking corrective control action. It could also be the disciplining part of supervising.

13. *Managing.* This is the measuring part of controlling.

14. *Managing.* This is communicating for purposes of control — assuming you do so to receive possible guidance and direction. Otherwise, it is plain communicating which anyone does whether or not he is a manager.

15. *Doing.* This is a public relations function. You are doing because you are not trying to get results through your people.

16. *Doing.* You may have to do it if there is no one else to do it, but this is a specialized methods engineering or systems and procedures function that can be performed by an individual doer.

17. *Managing.* You are developing your program when you consider which resources your people should utilize to achieve or exceed objectives.

18. *Managing.* You are planning: developing your budget. Putting the budget in its proper form would be clerical, a doing activity.

19. *Doing.* The stated purpose of your attendance is to learn *detailed* technical developments. Generally, only specialists (individual doers) need to know technical developments in detail.

20. *Doing.* This is a public relations function.

You can see that the distinction between managing and doing can be subtle in many instances. Indeed, two managers can *appear* to be performing identical activities; yet one manager would be doing and the other would be managing. For example, solving a technical problem for one of your people would be doing if you were primarily interested in solving the problem; it would be managing if you were primarily interested in training or supervising your subordinate.

It is not important whether you agree with all the suggested answers to the quiz. What is important is that you try to distinguish when you are managing and when you are doing in your day-to-day activities. In this way, you are more likely to improve your managing and to realize your potential as a manager.

JOB DESCRIPTION: RESPONSIBILITIES COMMON TO ALL MANAGERS

Many organizations have job descriptions for their managers. Generally, the emphasis is for the manager to achieve maximum production or maximum sales or maximum profit or minimum costs or the like. I have seen few job descriptions that make clear to the manager his responsibility for managing—i.e., for planning, directing, and controlling the activities of his subordinates. Figure 1-4 shows a job description that is designed to make clear to the manager his responsibility for *managing*.

FIGURE 1-4   Job Description: Responsibilities Common to All Managers

I. GENERAL RESPONSIBILITY

Plan, direct, and control the activities of subordinates to achieve or exceed objectives in assigned area of responsibility.

II. SPECIFIC RESPONSIBILITIES

A. *Planning*

1. Develop measurable objectives to be achieved or exceeded annually and for interim periods.
2. Develop program of major actions required to achieve or exceed objectives; this involves determining where and when to make effective use of available resources.
3. Make and report appropriate forecasts such as for production, sales, cash flow, or manpower requirements.
4. Recommend to immediate superior any changes in organization, i.e., the types and numbers of positions required.
5. Plan assignments to subordinates so objectives will be achieved or exceeded.
6. Prepare budget for achieving objectives at minimum short- and long-range cost.
7. Obtain management approval for plans and programs when scheduled.

B. *Directing*

1. Implement and supervise the carrying out of approved plans and programs.
2. Delegate duties, responsibility, and authority so each individual can make maximum use of his experience and skills.
3. Supervise subordinates so their activities will promote a mutually profitable, long-range relationship with those your organization serves.
4. See that claims, complaints, and inquiries from those your organization serves are handled capably and promptly.
5. Motivate subordinates to excel in job performance—especially in times of unusual stress.
6. Administer personnel policies; e.g., recruiting, hiring, compensating, disciplining, transferring, promoting, and discharging.
7. Conduct regular training of subordinates to develop the knowledge and skills that they need to excel in their jobs; encourage individual development to meet the future needs of your organization.
8. Use job rotation and other means to assure that trained replacements are maintained for all key positions.
9. Orient new personnel and supervise their training so that they reach satisfactory production as soon as possible.
10. Support your organization's policies and procedures among contacts both inside and outside of your organization.

C. *Controlling*

1. See that necessary records and reports are made so progress toward achieving objectives is known at all times.
2. Use management by exception to determine key problems and opportunities plus possible corrective actions.
3. Take corrective action in time to take advantage of unusually favorable trends or to correct any significant negative deviations from planned performance.
4. Recommend to immediate superior upward or downward changes in objectives when major unforeseen factors develop.
5. Submit necessary reports to management.

D. *Improving*

1. Keep informed about modern managing methods, changing needs of those your organization serves, industry trends, and competitive activities.
2. Make, or recommend to immediate superior as appropriate, improvements in managing methods.
3. Encourage and follow through on subordinates' suggestions for improving products, services, policies, procedures, and the like.

E. *Other*

1. Keep subordinates, associates, superiors, and others informed about appropriate plans, progress, and problems.

2. Work cooperatively with all personnel in your organization to help them fulfill their responsibilities.
3. Take an active part in trade, professional, governmental, community, and service organizations when such activity will contribute to the best interests of your organization.
4. Perform other duties, including nonmanaging duties, as assigned by immediate superior.

The job description can be summarized as follows:

Accomplish *planned* results *through* your people.

Throughout this chapter, I have emphasized the importance of your getting results *through* your people. The job description also highlights the importance of planning—so you can get *planned* results. How to accomplish this is the subject of subsequent chapters. At this point, however, you may wonder if you really need to improve your managing.

SIGNS THAT YOUR MANAGING MAY NEED IMPROVEMENT

You probably need to improve your managing if you had difficulty with the quiz in which you were asked to distinguish managing from doing. However, you will have further indications if you answer yes to one or more of the following questions.

1. *Unsatisfactory results*

- Do you feel you should be getting better results?
- Do your subordinates and/or superiors feel you should be getting better results?
- Are your customers, or others that you serve, dissatisfied with the results you are achieving for them?

2. *Frequent "fires"*

- Do you have frequent day-to-day emergencies?
- Do you have to resort to expensive short-range solutions—e.g., solutions that put you over your expense budget?
- Does your job control you more than you control it?

3. *Objectives not defined in numbers*

- Do you and your people lack measurable objectives that you are trying to achieve or exceed?
- Are your people in doubt about what they must accomplish to qualify for pay increases or promotions?
- Would you have difficulty proving past and potential contributions

to your organization if there were a significant change in your organization's top management or ownership?

4. *Turnover of good people*

- Do promising subordinates take the initiative to leave your organization or to transfer?
- Have you terminated or transferred subordinates who subsequently performed much better than you expected?
- Do you have more than average difficulty in attracting and hiring capable people?

5. *No trained replacement*

- Do you lack a qualified subordinate who could replace you if you were offered a transfer or promotion?
- Would your people be seriously handicapped in performing their jobs if you were to become unexpectedly ill or absent?
- Do you feel you are in competition with one or more subordinates who may want your job or who want to progress beyond you?

6. *Little innovation in methods or services*

- Do you lack specific objectives for improving methods, services, or the like?
- Are you apathetic about getting improvement suggestions from your people?
- Are there few, if any, improvements that have been implemented or installed *and* were suggested by your people?

These questions are not meant to be all-inclusive, but they are meant to help you determine the extent to which you accomplish *planned* results *through* your people.

If you feel you have significant room for improvement, why not resolve *now* to learn and apply the "technology" of managing so you can realize your potential in management? One way to begin implementing your resolution is to study each of the managing elements as related to planning, directing, and controlling.

SIGNS THAT YOUR MANAGING MAY NEED IMPROVEMENT

You have difficulty in distinguishing managing activities from doing activities and/or you have

1. Unsatisfactory results
2. Frequent "fires"

3. Objectives not defined in numbers
4. Turnover of good people
5. No trained replacement
6. Little innovation in methods or services

KEY POINT: *Accomplish* planned *results* through
your people.

REFERENCES

1. Robert T. Davis, *Performance and Development of Field Sales Managers,* Harvard Business School, Division of Research, Boston, 1957.
2. "What the Executive Reads about His Job," *Business Week,* Aug. 6, 1966, p. 129.

Part 2

PLANNING

2

PLANNING: AN OVERVIEW

PLANNING   *Determining what needs to be done,
by when and by whom, to fulfill one's assigned
responsibility.*

At this very moment, there are trends developing that will have a significant effect upon you within the next one to five years. In most instances, you can harness these trends — *if* you look and *if* you act. However, the trends are often insidious. They emerge so gradually that you may not realize their effect until something dramatic occurs, such as loss of a key account to competition. The effect is often negative, but it can be positive if you have done the kind of planning required of today's manager.

TRENDS THAT WILL AFFECT YOU

Examples of trends that you should be aware of are shown in Figure 2-1.

FIGURE 2-1   Which of These Trends Will Affect You?

____ 1. Technological changes (including those outside of your industry) that will make obsolete your present products, processes, and/or methods

____ 2. Increasing domestic and foreign competition that will force you to change the way you do business

____ 3. Increased use of computers and mathematical models that will make your present skills obsolete

____ 4. Increasing government regulation that can hamper or restrict your operations

____ 5. Economic and sociological changes (e.g., welfare programs, education, civil rights, unionization, availability of money) that will make your employees, customers, and suppliers less dependent on you

____ 6. Changes in those who control your organization (e.g., top management, owners, members, directors) and whose ideas may differ from yours

____ 7. Changes in the physical and mental health of superiors, key employees, associates, and others on whom you are dependent

You can either exploit, fight, or ignore these kinds of trends. You can react aggressively, defensively, or lethargically. Probably your best course of action is to try to exploit—and possibly even to originate— trends. If you can exert sufficient influence, it may be worthwhile for you to fight a trend. Probably your worst course of action is to do nothing until a trend erupts with serious consequences for you—e.g., termination, demotion, loss, bankruptcy, or failure.

PLANNING IS THE LEAST UNDERSTOOD PART OF MANAGING

No doubt you are *for* planning. You probably work from a weekly or monthly task list and you may even develop a budget. But to what extent do you

▪ Set measurable objectives to be achieved or exceeded for the next few months or a year?

▪ Develop a strategy, program, and schedule for accomplishing your objectives?

▪ Forecast production levels, space requirements, position openings, cost of money, developments by direct and indirect competitors, legislation, or the like to identify future problems and opportunities?

▪ Develop an improved organization structure or a realignment of duties and responsibilities to streamline the work flow?

- Develop new or improved policies and procedures so your people can make many of the decisions you now make?

- Develop measurable standards of performance for both hourly and salaried personnel so your people will know (rather than guess) what is expected of them?

These are planning actions that can help you harness the trends that affect you. For example, you are most likely to harness a trend toward automation in your area of responsibility if you forecast the impact of the trend and then develop objectives, programs, schedules, organization requirements, policies, procedures, performance standards, and budgets in time to help you exploit the trend before it erupts.

Unless you have, or have had, a boss who requires these kinds of planning actions, it is unlikely that you plan as much as you should for maximum effectiveness. You are likely to concentrate on current problems and "fires" because they are much more apparent than future problems and "fires." Without a good example to follow, you may find yourself in the position of the manager whose boss caught him with a clean desk and a pensive expression. His boss reacted: "If you want to think, think on your own time!"

Planning requires thinking about the future. The future is elusive, so you can never be completely right in what you predict or propose. Therefore, you may not want to commit yourself to objectives that you are responsible for achieving or exceeding, a program and schedule of planned accomplishments, or performance standards for your people. You may be afraid that you will lose face if you do not accomplish what you said you were going to accomplish. Furthermore, planning has an academic ring. Maybe this is because a large volume of planning has been done by staff people or others without the responsibility for, and commitment to, *making the plans work*.

In any event, if you are like most managers with whom I have dealt, you understand your responsibility for directing and controlling much better than you do your responsibility for planning.

WHY PLAN?

By doing the kind of planning necessary to harness the trends that will affect you, you help to ensure that you will realize three results.

1. *You will make things happen.* With sound planning, you can develop a new product, add a production line, develop an organization of qualified people, enter a new market, install a new system, or the like. And you can do so without neglecting your present operations. The

bigger and more complicated the project, however, the more lead time you will need.

At the top management level, you should do broad long-range planning—generally for at least five years into the future. At lower levels of management, you should do detailed short-range planning—generally for at least a year into the future.

What planning can do for a company has been demonstrated at Harris-Intertype under the managerial reins of George Dively. Over a twenty-year period, the company grew from $10 million sales to the sales and earnings position highest in the graphic arts equipment industry. In large measure, this was done through five-year plans, accurate one-year projections, and temporary operating plans for periods of economic stress—"boom type" and antirecessionary plans. In describing this company, *Business Week* reported:

> The corporate five-year plan—pegged to the development cycle of a printing press—is a "philosophical" guide, with broad objectives for growth, profit, finance, and management development. Divisional five-year plans are more specific: They peg realistic goals for shipments and earnings, based on intensive market research, and focus on one special problem area, such as management weaknesses. Both the corporate and divisional one-year plans are quite specific—and Dively expects them to be within a 7% tolerance in nine out of 10 years.[1]

Through these plans, the company's managers made things happen.

2. You will have a better framework for making current operating decisions. In hiring, should you seek someone primarily to meet your current production needs or should you seek someone on whom you can also build for the future? In establishing finished-goods inventory levels, should you stock primarily to meet the present needs of the market or stock to meet the future needs? In wage negotiations, should you grant above-industry increases to maintain current production or should you take a strike to minimize long-term labor costs?

The decisions that you make today should be dependent upon the overall plans that you have for your area of responsibility. Unfortunately, many managers make current operating decisions on the basis of: What makes us look best *this* year? As Carl Wente, former chairman of the board of the Bank of America, stated in a meeting that I attended: "Every year doesn't have to be a banner year."

One company that I know of needed to show better profits. There was such pressure for cost reduction that the responsible managers practically eliminated preventive maintenance on costly equipment. It wasn't long before the folly of this decision came back to haunt the managers in the form of repairs and downtime far more costly than the preventive maintenance would have been.

A sporting goods manufacturer took the opposite approach to current operating decisions. A few years ago, the company embarked upon a carefully developed expansion program. A year later, there was a general business decline and some of the company's managers were in favor of abandoning the expansion program. Top management had faith in its program, however, and the company was in a position to take advantage of a sharp increase in demand that occurred two years later.[2]

Sound planning will not always make clear to you what your current operating decisions should be, but it will normally make your decision making easier.

3. *You will control rather than be controlled.* In general, the best managers I know are those who plan carefully their personal careers. They set goals and timetables for the specific kinds of responsibility they want; then they plan and implement programs for personal development. They know that a good education, conscientious work, and past success will not guarantee their future success.

These managers carry this planning through in fulfilling their responsibilities as managers. They prefer to control where they are going versus being controlled by the inertia of the past and the unknown forces of the future.

Philosopher Henry David Thoreau once observed: "In the long run, men hit only what they aim at." This means that you have within you the forces with which to control your destiny—i.e., what you want to accomplish through your people and for yourself.

HOW TO PLAN

Following are six guidelines that are applicable to all the managing elements that require planning: your objectives, programs, schedules, budgets, forecasts, organization structure, policies, procedures, and standards.

1. *Schedule your planning.* You can do either too much or too little planning. If you are a "man of action," as most managers are, you probably do too little planning. Regardless, schedule yourself to do planning at least annually and monthly.

Develop an annual plan containing your objectives and your program of major accomplishments to be made throughout the year. Develop a monthly plan for carrying out your annual plan. Make whatever provision is necessary in your annual and monthly plans for developing objectives, programs, schedules, budgets, forecasts, organization structure, policies, procedures, and standards. In other words, plan to plan.

2. *Get the ideas and experience of others.*   When you plan major changes or are on unfamiliar ground, it is especially important that you get the ideas and experience of others. Contact your people, but also consider contacting your superior, your associates, and your staff specialists. In addition, consider getting external assistance such as from others in your industry or from management consultants.

Jay Monroe, president of Tensor Corporation, reported that his firm could have gone out of business if he and his people hadn't obtained outside assistance—even though they had a very successful product in their high-intensity 2-inch lamp. To help develop and implement necessary plans, the company relied upon ten outsiders including legal counsel, advertising agents, and consultants in the areas of production and engineering. In explaining why the firm went to outsiders for help, Mr. Monroe said:

> We failed completely in trying to set up production lines. We hired more people, bought more equipment. But all we got was confusion—everyone just getting in each other's way.
>
>   . . . It's silly to think that management has time to do all the things it should when you're moving so fast.[3]

Some managers at the top management level rely too heavily upon others for planning assistance. They leave the planning to the professional planners who can and should do a lot of the spade work but who cannot make critical decisions and are generally not responsible for implementing the plans. If you rely upon planning assistance, make sure you participate sufficiently in the planning so that you become personally committed to the decisions you make.

3. *Keep plans simple.*   The simpler you can make and state your plans, the more effective implementation is likely to be. One way for you to determine whether your plans are simple enough is review them for understanding with one or more of your people before you make a general announcement or formal presentation.

Some managers have adopted the so-called KISS formula: "Keep It Simple, Stupid." These managers will, for example, find out whether a new policy or procedure is clear to a stenographer, or a new employee, or someone else not directly affected.

4. *Put plans in writing.*   The best discipline that I know of for forcing one to think through his plans is to reduce them to writing—one page wherever possible. An unwritten plan is a mere intention that can easily be forgotten or disregarded. Studies show that most people remember only a small percentage of what they hear; therefore, anything as important as an objective or a policy, for example, should be put in writing for periodic reference by those affected.

5. *Consider use of tests or pilot runs.*   Often the way to torpedo a new program or a new policy or a new procedure or a new standard is to make it generally applicable before testing it out. Try it out in part of your organization just as some firms test new products in only parts of their total market. Or consider a parallel operation until debugging has been done—just as some firms do when they install computers; both the old and the new systems are run concurrently for a test period.

One sales manager in a metal company had outstanding success with a creative selling program. Later he was transferred to another division and he wanted to install a similar creative selling program. He recognized that there might be hidden problems, so he tested the program out among a few of those concerned. The result was that these persons helped sell the program to their associates in later meetings of all sales personnel.

6. *Obtain necessary approvals.*   Your organization probably requires that you obtain higher-up approval for major programs, budgets, basic policies, and major changes in organization structure. What may not be required, but may be just as important, is that you obtain prior approval (or at least the agreement) of your people and any others concerned. For example, if your key people do not participate in finalizing the budget request, they may feel that they have been shortchanged in the resources which they need to accomplish their objectives. If you plan to rely upon staff assistance to help you accomplish your objectives, it would be well for you to clear this with the responsible staff managers so that they support your plans and make their own plans to help you.

Perhaps I can summarize the six guidelines for planning with one key point: *Get the participation of your people when you plan.* If you are trying to get results through your people, then your people need to be committed to whatever it is they are to do.

For several years, one manufacturer had its headquarters staff people devote much time and money to develop plans that line managers were expected to implement. Line managers had little or no participation in the development of the plans, so they dragged their feet in making the plans work. In fact, some managers never even referred to the plans after the original presentations.

James F. Leisy, president of the Wadsworth Publishing Company, has a different approach to planning. In a recent speech, he said:

> Employees at all levels of responsibility participate in establishing both short and long range goals. Then, at least 50 per cent of our employees are involved in establishing individual budgets for meeting these goals. This

depth of participation in setting company-wide objectives results in a greater degree of commitment and responsibility for individual performance than, we believe, is possible under traditional management policies and practices. We believe this factor, more than any other, has led to the remarkable growth of our company.[4]

It would also appear that the managers in this company have been successful in harnessing the trends that affect them. Likewise, your people can help you, through planning, to harness the trends that affect you.

HOW TO PLAN

1. Schedule your planning.
2. Get the ideas and experience of others.
3. Keep plans simple.
4. Put plans in writing.
5. Consider use of tests or pilot runs.
6. Obtain necessary approvals.

KEY POINT: *Get the participation of your people when you plan.*

REFERENCES

1. "Why the Ink Is Black at Harris-Intertype," *Business Week,* Dec. 31, 1966, p. 35.
2. "Six Steps to Better Planning," *Nation's Business,* August, 1961.
3. "The Little Lamp That Grew Up," *Business Week,* Dec. 19, 1964, p. 64.
4. James F. Leisy, "The Wadsworth Story," *The Diary of Alpha Kappa Psi,* Summer, 1966, p. 4.

3

SETTING YOUR OBJECTIVES

OBJECTIVES *A goal, target, or quota to be achieved by a certain time.*

There is probably no element of managing that has greater importance than that of setting your objectives. Without sound objectives, you will find yourself thinking and acting: Let's all do as well as we can and hope for the best. You may survive, but then again you may not.

I know of one nonprofit organization with a management that believes that what it offers the public is good enough so that its only objective for growth is to "accept the growth that comes to it." The result is that this organization has stayed about the same size for the last several years and there is evidence (e.g., drastic cuts in operating budgets) that its position in its field is dwindling.

QUIZ: ARE THESE SOUND OBJECTIVES?

In recent years, many management authorities have promoted management by objectives. Yet I find that many managers have difficulty even in distinguishing what are clearly stated objectives.

29

Perhaps you'd like to test yourself. You can do so by taking the short quiz shown in Figure 3-1. Later in the chapter, I'll present my key to the quiz.

FIGURE 3-1   Are These Clearly Stated Objectives?

Yes *No*

1. Serve the public with competence and integrity.
2. Achieve maximum profit.
3. Develop a climate for personal growth and development.
4. Market only quality products.
5. Develop additional sources of supply.
6. Reduce number of employee grievances.
7. Establish research and development department.
8. Carry out assigned responsibilities within approved budget.
9. Maintain good housekeeping.
10. Install the XYZ System.

WHAT ARE THE OBJECTIVES OF YOUR REAL BOSS?

Whether you are the chief executive officer or a manager down the line, you have a boss on whom your *ultimate* success depends. He is your real boss. In a business, he is the ultimate consumer. In a government, he is the citizen. In a church, he is the parishioner. Unless you serve his interests, he will not buy, vote, approve, or act in other ways to support what you and your organization are trying to accomplish. This means that before setting your own objectives, you should consider the interests or objectives of your real boss.

To illustrate, let's consider the Marketing Concept. Formalized by the General Electric Company around 1950, the Marketing Concept has gained wide acceptance. Its essence is: Run your business from the viewpoint of the customer rather than from the viewpoint of the seller. The presumption is that in the long run the seller and the customer will benefit mutually even though the seller's profits, for example, may suffer in the short run.

If you are a typical seller, the question you are likely to ask yourself is: How can I sell the customer what *I've got?* However, when you apply the Marketing Concept you ask yourself: What does the customer *need* and how do I get it for him? Your answer to this question will affect the objectives you set and the actions you take to achieve your objectives. You may, for example, decide to obtain a license to make a new product developed by a competitor if the new product better serves the needs of the customer.

HOW TO SET YOUR OBJECTIVES

One intangible products company had a record of being the fastest growing in its field. Its growth was based primarily upon sales volume. Management had such a fixation on this kind of growth that it closed its eyes to the profitability of the business, to whether the existing business would repeat, and to whether there would even be enough working capital in the not too distant future. Furthermore, there weren't really objectives for sales volume; the company was relying upon costly financial incentives to accomplish the fast growth that management wanted. The day of reckoning was bound to come, and the company finally had to sell out. It should have had *measurable* objectives to ensure *balanced* results in all areas of *critical* importance.

Regardless of your level of responsibility, you, too, should *set measurable objectives to ensure balanced results in your critical areas of responsibility*. This involves six actions.

1. *Identify your most important opportunities and problems in all your areas of responsibility.* If you are starting up a new facility, your opportunities and problems are quite different from those you have when you are managing an activity that is already off the ground. For example, one of your key objectives in a start-up might be to keep product waste below 20 percent of output. For a going operation your objective may be to keep waste below 5 percent.

To help them identify their most important opportunities and problems, the production supervisors of one manufacturer consider the following:

a. Increase production, yield, equipment utilization, or other quantity of work.
b. Reduce costs such as waste, rejects, personnel turnover, absenteeism, learning time, overtime, downtime, maintenance, and repair.
c. Reduce medical aid and/or lost-time accidents.
d. Reduce number of employee grievances.
e. Obtain more suggestions for improving methods and procedures.
f. Reduce the number of claims and complaints.

Look at your areas of responsibility from both a "vertical" and "horizontal" viewpoint.

From a vertical viewpoint, consider setting both short- and long-range objectives. For example, in the short range you may have an objective to achieve a certain level of production; in the long range—say, beyond a year or two—you may have an objective to develop a trained replacement for yourself.

From a horizontal viewpoint, consider the breadth of your responsibilities. Use the checklist shown in Figure 3-2.

FIGURE 3-2   Checklist to Help You Set Objectives

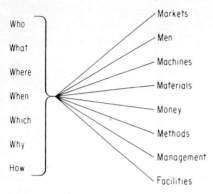

Who
What
Where
When
Which
Why
How

Markets
Men
Machines
Materials
Money
Methods
Management
Facilities

Use the key words to spark your thoughts as to where your most important opportunities and problems lie. For example, here are a few questions you might consider relative to each of your user and geographical *markets:*

Who are the potential customers in this market?
What are their needs—i.e., the objectives of our real boss?
Where are they located?
When do they have needs?
Which of them are we serving now?
Why shouldn't they stay with competition?
How might we test our potential?

Such questions can help you set sales and marketing objectives.

Here's one more example; these are questions that you might ask relative to *men:*

Who are our best and least qualified people?
What are our future needs for people—in quantity and quality?
Where can we obtain people to meet temporary and permanent needs?
When during the year will we have the most and the least needs for people?
Which persons are likely to stay and which are likely to leave voluntarily or involuntarily?
Why not use more females?
How can new people be attracted to our organization?

Such questions can help you to set hiring and training objectives.

2. *Set one to three primary objectives.* The next worst thing to your not having any objectives is having too many objectives. If you are a typical manager, you have so many activities going on about you that you can really keep your eye on only one or two or three balls.

One group of sales managers found this out. Altogether, they set sales objectives for a couple of hundred target accounts. A year later they found that they had scattered their attention and their objectives had been meaningless.

A corporate training manager did just the opposite. There were a dozen or more objectives that he could have set. He determined that his primary objective should be to help the line management of a new plant achieve rated production by the end of the year. In the subsequent months, he had many temptations to get overly involved in other accomplishments, but he was able to keep his eye on the ball and devote the necessary effort to accomplish his one primary objective.

There are many organizations that do a good job of helping their line managers set sound objectives, but these same organizations often overlook what their staff managers should have by way of objectives. Edward C. Schleh, author and management consultant, proposes that the staff man be held accountable for achieving the same results as the line people that he serves.[1] For example, give the controller the same cost-reduction objective that the line managers he works with are responsible for achieving.

One of the biggest mistakes that staff managers make is to become so involved in activities that they overlook the primary result they should be working toward. Consequently, staff departments are often the first to go when an organization has a crash program to reduce cost. Take management development. How many managers of management development can point to one or two clear-cut primary objectives that they have helped to achieve? One suitable annual objective for many organizations would be: X percentage of key openings to be filled with qualified internal candidates.

3. *Consider setting secondary objectives.* Secondary objectives can help you attain your primary objectives and provide you with the opportunity to make additional accomplishment beyond your primary goals. For example, if you are a sales manager, you may set a primary objective of 1,200 new-prospect calls to be made by your salesmen during the next year. Your secondary objectives may specify that a certain proportion of the calls be made in three or four industries or in three or four geographical locations. Or perhaps you wish to promote three or four different product lines. Additional objectives might be in the areas of sales by direct mail or a certain volume of sales for a new product.

Avoid setting objectives in areas of routine accomplishment such as for quality, customer service, or cost control. Once an accomplishment becomes routine, it should be a continuing standard.

Altogether, you should probably limit your total number of primary and secondary objectives to somewhere between five and ten. If your objectives are well thought out, you will be sufficiently busy taking the various actions required to accomplish these objectives.

4. *Make sure the attainment of your objectives is largely under your control.*   One general manager held an all-day sales meeting with his sales managers and admonished them to help achieve a 50 percent increase in profits by the end of the year. However, the sales managers were not given individual profit objectives. Further, they felt that the biggest problems affecting profits lay in the area of pricing policy (which was decided even above the level of the general manager) and in the area of production. What the general manager could have done was to establish with his sales managers profit-contribution objectives.

Profit contribution is generally defined as what is left in the sales dollar to cover overhead and profit after you subtract direct costs such as for labor and materials; however, you can also subtract those costs over which the sales managers have considerable control.

Suppose there is a $1,000 sale of a product that has an assumed profit contribution of 40 percent. The sales manager would get credit for $400 unless he or one of his people helped to incur costs such as price cuts, nonreimbursed overtime or make-overs, claims or credits, and expenses over budget. The dollars involved for any of these costs would be deducted from the $400 in calculating the profit contribution on the $1,000 sale.

You will never have complete control over the various factors that affect the attainment of your objectives. However, if it is clear that you will have major obstacles completely beyond your control, then you should seek to define your objectives so that you will have clearer, more attainable targets.

5. *Express your objectives in numbers.*   The best way to make your objectives measurable is to express them in numbers. Examples are shown in Figure 3-3.

Led by the example of Robert McNamara, former Secretary of Defense, the federal government's civilian agencies are now held responsible for establishing measurable objectives. As reported by *Business Week* magazine:

> "Quantification" is the theme. Bureaucrats must put numerical values on every program in their books—even where it seems impossible. They must spell out in complete detail the objectives they hope to accomplish with their

FIGURE 3-3   Examples of Measurable Objectives

Position	Year-end Objective
Sales Manager	Achieve $1,500,000 profit contribution (sales less direct costs).
Production superintendent	Make 95 percent on-time shipments to customers.
Supervisor, cost accounting	Reduce direct labor in Department B by 15 percent.
Personnel manager	Reduce annual rate of turnover for hourly employees to 20 percent.
Engineering manager	Produce 1,000 units of Product X.
General manager	Achieve 10 percent profit after taxes on total capital employed.
Chairman, program committee	Achieve net income from programs of $1,000.
Association president	Increase active members to 200.

programs over the next five years and the resources they will need to do the job.[2]

This is being done to give our government a better basis for approving budgets. It also means that progress toward objectives can be *measured;* for what good are objectives unless progress toward them can be ascertained?

Every manager has the same need to express his objectives in numbers, although each must determine how best to do it. Stating your objectives in numbers is how you can make them most meaningful to your people and to others concerned.

6. *Establish deadlines.*   Typically, the period for accomplishing your objectives will coincide with your budget. This is generally a year, but there is no reason why you can't use some other segment of time, such as six months. If your objectives are challenging enough, they will probably take you several months to accomplish—or several years if you have challenging, long-range objectives. Whatever your deadline is, make sure it is clear to you and your people. The importance of deadlines has often been cited as one of the basic reasons why managers in the United States have been able to accomplish more than managers in many other countries.

In the light of the preceding discussion, I believe you'll agree that none of the items in Figure 3-1 is measurable—either in terms of numbers or deadlines. It may be desirable to accomplish the items, but they are poor examples of objectives that can be communicated to, or understood by, those responsible for getting results. To have meaning, objectives must be measurable.

There are arguments against setting objectives as described in this chapter. I recall one manager who objected on the ground that he felt it would hurt morale if one manager were shown up to do a poorer job than another manager in relation to defined objectives. By now, I hope this manager sees that sound objectives are vital if managers are to challenge themselves and their people in relation to their potential and in relation to their opportunities and problems.

HOW TO SET OBJECTIVES

1. Identify your most important opportunities and problems in all your areas of responsibility.
2. Set one to three primary objectives.
3. Consider setting secondary objectives.
4. Make sure the attainment of your objectives is largely under your control.
5. Express your objectives in numbers.
6. Establish deadlines.

KEY POINT: *Set measurable objectives to ensure*
balanced results in your critical areas
of responsibility

REFERENCES

1. Edward C. Schleh, *Successful Executive Action*, Prentice-Hall, Inc., Englewood Cliffs, N.J., 1955, p. 128.
2. "Putting a Dollar Sign on Everything," *Business Week*, July 16, 1966, p. 123.

4

DEVELOPING YOUR PROGRAM

PROGRAM   *Strategy to be followed and major
actions to be taken to achieve or exceed objectives.*

Most likely you understand why a company needs a strategy for accomplishing its primary objectives—generally for sales and profits. But do you understand why *you* need a strategy for accomplishing your primary objectives? Do you have a managing strategy with the characteristics listed in Figure 4-1?

**FIGURE 4-1   Do You Have a Managing Strategy with
These Characteristics?**

($\checkmark$)

_____ 1. It is basic to the achievement of your primary objectives.
_____ 2. It is implemented through your people.
_____ 3. It is designed to make best use of your available resources.
_____ 4. It takes competition and other obstacles into account.
_____ 5. It makes provision for both the worst and the best that can happen.
_____ 6. It prevents you from trying to be all things to all people.

ARE YOU A STRATEGIST?

A certain controller was recently shocked to find himself replaced. When he first went into his job as controller, he made a number of improvements, such as the installation of a cost-accounting system and conversion of a number of accounting operations to electronic-data-processing methods. Then, as time went on, it became apparent that he was much more concerned with protecting the status quo than with meeting new needs such as faster ways to process the paper work on customer orders, better ways to evaluate actual return on capital expenditures, and better reports for management control. He developed no strategy or program for making accomplishments beyond the routine—apparently because he was busy and felt that his current activities were already critical to his organization. He even became oblivious to assignments and organization changes that would normally have fallen into his area of responsibility. The result was he "lost a war" that he may not have really realized he was in.

Right now you are "in a war" because you have competitors both within and outside of your organization.

Internally, you compete with other managers who are ambitious and try to excel in their areas of responsibility. In turn, they seek control over more of the available resources—including some of the same people and budget monies that you may wish to obtain or keep. Internally, there may well be one or more persons who aspire to your position— whether or not you get promoted, demoted, or transferred.

Externally, you compete with other managers who have responsibilities similar to yours. Unless you perform as well as they do, your superiors, associates, and subordinates may exert influence to have you replaced. Even as a chief executive, you have no security because outside interests may seek control of your organization if it appears that you are missing important opportunities such as for profit or sales.

If you see yourself as a strategist, you will find ways to compete effectively with those inside and outside of your organization. And you will do so on the basis of your performance rather than by detracting from what others may accomplish. You will find ways to accomplish more than the routine and to meet the changing needs of those you serve.

Perhaps you are now wondering: What specifically does a strategist do that is different from what a nonstrategist does?

WHAT DO YOU DO AS A STRATEGIST?

As a strategist, you set sound objectives such as I described in the last chapter. Next you develop a carefully thought out strategy: the basic method describing *how* you will achieve or exceed your objectives. Then you develop and carry out specific actions to implement your strategy *through your people*.

What this involves is perhaps best illustrated with a simple example.

Suppose that Dad (the manager) wants to take his family to the beach (his objective) and that he develops his plans as follows:

DAD: All right. It's decided. We'll go to the beach next Sunday.

MOTHER: When shall we go to avoid the traffic?

JOHN: Why don't we go early and come back early?

DAD: That's good thinking. Let's go about 8 A.M. and leave to come back at about 4 P.M.

MARY: What about eating?

JOHN: Can we eat breakfast at a restaurant on the way?

DAD: If we stop along the way, we might get caught in traffic. Aside from that, let's save our money in case the old station wagon breaks down. If everyone will help out, meals won't be too big a burden on anyone.

MARY: I can fix breakfast before we leave.

MOTHER: I'll prepare our lunches for the beach.

JOHN: I'll gather firewood so we'll be able to roast hot dogs.

DAD: That sounds fine. I'll have the station wagon serviced and do the driving. And if we have no expensive car trouble, I'll buy us supper when we get close to home. Remember, though, we have to get everything done in time to leave home by 8 A.M.

Dad's strategy is to go early and come back early — to avoid traffic (competition). His actions for implementing his strategy are described in the last four dialogue exchanges. With these actions, he utilizes his resources (people, station wagon, food supply, money); and he recognizes that there are potential problems — breakdown of station wagon, limited money, and the possibility that everyone won't complete his tasks to leave on time. Because of careful planning, however, he can expect to accomplish his objective and to enjoy his trip to the beach.

The nonstrategist might get to the beach also. But, there's a good chance that he will get caught in traffic or run out of money or have a miserable time.

Your strategy will be most effective if you try to *get a maximum return on a minimum investment* in time, effort, and money. In other words, you should optimize: Try to get the best utilization of your resources — neither too much nor too little — to achieve or exceed your objectives. In the skit above, for example, Dad divided the effort among the members of the family. Furthermore, he made provision for the worst that can happen and the best that can happen. If the old station wagon breaks down, he expects to have enough money to have it fixed or towed. If it performs well, he will take the family out to supper.

You will probably never have all the resources you'd like, so your challenge is generally to do the best you can with what you've got. As your success increases, so will your resources.

Your biggest temptation is probably to try to be all things to all people. In the skit, for example, Dad vetoed John's suggestion to eat breakfast in a restaurant. Sound strategy will prevent you from spreading yourself too thin and from yielding unwisely to the job pressures and distractions about you.

EXAMPLES OF MANAGING STRATEGY

Perhaps you, or managers you know, have been unusually successful in developing and implementing managing strategy. Here are some examples that I know about:

- A sales manager exceeded his sales and gross-profit objectives through a program wherein his salesmen helped customers to identify and solve business problems not necessarily related to the salesmen's products.
- A manufacturing manager exceeded his goal for cost reduction through a program of training his people in methods-engineering techniques that they could use to make their own methods improvements.
- A director of purchases reduced materials costs substantially through a program in which his people used value engineering to standardize and substitute materials.
- A credit manager helped his firm to increase profitable sales through a program of having his staff use credit services to get business rather than to turn down business.
- A traffic manager created large savings through a traffic research program in which his people found ways to reduce shipping rates negotiated with carriers.
- A plant start-up manager with many new people exceeded his objectives for scheduled production through a program wherein persons at each level of responsibility were trained to develop and conduct how-to-do-your-job training for the persons at the next level down.
- A personnel director reduced turnover by having his staff recruit college graduates with a few years of work experience rather than college graduates fresh out of school.
- A newly appointed general manager increased his division's profits remarkably by replacing several key managers with better-qualified people and by giving them increased authority and responsibility over what the previous managers had.

Note that in each of the above examples, the manager obtained results through his people. That is what makes each strategy a *managing* strategy in addition to perhaps also being a marketing strategy, a production strategy, or some other kind of functional-area strategy.

Note also that a manager can have a managing strategy regardless of his functional area and his level of managing responsibility.

HOW TO PLAN YOUR PROGRAM

Earlier in this chapter, I described generally what a strategist does. Now let's consider the subject in more depth; in other words, let's consider how to develop your program. I recommend five steps.

1. *Review your objectives.*   I find that most managers have difficulty in distinguishing objectives (results) from activities. Your objectives are the *whats;* they differ from the *hows* required in a program for accomplishing your objectives. For example: Your *what* may be to achieve a certain level of sales; your *how* may be to add some key distributors and/or to conduct a certain advertising and promotion campaign and/or to enter a new market and/or to introduce a new program for incentive compensation. If you have not made the what-how distinction in setting your objectives, you should do so; otherwise you may perform a great deal of activity without really pinpointing what the measurable results will be.

Make sure you distinguish which of your objectives have primary versus secondary priority. Most likely, you will want to invest the most time, effort, and money in attaining your primary objectives.

2. *Identify your resources.*   If you are perfectionistically inclined, you may be far more aware of your weaknesses than you are of your strengths. A strategist tries to optimize—by maximizing his strengths and minimizing his weaknesses. Therefore, you will want to identify all the important resources (strengths) that you have at your disposal. Chances are you have significantly more resources than you realize.

One way to identify these resources is to use a checklist developed around the headings: seven M's and an F. Figure 4-2 shows such a checklist—in this instance from a marketing viewpoint.

3. *Identify your obstacles.*   An item that is not a resource may be an obstacle that can prevent or hinder you from achieving your objectives. For example, if a major competitor has better-qualified people than you have, then you may have an obstacle that you will need to overcome.

To identify your obstacles, you can use the same checklist (Figure 4–2) that you used to identify your resources.

FIGURE 4-2 Checklist for Identifying Your Marketing Resources and Obstacles Relative to Your Competition

Markets:	Share of market
	Amount of new business
	Amount of old or repeat business
	Customer needs, attitudes, and habits
Men:	Qualifications of your people
	Locations
	Organization structure
	Training and development
Machines:	Production capacity, efficiency, and cost
	Versatility
	Delivery schedules
Materials:	Product design or formula
	Product quality and performance
	Packaging
	Dependability of sources for direct materials
	Diversity of product line
Money:	Working capital available
	Gross profit percentage by product
	Percentage return on total capital employed
	Money available for capital expenditures
	Sources for additional capital
Methods:	Distribution outlets
	Policies and procedures for pricing, discounts, credit, ordering, storing, shipping, guarantees, claims, allowances, trade relations, new markets and products, sales incentives
	Services to customers
	Advertising, promotion, publicity
	Compliance with, and exploitation of, laws and regulations: local, state, national, and foreign
Management:	Qualifications of managers at all levels
	Decision-making authority
	Locations and availability
Facilities:	Kinds for production, distribution, storage, and sales
	Locations
	Communications network

4. *Define your managing strategy.*   Your managing strategy describes the basic method that you will use to achieve or exceed your objectives; it should be based upon

   a. Your resources and obstacles—especially relative to any competition that your firm has *b.* Sound strategy for your functional area—e.g., marketing, production, engineering, accounting, personnel

Because of your background and/or current responsibility in a functional area, most likely you will think first of functional-area strategy. Accordingly, consider developing and maintaining a checklist containing items on which you might base your functional-area strategy. Such a checklist is shown in Figure 4-3—again for the functional area of marketing.

FIGURE 4-3   Checklist for Developing Your Marketing Strategy for What You Sell

Products or services	Customer services
Specialized	Design
Broad line	Selection counsel
Latest style	Delivery
Brand names	Installation
Impulse items	Packaging
Imported	Maintenance
Repeat	Repair
Quality of products or services	Claim and complaint
Price or dollar savings	Financing
Terms or allowances	Problem solving
Guarantees	User education
Time saving	Automated ordering (via electronic
Convenience (e.g., location, parking)	data processing)
Comfort	Psychological benefits
Health	Personal attention
Employee qualification	Social approval
Reputation	Prestige
Dependability	Sex appeal
	Accomplishment
	Freedom from fear and danger
	Welfare of loved ones
	Entertainment, pleasure, diversion

This checklist covers *what* you sell, but you can develop similar checklists for *whom, when,* and *how* you sell. Your marketing strategy can center around what, whom, when, or how you sell—or a combination. For example, McDonald's Corp. has become prominent through franchising quick-service food outlets located to serve young above-average-income families primarily during mealtimes.[1] Other companies have utilized marketing strategies such as blending product mix with market need, giving buyers an indispensable service, and establishing industry standards where none existed.[2]

If you have production responsibility, you might develop and maintain a checklist for production strategy covering, for example, ways to increase production, ways to improve quality control, ways to improve customer service, ways to improve inventory management, ways to maintain good employee relations, and ways to reduce production costs.

Your functional area of strategy may be technical in nature, so it must be integrated with what you want to accomplish through your people. If you are going to introduce a new product or service, for example, you will probably need to train your people how to perform new tasks related to the new product or service. As a minimum, you will need the cooperation and support of your people if they are affected by your functional-area strategy.

A broader checklist applicable to any functional area or to your organization as a whole is shown in Figure 4-4. Hence, this is a checklist for developing your *managing* strategy—assuming you must rely on your people to implement your strategy.

This checklist is not intended to be all-inclusive; but it and the previous checklist (Figure 4-3) are intended to indicate how many different kinds of managing strategy you can have. You have literally thousands

FIGURE 4-4   Checklist for Developing Your Managing Strategy

1. "Skim the cream" to obtain relatively easy and quick sales, savings, or other results.
2. Exploit existing services, products, or relationships; and/or develop or promote new services, products, or relationships.
3. Develop or promote products or services with high margin of profit; and/or develop or promote products or services with low margin of profit—to get volume.
4. Provide service of such quality that you will generate unsolicited referrals or requests.
5. Lead in making promising but unproved improvements in products, processes, and/or methods; and/or make those improvements already proved elsewhere.
6. Build up reserves (e.g., people, dollars, inventory) for future use.
7. Expand vertically and/or horizontally.
8. Expand through borrowed or shared resources or on a pay-as-you-go basis.
9. Standardize services, products, processes, or methods.
10. Automate operations.
11. Reduce seasonal or cyclical fluctuations of activity.
12. Eliminate unprofitable operations or activities.
13. Reduce the costs of major operations or activities.
14. Take advantage of new legislation and/or overlooked laws.
15. Utilize and/or improve staffing, training, policies, procedures, standards, organization structure, and/or other managing elements especially important to the achievement of your objectives.

of choices. That is why you should define and communicate to your people the managing strategy that is basic to the achievement of your objectives. Otherwise, you will spread yourself in too many directions or you will make only routine accomplishment.

There is no reason why you can't have the same managing strategy from one year to the next. However, when you have been successful with a certain managing strategy (by achieving or exceeding your objectives), you may wish to standardize on it and put your emphasis on something else. If, for example, staffing is the most important thing you can do to achieve this year's objectives, you should probably base your managing strategy on something else next year—even though staffing will always be very important. In general, as your objectives and problems change from year to year, so should your managing strategy.

5. *Develop six to twelve major actions.*   After you have defined your managing strategy, you need to develop the major actions that you will take to implement your strategy and to achieve or exceed your objectives.

I suggest only six to twelve major actions because I find that most managers get bogged down when they try to keep their eyes on too many balls. Major actions (e.g., develop and conduct training for your people) will generally help you achieve or exceed several of your objectives. In addition, your major actions should

   a. Center upon what you will accomplish through your people— assuming you wish to function more as a manager than as a specialist in one or more functional areas.
   b. Take into account both the best and the worst that can happen. For example, if there is a high volume of sales, can your people and your firm handle the business? (One savings and loan association was so successful in its promotional campaign to attract savings that it was unable to locate and make sufficient investments of the savings.) If there is a low volume of sales, can you increase the marketing effort and/or reduce costs?

One president of a retail chain does an excellent job of developing and implementing an annual plan of accomplishment. He helps each of his key people develop individual programs; then he summarizes their programs into an overall program. Recently, his primary objectives for the year were to increase sales by 15 percent and pretax earnings by 68 percent. He and his people established the managing strategy of providing customers in selected market areas with maximum savings primarily through low-margin pricing, high-quality private-label products, and efficient operations. Figure 4-5 shows eight items in his program for the year.

**FIGURE 4-5   Eight Items in a Twelve-month Program
Developed by the President of a Retail Chain**

---

1. Increase sales in each store a minimum of 10 percent by significantly improving the store's "in-stock" position through the installation and adherence to the new "stock count" ordering procedure.
2. Increase gross margins by 1.1 percent without increasing initial markup or changing warehouse discount.
   a. Dropping slow-moving, low-margin items
   b. A reduction of the markdowns through better care of merchandise and seasonal planning
   c. Proper schematics and display of high-gross items
   d. Proper markup and pricing of local purchases
   e. Reduction of overall company shrinkage to not more than 1.5 percent
3. Introduce thirty-three additional categories of private label.
4. Evolve further an advertising program specifically geared to
   a. Develop in our present and potential customers an awareness of the fact that we are a quality retailer affording them tremendous savings.
   b. Obtain maximum value from our advertising expenditures by identifying and appealing to the age and ethnic groups that constitute the majority of a given store's potential customers.
5. Continue evaluation of freight-in expense and seek more economical methods of moving merchandise.
6. Develop and install each area's management information and control requirements.
7. Develop and install a management development program.
8. Install effective store management and executive management incentive plans to maximize motivation for achievement of corporate objectives.

This president also shows for each item in his program the project chairman, committee members, start date, and reporting and completion dates. In this way, he makes clear that he expects to accomplish his objectives through his people.

Developing your program is not an easy task, but your task will be simplified if you visualize yourself as a strategist throughout the year. Then you will get into the habit of trying to get a maximum return on a minimum investment in time, effort, and money—the most important requirement for developing a sound program to achieve or exceed your objectives. Furthermore, you will have a better strategy than a certain gas station operator who, when asked how business was, replied: "Suits me fine. I've never made enough money to quit and I've never made enough money for anybody to want to buy me out."

HOW TO PLAN YOUR PROGRAM

1. Review your objectives.
2. Identify your resources.
3. Identify your obstacles.
4. Define your managing strategy.
5. Develop six to twelve major actions.

KEY POINT: *Visualize yourself as a strategist —*
to get a maximum return on a minimum
investment.

REFERENCES

1. "McDonald's Makes Franchising Sizzle," *Business Week,* June 15, 1968, p. 102.
2. "Four Marketing Strategies That Turn Followers into Leaders," *Business Management,* December, 1965, pp. 67–69.

5

DEVELOPING YOUR SCHEDULE

SCHEDULE   *A plan showing when individual or
group activities or accomplishments will be started
and/or completed.*

If you have *whats* as objectives and *hows* as major actions in a program,
there will still be a missing ingredient before you have a complete plan:
the *whens*. That's the purpose of your schedule: to provide you with
whens for implementing your program.

Many managers devote much time and effort in planning their *whats*
and their *hows,* then, for some strange reason, slight the *whens*. Consider the following examples:

A manufacturing manager waited to hire and train 300 new employees
for a production expansion. The result was poor training, high personnel
turnover, and a year of costly substandard production.

A sales manager announced a first-quarter sales contest two weeks
before the end of the previous fiscal year. The result was that the salesmen saved up orders to get off to a fast start in the sales contest and the
sales manager missed his sales objective for the previous year.

48

A personnel manager waited to make college and university arrangements for recruiting scarce engineering and business graduates. The result was that his recruiters had to limit their recruiting efforts to a few small colleges and he missed his hiring objective by a large margin.

A president waited to get tax counsel until almost the end of the fiscal year. The result was his firm had insufficient time to take actions that could have resulted in significant tax savings.

In each of the above instances, the manager did poor scheduling to accomplish what he knew several months in advance had to be done and what was otherwise sound action.

HOW WELL DO YOU SCHEDULE?

There are a number of ways to do *poor* scheduling. Six symptoms that are indicative of poor scheduling are shown in Figure 5-1. An explanation of each symptom follows.

FIGURE 5-1 Do You Have Any of These Symptoms of Poor Scheduling?

Yes	No	
——	——	1. You use a calendar as your only scheduling document.
——	——	2. You rely mostly on short-term schedules such as for a week or a month.
——	——	3. You have schedules for individual projects or major actions but you have no master schedule.
——	——	4. You find that the activities of other people or departments interfere with your planned activities.
——	——	5. You get tied up with unforeseen problems or assignments and aren't able to make your planned accomplishments.
——	——	6. You get unexpected unfavorable reaction from those affected when you begin to implement your plans.

Symptom No. 1: A calendar has dates, so it is an indispensable scheduling document. However, you are limited in what you can show on a calendar. For example, it is generally difficult to show what must be accomplished concurrently from one week or month to the next. Also, you will find it difficult to provide your superior or your people with a copy of your schedule if it consists only of what you record on a calendar.

Symptom No. 2: You may have a list of the major actions that you wish to take throughout the year; but if you schedule them only a week or a month into the future, it is unlikely that you will accomplish all of them. Schedules for relatively short periods of time should be integrated into a master (overall) schedule showing what you plan to accomplish throughout the year. Otherwise you may spend a disproportionate amount of time on some activity simply because you have not thought through what might be involved in accomplishing activities not yet started.

Symptom No. 3: One manager recently complained to me that he had too many schedules. He said that he had schedules from each of his people—including schedules for each of the major projects for which his people were responsible. In spite of all these schedules, it developed that he had no schedule for himself, i.e., a master schedule which integrated all major activities in a digestible form. The result was he was able to see the trees far more clearly than he was able to see the forest. I find that this kind of problem is prevalent mostly among technically oriented managers who, as managers, are often just as concerned with detailed activities as they were when they were individual doers.

Symptom No. 4: If you become engrossed in your own planning activities, you may overlook the planned activities of other people or departments on whom you are dependent. Many staff managers, for example, have had to delay implementing their plans because line managers with whom they had to work were tied up with other commitments.

Symptom No. 5: Every manager has unforeseen problems or assignments related, for example, to competitive actions or personnel changes. A schedule of planned activities will help you get back on the track as soon as possible. However, you can also overcommit yourself and your people if you do not have in your schedule some provision for the time it may take to handle the unforeseen problems or assignments.

Symptom No. 6: Probably the most significant problem of poor scheduling is indicated when you take a planned action and get unexpected unfavorable reaction from those affected. The cause is often poor timing. For example, your people may support a performance-evaluation program, but they may react unfavorably if you schedule performance appraisals to be made during a seasonal or cyclical period of peak production. Your people may support a certain kind of training, but they may react unfavorably if you schedule the training during the summer-vacation period when they are working overtime and substituting for their fellow employees. No matter how well-conceived your major actions are, they may turn out to be fiascoes unless you time and schedule them carefully to get maximum acceptance by your people and any others affected.

How to schedule—how to alleviate symptoms of poor scheduling—is covered later in the chapter. First, let's consider three kinds of schedules that managers use.

THREE KINDS OF SCHEDULES FOR MANAGERS

Most managers use some form of *calendar* schedule; some managers use some form of *Gantt* schedule; and a few managers use some form of *network* schedule. Each kind of schedule has its own application.

A calendar schedule is the easiest to prepare. You list merely what you plan to do and record opposite each item when you plan to get it done. This kind of schedule is easy to communicate to your superior and to any others affected. An example is shown in Figure 5-2.

FIGURE 5-2 Calendar Schedule of a Training Manager's Twelve-month Program for a Packaging and Building Materials Company

	A. PRIMARY PRIORITY
	1. Packaging sales training—37 weekly sessions
Jan.–Oct.	*a.* Conduct pilot program.
Jan.–Dec.	*b.* Conduct program in other districts.
Jan.–Feb.	2. Individual development conference training for all supervisory personnel—2 hours
	3. Building materials sales training
Feb.	*a.* Plaster—2 days
May and Aug.	*b.* Gypsum—4 days
Apr. and July	*c.* Roofing—4 days
Apr.	*d.* Floor covering—2 days
Apr.	*e.* Paint—2 days
	B. SECONDARY PRIORITY
July–Sept.	1. Development of reference manual for techniques of supervision
Oct.–Nov.	2. Preparation of course and reading references for management development program
Feb.–Dec.	3. Administration of educational-assistance program

The Gantt schedule gets its name from Henry L. Gantt, one of the pioneers in scientific management. A Gantt schedule can be made up in many different ways, but it generally shows in graphic form what activities must be accomplished concurrently and in relation to the total time available. An example of such a schedule is shown in Figure 5-3.

This schedule shows that five items of primary priority are to be accomplished in January; viz., items 1b, 2, 3, 4, and 5. As shown at the bottom of the schedule, you can also indicate percentage of accomplishment for each item on the schedule.

A network schedule such as PERT or CPM is applicable when you

FIGURE 5-3   Gantt Schedule of a Marketing Manager's Twelve-month Program for a Printing Plates Company

Bottom bar shows scheduled accomplishment; top bar shows approximate percent of completion.

Activity	Jan.	Feb.	Mar.	Apr.	May	June	July	Aug.	Sept.	Oct.	Nov.	Dec.
A. Primary Priority												
1. Conduct mail campaigns												
a. Deep die plates												
b. Magnesium engravings, mats, electros												
c. Dycril pantographic plates												
2. Sell designated products to target accounts; sell and service existing business												
3. Install, evaluate, and revise sales incentive program												
4. Develop, print, and distribute sales brochure												
5. Hold planned sales meetings												
6. Revise and extend marketing plan six months												
B. Secondary Priority												
1. Promote additional sales of designated products through mailings and sales calls												
a. Printers												
b. Converters												
2. Conduct feasibility studies												
a. Dycril sales in chemical milling field												
b. Night shift without overtime charges												

have many activities that must be accomplished at minimum time and/or minimum cost. PERT (Program Evaluation and Review Technique) was developed for use by the United States Navy and was credited with slashing the estimated completion time of the Polaris program by about two years. CPM (Critical Path Method) is similar to PERT but it was developed in industry. The Du Pont Company spearheaded the development of CPM and used it to save $1 million during the construction of a $10 million chemical plant.[1]

Figure 5-4 shows a simplified version of a PERT/CPM network.

FIGURE 5-4   PERT/CPM Network

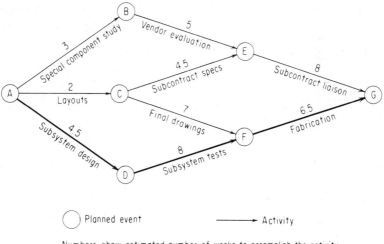

Planned event   ⟶ Activity

Numbers show estimated number of weeks to accomplish the activity.
Dark arrows show critical path.

The network plan seeks, through a graphic flow chart, to show how the various parts of a project depend on each other and how certain tasks must be finished before others can be started. The critical path is the most vital series of interlocking activities in a project. The other activities arise from and depend upon the execution of these on the critical path. The length of time required to accomplish the entire project is directly related to the length of time required by activities on the critical path. Each step on the critical path must be completed in sequence and in the time alloted or else the whole project will be thrown out of order. The critical path is the longest time sequence in the network and it is the key to time control.[2]

PERT/CPM has been used very successfully to schedule and control construction, maintenance, production and retooling programs, new-product introductions, and many other projects. If you are not familiar with PERT/CPM, you should learn enough about it so that you can at least recognize its application in the scheduling and control of your activities. Then you can take steps to get whatever help you may need.

HOW TO SCHEDULE

You may use one kind of schedule to show when you will take each of the major actions in your twelve-month program to achieve or exceed your objectives. You may use another kind of schedule to show what you will accomplish monthly or to detail the actions required to carry out a project in your twelve-month program. In any event, I recommend that you take the following steps whenever you develop a schedule.

1. *Estimate time required for each major action.*   This may sound like a simple and obvious thing to do. However, you probably have in your program certain actions that you have never taken in the past. If so, it is likely that you will underestimate what is involved. For example, if you want to recruit and hire a person with technical skills, it may take six months as compared with one or two months to recruit and hire persons with other kinds of qualifications. In your overall schedule, your time estimates need only be approximate—the number of weeks or months required to carry out a major action.

2. *Allow time for handling routine responsibilities.*   When you develop your schedule, you are normally concentrating on several new actions that you will take to achieve or exceed your objectives. Therefore you may overlook the time involved in helping you maintain your present level of accomplishment. For example, if you are a sales manager, you may feel that your salesmen are effective in making their sales calls. But unless you make periodic field visits with your salesmen, it is likely that the quality of sales calls will begin to deteriorate before there is a clear indication of this in the sales figures.

3. *Make provision for unforeseeables.*   Some managers spend the time to develop contingency plans so they can take quick action in the event of unforeseeables such as strikes, competitive actions, and acts of God. Whether or not you formalize contingency plans, you should certainly plan on having some disruptions due to unforeseeables. If you are a production manager, for example, you may wish to order certain critical equipment to be delivered and installed a month or two before you actually need it. If you are a marketing manager, you may wish to schedule periodic checks with your product development and manufacturing people to make sure that any new products have been

performance-tested and will be available by the time you implement your advertising and promotion plans.

4. *Establish deadlines for starting and completing each major action.* Some managers show only completion dates in their schedules. I believe it is just as important for you to show starting dates. If you do not start an action on time, it is unlikely that you will meet your completion date. Your deadlines should also take into account the priorities of your major actions. Those actions that will help you accomplish your major objectives should be given primary priority. Unless you separate your actions by primary and secondary priority, you may be tempted to spend a disproportionate amount of time on items of secondary authority because they are easier to accomplish or may hold greater personal interest for you.

Probably the most important thing for you to keep in mind when you develop your schedule is to try to *time each major action to get maximum acceptance by those affected.* This is easier said than done because when you are developing your schedule, you are concentrating on what *you* want to accomplish. Yet others on whom you are dependent, or who can affect what you are trying to accomplish, have their own plans and ideas for what they wish to accomplish. To help you think beyond yourself, see Figure 5-5 for some factors that can affect the timing of your major actions.

FIGURE 5-5 Some Factors That Can Affect the Timing of Your Major Actions

1. Planned activities of superiors, subordinates, associates, unions, customers, competitors, stockholders, legislators, or others who can have a positive or negative effect on what you are trying to accomplish. For example, will you be affected by others' plans for
   Meetings?
   Vacations and holidays?
   Trips?
   Contract negotiations?
   Expansions?
   Introduction or installation of new products, services, policies, people, processes, equipment, facilities, etc?
   Legislation?
2. Peak and trough periods of activity—internal and external.
3. Availability of funds—internal or external.
4. Tradition, custom, habits—internal and external. For example, many organizations concentrate on budget preparation during a certain period of the year.

Perhaps your immediate superior can help you to evaluate the relevance of the factors. In any event, do whatever is required to satisfy yourself that you have timed and scheduled your major actions to get the acceptance that you need by those affected.

Sound action poorly timed may be ineffective; poor action properly timed may be effective; sound action properly timed is generally very effective.

HOW TO SCHEDULE

1. Estimate time required for each major action.
2. Allow time for handling routine responsibilities.
3. Make provision for unforeseeables.
4. Establish deadlines for starting and completing each major action.

KEY POINT: *Time each major action to get*
maximum acceptance by those affected.

REFERENCES

1. Robert K. Stern, "The 'Critical Path' to Management Control," *Dun's Review and Modern Industry,* March, 1966, p. 208.
2. "PERT/CPM Management System for the Small Subcontractor," *Technical Aids for Small Manufacturers,* no. 86, Small Business Administration, Washington.

6

DEVELOPING YOUR BUDGET

BUDGET *Planned expenditures required to achieve or exceed objectives.*

Many a manager reacts to budgets as many a teenager does to his parents: He doesn't like 'em, but he needs 'em.

DO YOU LIKE BUDGETS?

In Figure 6-1, which line is longer: Line A or Line B?

FIGURE 6-1   Which Line Is Longer?

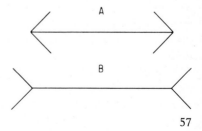

A ruler will show that Lines A and B are identical in length. A manager's view of budgets can also be misleading.

Whether or not you like budgets depends on your background and experience with them. If you are favorably disposed toward them, the chances are good that you know how to develop and use them effectively. If you are not favorably disposed toward them, you probably do not develop and use them as well as you might.

A vice-president and controller of a major firm once summarized what I believe is the view that managers should have toward their budgets:

> Like all other techniques of business, the budget should be a door open to more satisfying and profitable work—not an instrument of torture.
>
> Then it will be known that what you can do without a budget you can do better with one. It will be seen that the entire planning and control procedure, under whatever name, is a device for freeing men to do their best work—not a machine of restriction and condemnation.[1]

While this quotation makes a positive point, it also suggests that there are problems associated with budgets.

BUDGET MALADIES

Budget problems in many organizations are serious enough to be called "budget maladies." But if you recognize them as such, perhaps you can do something about them—e.g., by making recommendations to your immediate superior or by getting specialized assistance.

There are at least four budget maladies.

Malady No. 1: *Budget is based on past expenditures rather than on program for future.*   This is probably the most serious malady. In many organizations, the budget is the plan. The manager who develops his budget in place of, or before, developing his annual objectives, program, and schedule has in effect developed his annual plan. He has given far more attention to how much money he thinks he will need than to the use for the money. Generally, he is guided primarily by past expenditures. Later he has to figure out how to make the money fit what he wants to do.

Often the reason a manager bases his budget primarily on past expenditures is because his firm's financial people ask him to develop a budget before he has gotten around to thinking about his program for the future. In other words, his financial people are more on the ball than he is.

Malady No. 2: *Responsibility for budget development is abdicated to financial department.*   You probably receive assistance from a representative of the financial department when you prepare your budget.

He probably provides you with forms and procedures and is able to answer questions that you may have. If he has a strong personality, you may be tempted to rely on him too much—especially if you do not like to work with figures and have an aversion to budgets. But he probably does not understand your operation; and even if he does, he has no responsibility for the results that you are expected to achieve.

Malady No. 3: *Significant underspending or overspending is allowed.* In some organizations, significant overspending is allowed and the budget is not taken too seriously. The result is that managers do not give much time and attention to the preparation of their budgets and they do not realize the benefits that budgets can provide. In other organizations, significant underspending is allowed—even to the point of basing management incentive payments on underspending. The result is that managers overrequest the money they need and are often able to tie up dollars that could serve much better purposes. Furthermore, some managers neglect to spend the money they should on important needs—especially if the resulting cost will be charged to another department. While economizing on maintenance, for example, a maintenance department manager can cause the production department to incur significant costs through excessive downtime or impeded production.

Malady No. 4: *Budget is held to be sacred and fixed.*   Many managers hold the budget in such awe that they are afraid to exceed it even when there is a good reason to do so. For example, many managers are afraid to recommend an unbudgeted raise in pay for a subordinate who has performed unusually well. The result is often unnecessary and expensive personnel turnover.

A manager should certainly do a careful job in developing his budget, but he shouldn't have to worry about whether or not he has included everything. I don't know a single manager who is clairvoyant enough to foresee all his opportunities and needs for a budget period. Do you?

Before you can take action to correct budget maladies such as the four we have just reviewed, you need to have clear guidelines for developing your budget.

HOW TO BUDGET

Perhaps the most important guideline is: *Develop your budget to support your program.* If you have a sound program, you have a much better chance of getting the budget money you need for operations as well as for capital expenditures. This is true at all levels of management.

At the top management level, many managers forecast how much money they will or can raise; then they plan their growth around this cash. The top management of Clark Equipment Company has a much sounder approach. It plans its operations and expansion first and then tells its financial vice-president how much money it will need.[2]

One way to show that your budget supports your program is to show a summary of your budget with your program. For example, for each month of the year, you might show at the bottom of your program your budget for income, fixed expenses, variable expenses, and gross profit.

Following are four other guidelines for developing your budget.

1. *Develop a budget that will be variable in relation to actual accomplishment.*   A sure way to upset your people is to hold them to fixed amounts of budgeted expenditures even though they have far exceeded planned accomplishment. A tool that many organizations use to avoid this problem is the flexible budget.

If you are a production manager, for example, you can set up a budget for various levels of production. By using a unit such as cost per man-hour or cost per machine-hour, you can budget for costs such as raw materials, direct labor, indirect labor, and variable overhead — e.g., electricity. Then you can determine your cost for various levels of production. You can see whether you are operating according to the budget in the seasonal valleys as well as in the seasonal peaks. This procedure can help you operate at a profit at any given production level.

2. *Include only controllable expenses.*   Some managers have in their budgets expenses over which they have no control. This occurs, for example, when overhead is allocated to a department or an operation. Such an allocation may be satisfying to an accountant, but it is frustrating to the manager who can do nothing about depreciation, insurance, taxes, and other overhead expenses. An organization cannot overlook overhead expense, but such expense should be charged to the budgets of those managers who can do something about it.

3. *Specify how to handle unplanned expenditures.*   What if a manager has the opportunity to hire an unusually good man, or to capitalize on a special market situation, or to purchase an important piece of equipment at a bargain price? If the money he needs to take advantage of such opportunities is not in his budget, there should be a simple procedure whereby he can request the money he needs. You should have this understanding up the line, and you should make it clear to any of the people who report to you.

I recall a certain production manager in a food-processing plant. Rats invaded the plant and he spent over a thousand dollars to get rid of them even though the money was not in his budget. Some of his fellow managers expected him to be criticized for not getting prior approval for the expenditure. They were somewhat surprised when he was commended. This incident helped to make clear to all managers in the plant that there are instances when it is good judgment to exceed the budget — even when there is provision for making requests outside of budget.

4. *Let each of your key people decide on his budget.* If you are to manage more by doing less, you need to rely on your key people to help you achieve your objectives. They will do a much better job for you if they have the conviction that they have the resources that they need to do their part. In large measure, their resources come from the budget. Therefore, do everything you can to let each of your key people make the decision for the budget with which he will have to work. With this approach, your people will generally be understanding and reasonable even when there is less budget money available than you and they would like.

If you don't already like budgets, I can't guarantee that you will get to like them by following the guidelines I have presented or by eliminating any budget maladies that you may face. However, I believe I can guarantee that you will be on friendlier terms with your budget.

HOW TO BUDGET

1. Develop a budget that will be variable in relation to actual accomplishment.
2. Include only controllable expenses.
3. Specify how to handle unplanned expenditures.
4. Let each of your key people decide on his budget.

KEY POINT: *Develop your budget to support your program.*

REFERENCES

1. James L. Peirce, "The Budget Comes of Age," *Harvard Business Review,* May-June, 1954, p. 66.
2. "He Oils the Wheels at Clark Equipment," *Business Week,* Apr. 15, 1967, p. 70.

7

DEVELOPING YOUR FORECAST

FORECAST *A projection of what will happen by a certain time.*

Perhaps you've heard the story of the man who set up a hot dog stand. He located it well, gave his customers their money's worth, and served his customers with a smile. Gradually, his business grew to the point where he made enough money to send his son off to college. While his son was away, he expanded his business, got a larger sign, and prospered more than ever.

One day his son came home. He saw what his father had done and exclaimed, "Father, haven't you heard about the downturn in business that's coming?" His father thought, "Now that my son has been away to college, he certainly knows more than I. He must be right."

The man took down the big sign, economized by reducing the size of his hot dogs, and wore a worried look. Gradually, his business went downhill. Finally, he closed his hot dog stand and concluded, "My son was right. There was a business downturn."

It is easy to see that this man would have been better off if he had never heard of the projected downturn in business. Does this mean that forecasts *can* do more harm than good?

WHY FORECAST?

It is true that a forecast—whether optimistic or pessimistic—can hurt your performance as a manager. You are likely to hurt your performance if you allow yourself to be controlled by a forecast that you should do something about. However, you can also suffer serious consequences if you do not forecast. To identify some of the things that can happen when you don't forecast, perhaps you'd like to take the exercise shown in Figure 7-1.

FIGURE 7-1   What Can Happen If You Don't Forecast?

(✔)	*Consequence*
____	1. You may set unrealistic objectives.
____	2. You may pay higher prices than necessary for goods, services, or money.
____	3. You may maintain or reduce the size of your operations when you should expand.
____	4. You may lose trained employees.
____	5. You may lose your share of market even though your sales increase.
____	6. You may have costly unutilized equipment.
____	7. You may have a costly finished-goods inventory.
____	8. You may miss delivery commitments or other important deadlines.
____	9. You may have inadequate cash.
____	10. You may not achieve attainable objectives.

Let's examine further each of the ten consequences.

Consequence No. 1 is likely if you set objectives that do not take into account indicators on which your performance is directly dependent. If you are in the construction business, for example, what you can accomplish may be directly related to the number of building permits issued within the geographical area that you serve. Your forecast need not be the same as your objectives, incidentally. In general, your objectives should be higher then your forecast.

Consequence No. 2 is likely if you are unaware that the prices of goods, services, or money that you will need in substantial quantity are going to go up. Some firms, for example, make borrowing arrangements for money before they actually need it because they believe that interest rates are going to rise.

Consequence No. 3 is likely when you are unaware of your opportunities or when you are going to have a significant increased level of activity that you could have foreseen. Many production managers, for example, have been caught short because they did not gear up for production surges that they could have predicted by working more closely with the sales department.

Consequence No. 4 is likely when you have frequent or extended employee layoffs. Many managers avoid employee layoffs by predicting future needs for production and by using slack periods to build up inventory or to accomplish other activities that will be needed later.

Consequence No. 5 is likely if you are unaware of the projected total volume of business that will be done in the market you serve. Many a manager has been surprised to find that his firm's position in the market it serves has dwindled even though the firm's annual sales had increased at an annual rate of 10 percent. What happened was that total sales in the market had increased at an annual rate of 20 percent.

Consequence No. 6 is likely if you purchase expensive equipment, perhaps to meet a current need, without projecting what the future need will be for the equipment. For example, many firms have had computer installations made without thinking through how the computer would be utilized. The result has been poor utilization of computer equipment and excessive cost—often to do little more than was done previously with less sophisticated methods.

Consequence No. 7 is likely if you produce goods without an adequate knowledge of whether they will be sold. This is a particular problem for firms that distribute through middlemen such as wholesalers or dealers. Just because goods are being purchased by middlemen does not mean that they are being purchased by the ultimate consumer. The result can be a buildup of finished-goods inventory that has expensive carrying costs and that may have to be sold at reduced prices.

Consequence No. 8 is likely if you do not predict the number of rush orders that you will get for goods or services. Your production schedule will be in a continual state of upheaval if you do not make standard provision for a certain number of rush orders that are often predictable, for example, through an analysis of past records.

Consequence No. 9 is likely if you have slow-paying accounts receivable or if you have to make a large expenditure to produce goods and services for unusually large orders. Many firms have shown excellent profits on their financial statements but have had to sell out or go out of business because of inadequate cash.

Consequence No. 10 is likely if you do not keep abreast of changing internal and external conditions that affect whether you attain your objectives. If, for example, you have traffic responsibility and it develops that your main carrier faces the possibility of a labor strike, you should predict how you will be affected. Then, perhaps you can make alternative arrangements with other carriers or develop some other solution that will still enable you to attain your objectives for delivery service to customers.

Sound forecasting can help you to avoid the kinds of consequences described above. However, you have no guarantee of success; business is always a gamble. The purpose of your forecast is to help increase the odds in your favor. Forecast to plan the controllable and to identify what will happen if you don't, or if you do, take certain actions. In short, *forecast with a view to what you can make happen.*

HOW TO FORECAST

At some point, there's a fine line between forecasting and guessing. I'd say you're guessing if you buy an expensive piece of equipment based upon intuition or feel for what you believe will be the future need for the equipment. I'd say you're forecasting if you buy the equipment based upon a systematic attempt to identify just how much application the equipment will have. On the assumption that you want to do your forecasting on a systematic basis, I recommend that you follow the guidelines which follow.

1. *Identify one or more factors that have a critical effect on whether you achieve your objectives.*   Probably every manager should forecast his anticipated work load, his requirements for manpower, and his costs; these factors are generally critical to what any manager wants to achieve. Most managers have additional needs for forecasting. For example, a methods engineer once studied the production planning system of a container plant. In his report he stated:

> Plant management is recognizing the serious need for forecasting probable order input volumes in addition to analyzing data on orders already received before making decisions to adjust manufacturing activities. Effective forecasting can provide a "load cushion" whereby more short lead-time orders can be processed through the plant with fewer interruptions and set-backs of existing orders. Plant management is presently working toward the development of sound forecasting techniques.

The study contained recommendations for a forecasting method that the responsible manager adopted; the result was a considerable improvement in delivery service to customers.

One way for you to identify those factors that have a critical effect on whether you achieve your objectives is to develop and use a checklist under the headings: 7 M's and an F. Such a checklist is shown in Figure 7-2. Generally, it will be unnecessary for you to do forecasting in connection with those factors that have a noncritical effect on whether you achieve your objectives. For example, forecasting your needs for specific materials may not be necessary if the materials are readily available or if you can get along with substitutes.

FIGURE 7-2   What Should You Forecast?

Note: "Basis for" column shows only one example of how a particular forecast is used.

MARKETS	Basis for:
____ Total sales	Setting profit objectives
____ Sales by product	Planning or revising product line
____ Sales by industry	Making field sales assignments
____ Sales by geographical area	Establishing or revising methods of distribution
____ Sales by salesman	Setting sales quotas (objectives)
____ Sales for new product	Planning advertising expenditure
____ Sales by season or cycle	Planning special marketing efforts during low-sales periods
____ Share of market	Planning research and development effort
____ Number of customer orders	Planning new system of order processing
____ Price levels	Expanding or contracting sales organization
____ What competitors will do	Planning programs for fast counteraction

MEN	Basis for:
____ Number of new employees required	Planning recruiting effort
____ Number of quits	Developing and conducting a training program
____ Number of absences	Planning job coverage
____ Length of learning time	Determining hiring dates
____ Number of lost-time accidents	Improving working conditions
____ Amount of overtime required	Adding another shift
____ Number of persons to be laid off	Planning work assignments
____ Possibility of strike	Stockpiling or curtailing production
____ Number of meeting attendees	Making meeting arrangements

MACHINES	Basis for:
____ Number of new machines required	Planning production capacity
____ Number of breakdowns	Making shift maintenance assignments

——— Amount of maintenance required

Contracting outside maintenance service

——— Equipment   utilization

Seeking business to utilize un-used capacity

——— Number of orders with short lead time

Allocating productive capacity

——— Number of orders with long runs

Developing delivery schedule

MATERIALS

Basis for:

——— Amount of direct material needed

Planning lead times for pur-chases

——— Amount of finished-goods inven-tory required

Developing production schedule

——— Amount of in-process inventory

Purchasing   material-handling equipment

——— Production from crops

Negotiating purchase prices

——— Number of new-product intro-ductions

Hiring additional production en-gineers

——— Product mix

Planning packaging requirements

MONEY

Basis for:

——— Cash flow

Making arrangements for short-term borrowing

——— Profit

Deciding amount of quarterly dividend

——— Cost of money

Determining when to float a bond issue

——— Labor cost

Developing price of long-term contract

——— Inventory   investment

Determining selling prices

——— Selling price of stock

Planning acquisition program

METHODS

Basis for:

——— Reaction to new policy, pro-cedure, organization change, or other management action

Planning how to get necessary acceptance

——— How long present system will handle work load

Conducting feasibility study for new system

——— Outcome of legal action

Deciding whether to continue present business method

——— Success of competitive program

Deciding whether to follow suit

MANAGEMENT

Basis for:

——— Number of new managers re-quired

Utilizing a psychological ap-praisal service

___ Number of trained replacements required	Installing a management development program
___ Number of quits	Developing a revised compensation plan
___ Number of managers needed with specialized skills	Installing an educational-assistance program
FACILITIES	*Basis for:*
___ Production space required	Planning new construction
___ Warehouse space required	Initiating inventory management study
___ Number of freight cars required	Making long-term arrangements with carriers
___ Amount of utility services required	Negotiating prices for utility services
___ Whether contractor's construction schedule will be met	Determining when to hire and train new employees

2. *Determine how often you need your forecast.*   Most managers need to develop both regular and special forecasts.

You should probably develop *regular* forecasts when you

 a. Set your objectives. A forecast can help you identify industry trends or other major influences on what you can accomplish.

 b. Have responsibility for a high-volume or high-cost activity. Order processing, production planning, and customer service are examples of such activities. You may require weekly or even daily forecasts so you can allocate your people, equipment, facilities, or other resources as effectively and efficiently as possible.

You should probably make *special* forecasts when you

 a. Must make decisions that have significant cost implications. Before finalizing decisions, you should normally forecast the effects of major purchases of materials or equipment, major installations of systems, major construction, major expansion or contraction, major expenditures for research and development, major orders or contracts, and negotiations for labor agreements.

 b. Must contend with unexpected internal or external events that can have a significant effect on the attainment of your objectives. Normally you should forecast the effects of unexpected internal events such as strikes, acts of God, mergers, and unscheduled availability of new products or services. Likewise, you should forecast the effects of unexpected external events such as loss or addition of major accounts, competitive actions and government legislation.

Many managers think of a forecast primarily in terms of a sales forecast. If this has been your view, I hope I have made clear that there are many other occasions throughout the year when you can use a forecast to help you improve your performance.

3. *Use a forecasting method that balances accuracy, timeliness, and economy.* This means that you shouldn't invest any more in a forecast than it's worth.

Take sales forecasting. Large firms can generally afford to spend much more money to develop a sales forecast than a small firm can. One study[1] shows that the approach to forecasting used by many large firms is:

a. Forecast general business conditions for the entire economy.
b. From that forecast and other data, forecast the sales volume of the industry.
c. Estimate what share of the industry sales volume the individual firm can obtain.

Some large firms utilize electronic computers to assess the interactions of many different indicators and their influence on sales volume.[2] For example, computers are used for input-output analysis to forecast markets by tracing buying and selling relationships between industries.[3]

Most large firms utilize a combination of forecasting techniques such as those shown in Figure 7-3.

FIGURE 7-3 Techniques Used in Forecasting Chemical Market Volume[4]

1. *Quantitative Types*
   a. Statistical Trend Analysis
   b. Consumption Pattern Analysis
   c. Correlation Analysis
   d. Historical Analogy
   e. Customer Consumption Pattern

2. *Qualitative Types*
   a. Sample of Industry Opinion
   b. Consensus of Management Opinion
   c. Marketing Department Estimates

The typical approach to forecasting used by small firms is:
a. Project the firm's sales, either by individual products or in total.
b. Modify their projection as required by information on market trends.

The small firm's sales figures are easily and cheaply available. Forecasts of general business conditions and of industry sales require outside data and are more likely to be expensive. The small firm can modify projection of its sales figures from knowledge about its principal customers. It may serve too small a portion of the industry market, or may be selling a product not easily identified with a well-defined industry, so that its market share has little meaning.

Sales forecasting methods are usually fairly well defined in both large and small firms because sales forecasting is generally done on a regular basis. However, special forecasts may require new or modified approaches. For example, I once worked with a newspaper that had about outgrown its current facilities and had to decide how to expand. Here are the steps that we followed:

a. We forecast the population and number of households for the next thirty years in the newspaper's marketing area.

b. Based upon this information, we forecast the daily and Sunday newspaper circulation for the next thirty years.

c. Based upon the circulation forecast and management's policies for advertising linage and for the newspaper's total number of pages, we forecast newsprint tonnage requirements plus personnel and space needs.

With this information, we identified and evaluated various alternatives for expanding facilities. Then the publisher made a decision about the best alternative which served as the basis for plans to purchase property, design and construct new facilities, order and install new equipment, order critical materials, and integrate the existing operation into the new operation. The various forecasts took only about six weeks to develop; fortunately, they were timed to provide a lead time of about two years for developing and implementing plans to complete the expansion.

Long-term forecasts are often quite inaccurate; nevertheless, they still provide managers with better guidelines for decisions than the managers would have otherwise. Short-term forecasts can be quite accurate if you spend the time and money to develop a sound forecasting method. For example, many firms find that they can forecast sales within a 5 percent average deviation between forecasted and actual sales results.[5] Before you develop your forecast, however, make sure you determine how accurate it needs to be. Then you will have a basis for deciding whether you should spend an hour, a day, a week, or a month on your forecast. This is not necessarily time that you must personally spend on the forecast. As a manager, you can delegate the task of developing the forecast or you can seek specialized assistance; however, you must accept responsibility for the forecast and the way it is used.

Regardless of the forecasting method that you use, make sure you *forecast with a view to what you can make happen.* There is little point in forecasting if you are going to resign yourself to what you consider to be the inevitable. Time and use your forecast to determine what you can do to help you get the results you want.

HOW TO FORECAST

1. Identify one or more factors that have a critical effect on whether you achieve your objectives.

2. Determine how often you need your forecast.

3. Use a forecasting method that balances accuracy, timeliness, and economy.

KEY POINT: *Forecast with a view to what you can make happen.*

REFERENCES

1. "Forecasting in Small Business Planning," *Management Research Summary,* Small Business Administration, Washington, April, 1961.
2. *Forecasting Sales,* Business Policy Study, no. 106, National Industrial Conference Board, Inc., New York, 1963, p. 82.
3. "Input-Output Searches the Seventies," *Sales Management,* Aug. 1, 1968, p. 27.
4. K. J. Van Arnum, "Measuring and Forecasting Markets," *Chemical Engineering Progress,* December, 1964, pp. 18-22.
5. "Sales Forecasting: Is 5% Error Good Enough?" *Sales Management,* Dec. 15, 1967, p. 42.

8

DEVELOPING YOUR ORGANIZATION STRUCTURE

ORGANIZATION   *Design of the number and kinds
of positions, along with corresponding duties and
responsibilities, required to achieve or exceed
objectives.*

You won't manage as much as you should if you let your organization
grow like Topsy.

DESIGN IS IMPORTANT

Many managers suffer waste, frustration, high costs, and delay simply
because they give inadequate attention to their organization structures.
They seem oblivious of the fact that organization makes its own contribution to the success of an enterprise. The contribution of organization is *separate and distinct from that made by people.*

   Recently I worked with a pulp and paper company in connection
with a major expansion of production facilities. Maintenance management gave special attention to the design of its organization structure,
and as a result, was able to establish multicraft mechanic positions

rather than have separate positions for millwrights, pipefitters, welders, and so on. This has simplified administration of maintenance and has produced annual cost savings estimated at 25 percent as compared with conventional maintenance organization. Furthermore, the mechanics like being able to develop their skills and to work in more than one craft.

The design of an organization structure can be compared to the design of a building. I doubt whether you'd construct a building without having a carefully thought out design. The design is what determines whether your building will meet your present and future needs. So it is with your organization structure. If you add positions or establish organizational relationships without a carefully thought out design, it is likely that the organization structure will be inadequate for your present and future needs. As a building can collapse, so can your organization. By the same token, either your building or your organization structure can be too expensive. If you add a position, for example, you should make sure that you will get adequate return on that position. A position that costs $10,000 per year utilizes the gross profit (sales less cost of goods sold) on $30,000 in sales if the gross profit is 33.3 percent of sales.

SOME ORGANIZATION WEAKNESSES

Some of the commonest organization weaknesses are shown in Figure 8-1. Try testing your own company or department for these symptoms.

FIGURE 8-1   Do You Have Any of These Weaknesses in Your Organization Structure?

Yes	*No*	
___	___	1. Your position or others must be filled by persons with unique combinations of abilities.
___	___	2. You lack written job descriptions for yourself and your people.
___	___	3. You have people who are not sure to whom they report.
___	___	4. You have dead-ended positions.
___	___	5. You have people who complain about the amount of time they spend in committee meetings.
___	___	6. You have "assistant" positions.
___	___	7. You or your people could handle more responsibility.

Weakness No. 1: Perhaps you are a Jack-of-all-trades in that you have a unique combination of abilities. If you require your successor to have similar qualifications, your position may be improperly designed. Just because you can develop new products or services in addition to managing your operation, for example, is no reason to assume that someone else should be expected to have this same combination of abilities.

Entrepreneurs often have this organization weakness, and consequently do not develop replacements for themselves.

You also have an organization weakness if one or more of the positions that your people hold require unique combinations of abilities. Some salesmen, for example, have excellent ability to open new accounts but poor ability to provide routine service to existing accounts. To resolve this problem, some firms have two kinds of sales positions: one with responsibility primarily for new business and the other with responsibility primarily for servicing existing business. In production, some managers have excellent ability to start up new facilities but poor ability to manage a going operation. To resolve this problem, some firms establish two kinds of production management positions: one with responsibility for start-up activities (and other special projects) and the other with responsibility for managing a going operation.

If you are with a nonprofit organization, you may face a similar weakness in your organization structure. For example, clergymen are often expected to function both as ministers and as administrators even though they may have little interest or training in administration. In universities, professors are sometimes expected to be both excellent teachers and excellent researchers.

Weakness No. 2: Unless you have written job descriptions for yourself and your people, it is unlikely that you have thought through the design of your organization structure. It is also unlikely that you and your people have common understanding about who is responsible for what.

Weakness No. 3: Chances are one or more of your people do work for, or take direction from, more than one person. The result can be confusion about who reports to whom. I have found this situation in both large and small organizations.

Weakness No. 4: Dead-ended positions cause turnover of good people and attract mediocre people who may not be able to get better jobs elsewhere. Not everyone has the ability to progress to positions of greater responsibility, but each person should certainly be in a line of progression from among one or more lines that have been carefully thought out for every position in your organization. Your lines of progression can, of course, include lateral moves, and some positions may have more than one line of progression.

Weakness No. 5: Committees can serve a very useful purpose if their functions are carefully defined and understood. However, some managers rely entirely too much on committees and waste the time of all participants. I recall one group of department heads that spent more than a third of their time in various committee meetings. The president assigned responsibilities to committees that he should have assigned to individual department heads.

Weakness No. 6: The person who holds an "assistant" position often does not really know what his own responsibilities are, and those with whom he works are generally even more in doubt. An assistant may substitute for his boss or he may do detail work or he may carry out special projects or he may have clear-cut managerial responsibility. Too often an assistant functions at the pleasure of his boss. I know one firm that has several "assistant manager" positions each of which is supposed to have similar duties and responsibilities. In some instances the assistant is training to replace his boss and has line authority; in other instances, the assistant functions in a staff capacity by doing his boss's paper work. A good secretary can often perform most of the duties of the so-called "assistant manager."

Weakness No. 7: Many sales managers want a separate sales force for every product line. Yet present salesmen could handle additional product lines if they were organized according to markets rather than products. Other sales managers organize their salesmen by geographical territory, and their skilled salesmen spend over half of their time calling on small accounts and performing duties that are way beneath their level of skill and experience.

These are two examples where salesmen could handle additional responsibility if the sales managers were to organize differently. Managers in other functional areas also have similar opportunities to increase the responsibility that some of their people have, and at the same time justify increased compensation for these people.

You may have a similar opportunity for your own position. Perhaps you could spend more time on your more important responsibilities if you delegated more of your less important responsibilities. In addition, perhaps you should seek responsibility for functions that are not now being assigned to anyone. For example, I once had responsibility for corporate training and saw the need for my firm to research and develop improved methods of managing for its own use. I proposed that my firm establish the position of director of management services. Later I was asked to fill this position, which was also designed to include responsibility for corporate training.

Whether or not you have any of the organizational weaknesses that I have described, you should know how to avoid them.

HOW TO DEVELOP YOUR ORGANIZATION STRUCTURE

Perhaps your organization has someone who specializes in organization planning. If so, he can help you identify and solve your organization problems. However, he is still dependent upon you and all other managers because he cannot do the whole job himself. In any event, if you want to get results more through your people than through yourself, you must give adequate attention to your organization structure. I propose that you follow eight guidelines.

1. *Review your program and objectives.* You should take an in-depth look at your organization structure at least once a year. A logical time to do this is when you set your objectives and develop your program for accomplishing your objectives. If you plan to make significant changes in sales, production, costs, or profit, you will probably include organization changes as items in your program. For example, if you wish to take greater advantage of the computer capability available to you, perhaps you will need to add a computer specialist or establish a committee to conduct feasibility studies. In any event, there are probably some organizational changes that you should consider making—including any realignments in the duties and responsibilities of the positions that currently report to you.

2. *Design each position so a short label describes its main responsibility.* One way to make your organization structure function smoothly is to give your positions titles that are both descriptive and short enough to use in normal conversation. Try to avoid the use of titles that have "assistant" in them. Also, avoid euphemisms. If the main responsibility of a "customer relations representative" is to sell, for example, then perhaps he should be called "salesman" or "sales representative" if you want your customers to understand what he does.

3. *Assign to each position clear-cut duties, responsibility, and authority so each position holder will have freedom to act.* The best way to do this is to put it in writing. Some managers say they don't wish to give an employee a written job description because they want flexibility and can't think of everything that they may want him to do. This is easily handled, however, with a "perform other duties as assigned" statement at the bottom of the job description.

A position description for a manager in a religious organization is shown in Figure 8-2. The format is applicable to most organizations. The "responsibilities common to administrators" refers to the kinds of responsibilities that all managers have. (See Figure 1-4.)

A sample job description for a production employee is shown in Figure 8-3. It clarifies to whom the employee reports, the main purpose of the job, the equipment for which he is responsible, and his specific duties and responsibilities. Also note how simple and easy to understand it is.

When a person knows what he is responsible for and exactly to whom he reports, he can concentrate on getting things done rather than on whether he is infringing on somebody else's prerogatives.

FIGURE 8-2   Position Description for Diocesan Director of Charity

---

FUNCTION:

Provide overall planning and direction for Catholic Charities activities within the Diocese so that health and welfare needs are met as effectively and economically as possible and in accordance with the "Philosophy of Catholic Charities" and approved basic policies and plans.

ACCOUNTABILITY: The Most Reverend Bishop

SPECIFIC DUTIES AND RESPONSIBILITIES: Perform duties shown on "Responsibilities Common to Administrators of The Catholic Charities of the Diocese" and as follows:

1. Approve annual plans for agencies, institutions, voluntary groups, and Diocesan Office departments of Catholic Charities within the Diocese; prepare and submit for approval by the Bishop an integrated summary plan.
2. See that approved annual plans are carried out.
3. See that approved allocations of funds are made to each agency, institution, or group of Catholic Charities.
4. Plan, direct, and supervise the activities of the staff of the Diocesan Office of Charity.
5. Review administrators' proposals for new or improved facilities; forward to Diocesan Building Committee as appropriate.
6. Approve administrators' requests for funds to meet emergency health and welfare needs.
7. See that there is representation and participation of Catholic Charities in appropriate Catholic, professional, community, government, and legislative organizations and programs concerned with health and welfare.
8. Review progress of all Catholic Charities activities at least quarterly.
9. Plan and conduct meetings of administrators at least quarterly.
10. Approve research and development projects or, if appropriate, request approval from the Bishop.
11. Serve as ex-officio member of governing boards or bodies for agencies, institutions, and volunteer groups of Catholic Charities within the Diocese.
12. Arrange for annual financial audit of each Catholic Charities agency or institution.

---

4. *Establish line and staff positions that will enable you to realize the advantages of both centralization and decentralization.* The higher up you are in management the more you have to be concerned about the number and kinds of line and staff positions that you have. A line position, such as in production or sales, contributes directly to the purpose of the enterprise; a staff position, such as in personnel or accounting, contributes indirectly by providing specialized service and/or functional direction to line positions. In both line and staff positions, you can have too much centralization or too much decentralization of authority and responsibility. For example, if a salesman has to get clearance from the

FIGURE 8-3   Job Description for J-2 Operator

Responsible to: Shift Foreman

Job Purpose: Cook, extrude, and cut dough into pellets to produce quality snack product.

Area of Responsibility: All equipment from Merchen Feeder Surge Bin through the entrance of pellet air conveying line.

Duties and Responsibilities: According to approved policies, procedures, and schedules:

1. Maintain proper feed rates to J-2 Cooker.
2. Keep cooker fill at prescribed level.
3. Check pellet moisture and adjust to standard.
4. Maintain steady Esterline kilowatt recording.
5. Adjust Sterlco units to hold even extrusion pressure.
6. Sample the pellet quality and make necessary adjustments.
7. Adjust, clean, or replace face cutter blades as pellet quality requires.
8. Remove and install clean dies when necessary.
9. Abide by housekeeping and safety rules of the department.
10. Work cooperatively with other employees; e.g., dryer operator and maintenance men.
11. Give your relief man all necessary information to enable him to do his job effectively.
12. Make suggestions to shift foreman that may help cut costs, improve quality, make your job easier, and the like.
13. Perform other duties as assigned by shift foreman.

national sales manager every time he wants to make a concession to a customer, there may be too much centralization in the line. By the same token, if the salesman can make significant concessions to customers without checking with higher authority, there may be too much decentralization in the line. If each division of a company has its own independently functioning staff, there may be too much decentralization of staff positions. If most of the staff positions are located at headquarters with very few such positions in divisions, there may be too much centralization of staff. I know of one company that was crippled for years because there was too much centralization of staff. The staff heads were officers and outranked the general managers of the divisions. When a general manager wanted to make an important decision, he generally had to get clearance from each of the staff heads.

The computer has been a major factor in the trend toward centralization of many functions. Today, for example, a number of firms have a corporate director of physical distribution with responsibility for traffic and transportation, warehousing, materials handling, protective packaging, order processing, production planning, inventory control, customer service, market forecasting, and plant and warehouse site selection. Many of these functions formerly were decentralized.[1]

Centralization-decentralization studies are often complicated and may be beyond the scope of your authority and responsibility. However, you may be able to initiate such studies where you feel there might be significant advantages either to centralize more or to decentralize more. In any event, you can lend your support to this kind of organization planning effort.

5. *Establish each position on the basis of the knowledge and skills likely to be found in an individual.* As you evaluate your organization structure, make sure you look at your positions and not the people in them. This will help you think in terms of the knowledge and skills required for each of your positions rather than in terms of unusual combinations of knowledge and skills that some of your people may have. Don't forget to evaluate your own position on the same basis.

6. *Design each position so each position holder can make maximum use of his knowledge and skills.* When you spend your time doing tasks such as processing routine paper work, your production is worth only what a clerk gets paid. When you spend your time on managing tasks, your production is worth at least what you are being paid. Therefore, your position should be designed so you can concentrate on your managing tasks. The same is true for all your people. If you can design their positions so they can utilize their highest level of knowledge and skills most of the time, you will get a far better return on what you invest in your people, and they are likely to be much happier than otherwise. At the same time, you can design a line of progression for each of your positions so there is at least one path for each of your people to follow in achieving the highest level of responsibility that his abilities and ambition will allow.

In the production area, many firms today no longer rely upon the industrial engineer to do the bulk of work measurement and standards setting. For this purpose, they have established the position of analyst or technician that can be filled by a high school graduate with proper training in the required techniques. This frees the industrial engineer so he can concentrate on major cost-reduction or methods-improvement projects that require a higher level of knowledge and skills.

7. *Design positions so decision-making authority is as close as possible to the scene of action.* If your people must get your approval for routine decisions, you are wasting their time and yours. Try to design your positions so you delegate as much authority and responsibility to your people

as possible. Many managers let their people settle customer complaints, reschedule production, buy supplies from outside vendors, and inspect their own production to see that it is within quality-control limits.

Generally speaking, you should avoid giving committees decision-making authority and responsibility. Use committees to study and advise but hold one person responsible for decisions arising from a committee's efforts. For example, hold your production superintendent responsible for decisions affecting the safety of your employees even though he may use a safety committee to help him develop and implement safety programs.

8. *Give managerial positions responsibility for as many positions as possible.*   I am not recommending empire building for managers who judge their importance on the basis of the number of positions they have reporting to them. Rather, I am recommending that you develop as efficient and economical an organization structure as you can. This means to have no more positions than you really need and to avoid reliance upon rules of thumb about how many people a manager can supervise.

One study shows that technology has a significant effect on organization. In decribing this study, Dr. Leonard Sayles of the Graduate School of Business, Columbia University, says:

> In the unit-production firms sampled, the first-line supervisor had an average span of control of between 21 and 30 employees, but in the process-production concerns his span declined to between 11 and 20, while in batch-or-mass-production companies it went as high as 41 to 50. Similarly the number of people reporting to the top executive varied from a median of four in unit production, to seven in mass production, to 10 in process firms. The average number of levels of management used by the sampled firms ranged from three in unit-production to six in process companies; mass-production firms typically used four.[2]

In designing your organization structure, you may have difficulty evaluating the effect of technology per se, but you can evaluate your positions in terms of factors such as similarity of responsibility, complexity of duties, geographical locations of positions, and communication required between positions. If, for example, a manager has responsibility for positions that require a great deal of personal direction, he can handle fewer of such positions than he could handle if he were responsible for less demanding positions.

While a manager should have responsibility for as many positions as possible, he can also have too many positions reporting to him. Many a president has this problem—in many instances due to the number of staff heads that he has reporting directly to him. One solution for a single-division manufacturing company is shown in Figure 8-4.

FIGURE 8-4   An Organization Structure for a Manufacturing Company with Corporate Staff Services under Administration

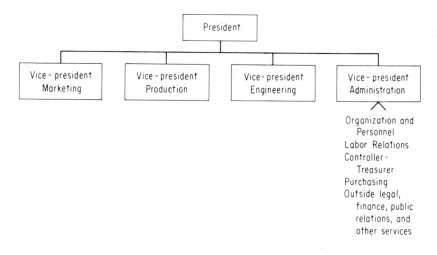

A vice-president of administration can relieve the president who has too many positions reporting to him and can see that the efforts of various staff functions are properly integrated and coordinated in serving the line.

If, as I have tried to show, organization makes a separate and distinct contribution to your effectiveness as a manager, you should develop your organization structure as objectively as possible. It is people who fill positions, but their effectiveness is a function of the kinds of duties and responsibilities that they have. Therefore, the key point of this chapter is: *Organize around necessary activities rather than around people.* When you have done this, you may find that you have too few or too many people, or that you lack people with necessary knowledge and skills. This is the point at which you may have to compromise and settle for less than you need. But your organization structure will still represent a blueprint toward which you can work.

HOW TO DEVELOP YOUR ORGANIZATION STRUCTURE

1. Review your program and objectives.
2. Design each position so a short label describes its main responsibility.

3. Assign to each position clear-cut duties, responsibility, and authority so each position holder will have freedom to act.

4. Establish line and staff positions that will enable you to realize the advantages of both centralization and decentralization.

5. Establish each position on the basis of the knowledge and skills likely to be found in an individual.

6. Design each position so each position holder can make maximum use of his knowledge and skills.

7. Design positions so decision-making authority is as close as possible to the scene of action.

8. Give managerial positions responsibility for as many positions as possible.

KEY POINT: *Organize around necessary activities*
rather than around people.

REFERENCES

1. "New Strategies to Move Goods," *Business Week,* Sept. 24, 1966, p. 112.
2. Leonard R. Sayles, "Managing Organizations: Old Textbooks Do Die!" *Columbia Journal of World Business,* Fall, 1966, p. 84.

9

DEVELOPING YOUR POLICIES

POLICY *A general guide for decision making and individual actions.*

A manager who spends his time *doing* rarely has defined policies. Often he tends to think, "If I pinpoint what our policies are, my people can make the decisions and I won't be needed as much around here."

It isn't hard to see the fallacy in this kind of thinking. Yet it appears to be prevalent. Other managers don't understand their responsibility for developing policies. They believe that only an organization's officers are responsible for developing policies. But this is a responsibility of every manager—at least insofar as his own area of responsibility is concerned.

Regardless of your level of responsibility, do you have defined policies in the areas listed in Figure 9-1?

If you don't have defined policies in each of the eight areas, you should certainly consider developing (or initiating) them.

FIGURE 9-1   Do You Have Defined Policies in These Areas?

Yes	No	
___	___	1. Scope of your products or services
___	___	2. Whom you will serve internally and externally
___	___	3. Quality level of products or services provided
___	___	4. Sources and determination of income
___	___	5. Determination of expenditures and costs
___	___	6. Scheduling of orders for products or services
___	___	7. Resolving claims and complaints from those served or affected
___	___	8. Personnel administration (e.g., selection and hiring, placement, compensation, absence)

WHY DEFINE POLICIES

There are at least three reasons why you should have defined policies.

1. *To improve decisions.*   The degree of success that you have as a manager is directly dependent upon the decisions that you and your people make. If, for example, decisions about customer complaints are wrong, inconsistent, or delayed, your performance suffers. On the other hand, defined policies about how to handle customer complaints will help both your experienced and new people to make sound, consistent, and prompt decisions.

2. *To develop your people.*   Defined policies help you delegate because they provide your people with the same kinds of guidelines that you would use if you were making the decisions. If, for example, you have defined your overtime policies, your first-line supervisors may be able to make their own judgements about when to authorize overtime. The more responsibility that your people have for making decisions, the more they must rely upon themselves and the more they develop themselves for handling increased responsibility.

3. *To save your time.*   Some managers bog themselves down with routine decisions—often subconsciously—because they want to be involved in the action. They claim that they cannot define their policies because each decision is different and they must have flexibility. Generally, however, these managers have spent little time trying to define their policies and they don't really wish to save time by having their people make more of the decisions. If, on the other hand, you are the kind of manager who has more constructive things to do, defining your policies is one way to free yourself from having to make routine decisions.

KINDS OF POLICIES

Policies can be classified by functional area (e.g., marketing, production, personnel, finance) and by organizational unit (e.g., corporate, group, divisional, departmental). The most significant policies are those defined at the top organizational unit, because they represent top management's guidelines for the operation of the entire enterprise. Examples of such policies in the case of a newspaper are those printed on the "editorials and opinions" page of the *Minneapolis Tribune:*

1. Report the news fully and impartially in the news columns.
2. Express the opinions of the *Tribune* in—but only in—editorials on the editorial/opinion pages.
3. Publish all sides of important controversial issues.

Examples of marketing policies (guidelines) that one division of a major company developed are shown in Figure 9-2.

FIGURE 9-2 Marketing Guidelines Developed by One Division of a Major Company

1. *Development of New Products*
   We will develop new products to meet the needs of the consumer rather than develop products which are easiest for the company to produce and sell.

2. *Test Marketing*
   We will test-market new products when the risk (potential loss) of national introduction, including capital investment, is greater than the test-marketing cost.

3. *Established Product Line*
   We will keep each product, size, and flavor in the product line only as long as it makes a contribution to profit.

4. *Marketing Group Function*
   We will organize to delegate accountability for all aspects of a given product to one individual who will have profit responsibility for that product.

5. *Sales Function*
   We will organize to achieve planned volume objectives by selling effectively distribution and promotional programs to the trade.

6. *Development of Distribution and Promotional Programs*
   We will develop distribution and promotional programs tailored to the requirements of individual market areas and based upon all pertinent factors including full input from field sales about current trade attitudes, effectiveness of previous programs, and competitive activity.

7. *Trade Relations*
   We will maintain a function independent of the sales organization to identify future trends, opportunities, and potential problems in the grocery business.

8. *Marketing Planning and Implementation*
We will develop and implement our marketing plans to meet the needs of the ultimate consumer and based on a "mix" of marketing elements that are given different weights depending on the product, category, consumer demand, and competitive considerations. The main elements in the marketing "mix" are: consumer perception of product quality and use characteristics, price, advertising message (copy), media target, consumer promotion, trade and price promotion, and packaging.

Note how Policy No. 8 defines the flexibility that a marketing manager has to develop and implement marketing plans. Some managers feel that policies restrict, when in reality, they can also be used to provide flexibility and freedom.

If your organization has not devoted the same kind of attention to the development of its policies, perhaps you can set the example by making sure that you have defined the policies that you need for your area of responsibility.

HOW TO DEVELOP YOUR POLICIES

These are actions that you can take to develop your policies.

1. *Define your long-range purpose.*   If you are in top management, make sure you have a clear concept about the business you are in. Otherwise, you and your organization may become unfortunate victims of new technology and better methods.

Professor Theodore Levitt of the Harvard Business School once startled a group of publishing executives by telling them that their competition was Xerox Corporation. He told them that they were not in the publishing business but, like Xerox, were in the business of communicating information.[1]

A recent ad of one major manufacturer of computers explains the company's interest in the laser beam. Reason: This company is interested in anything that makes information more useful for people. Do you have as enlightened a concept of your business in terms of the products or services that you provide?

If you are with a business organization, I hope you do not state your firm's purpose in terms of profit, return on investment, or money. These are fine units of measure for objectives, but they are a *result* of your being in a business that serves a meaningful purpose in our society. I like what one creative entrepreneur in the insurance field says:

> You can't work for money! Very few people will give you money unless you fulfill their needs. This means you need a higher purpose than that of making money.

One company that has done an excellent job of defining its long-range purpose is General Mills, Inc. Furthermore, the company makes this clear to all its people. In a recent issue of the company's magazine, *The Modern Millwheel,* this statement appears:

> We are determined to think of ourselves as experts in the creation, marketing and advertising primarily of consumer goods. Today, this largely means package foods, but what of tomorrow?[2]

At lower levels of management, you may also wish to define your long-range purpose. If, for example, you are an accounting manager, is your long-range purpose to provide management with economical and timely accounting data or is it to provide management with a modern management information and control system?

2. *Define your managing philosophy.*   The higher your level of responsibility in management, the more important it is that you define your managing philosophy. With such a philosophy, your managers have the assurance of knowing that there is supposed to be some order to the managing methods used throughout your organization. As a matter of fact, your managing methods should provide you with your most important competitive advantage over the long run.

Your managing philosophy should reflect what you and your managers feel is important, and it should be stated as simply as possible. Examples are shown in Figures 9-3 and 9-4.

FIGURE 9-3   The Managing Philosophy Developed by a Division of a Major Company

1. We believe in managing by objectives.

2. We believe that our company's future is directly dependent upon the kind of people we attract and develop.

3. We believe in promoting individuals on the basis of performance, personal growth, and potential.

4. We believe that managers should be sensitive to the individual needs of their people.

5. We believe that managers should encourage constructive controversy.

6. We believe that each manager should have some freedom in his managing methods.

7. We believe in achieving a balance between short-range and long-range results.

8. We believe in leading in the application of modern management tools such as the computer.

9. We believe in management by exception.

10. We believe in developing professional managers.

FIGURE 9-4   Basic Management Doctrine of the Department of the Navy[3]

1. CLEAR FUNDAMENTAL OBJECTIVES
2. CENTRALIZED POLICY DIRECTION
3. CLEAR EXECUTIVE AUTHORITY AND RESPONSIBILITY
4. MAXIMUM DECENTRALIZATION OF EXECUTION
5. MANAGEMENT BY EXCEPTION

3. *Define policies in those areas where you or your people make repeated decisions.* If you have purchasing responsibility, you and your people will make repeated buying decisions. If you have personnel responsibility, you and your people will make many selection and hiring decisions. You must determine for your own activity the kinds of decisions that are required most often. Then, if you don't already have policies, try to define some that will enable the decision making to be made as far down the line as possible.

4. *Determine how each policy will be enforced.* Some managers develop and announce a policy, then fail to enforce it. I recall a sales manager who announced the policy that raises would be given to salesmen strictly on a merit basis. During the following six months, three salesmen resigned, and in each instance, the sales manager tried to use salary increases to entice them to stay.

Generally, you should test a policy for a while before you announce it. However, when you do announce it, plan to enforce it if you want it to have meaning. In situations where you are not close enough to the scene to tell whether a new policy is being carried out, you might ask your people to report on its effectiveness within a month or two after it goes into effect. If you have an internal audit department, you might ask that the effectiveness of your policies be evaluated whenever there is a regular audit of your operation. In addition, you probably receive regular reports that will give you an indication as to how well your policies are being carried out. For example, your report on budget compliance should give you an indication as to whether your people are spending money according to approved policies.

5. *Specify how exceptions to policy are to be handled.* Probably no policy has ever been developed that took into account all possible situations. Therefore, you should avoid having policies that are completely inflexible.

Suppose you have the policy that all promotions are to be made from within your organization. Then suppose that you have the opportunity to fill a vacant position with an outsider who has knowledge and skills that you had never before visualized being needed in your organization. Should you make an exception to your promotion policy and hire him?

You and your people should have common understanding about the reasoning behind your present policies and about what to do when a current policy does not seem to be in the best interests of your organization. Generally, the person who made the original policy, or his successor, is the one who should authorize any exceptions to it. Probably he is also the one to cancel or revise any existing policies and to add any related policies.

Throughout this chapter, I hope I have made clear that your policies can be an important vehicle for your getting results through your people. I believe we can summarize with a key point: *Define your policies so your people can make most decisions.* Your policies are of little value unless somebody can act on them. If your people can do so, you probably have policies that are well conceived, understood, and effective.

HOW TO DEVELOP YOUR POLICIES

1. Define your long-range purpose.
2. Define your managing philosophy.
3. Define policies in those areas where you or your people make repeated decisions.
4. Determine how each policy will be enforced.
5. Specify how exceptions to policy are to be handled.

KEY POINT: *Define your policies so your people can make most decisions.*

REFERENCES

1. "What Business Are You Really In?" *Business Week,* Mar. 11, 1967, p. 179.
2. "Philosophy & Strategy," *The Modern Millwheel,* January, 1967, p. 16.
3. "New General Order Will Clarify Objectives and Responsibilities," *Navy Management Review,* July, 1963, p. 7.

10

DEVELOPING YOUR PROCEDURES

PROCEDURE   *A detailed method for carrying out a policy.*

To carry out your policies and to get things done, your people must have procedures or methods. You can either define how your people are to perform their activities or let each person develop his own ways of doing things. This poses a dilemma for many managers.

Suppose you have a sales policy to provide your salesmen with modern selling aids. Either you can develop standard procedures that you expect your salesmen to follow in using such aids, or you can let each salesman develop his own methods for using the aids. Take the situation described in Figure 10-1. What would you decide?

I know a national sales manager who faced the situation described in Figure 10-1. He decided to go ahead with the standard procedure, but it was a poor decision. His sales people had been used to having the freedom to develop their own selling methods, and they resented what appeared to be an effort to regiment them. Furthermore, some of his people felt that it was unsound for them to describe their company to a buyer before they had identified specific buyer interests.

90

FIGURE 10-1 Is a Standard Procedure Applicable Here?

You are a sales manager for a company that plans to expand into new markets. You are considering the development of a sales aid that will help your salesmen introduce the company to prospective buyers. You have in mind a "This Is Our Company" presentation piece that would take about ten minutes for each salesman to go through as a prelude to his exploring specific needs that a buyer might have. The investment in such a sales aid is relatively large, so you want to be sure the aid will be used. Should you develop a standard procedure to ensure that your salesmen will use the aid?

THE CASE AGAINST STANDARD PROCEDURES

There are at least three arguments against your use of standard procedures.

1. *You discourage initiative and imagination.*   Salesmen, engineers, researchers, and others with a great deal of creative responsibility tend to look upon standard procedures as restrictions. Even persons without much creative responsibility sometimes feel hemmed in by standard procedures. For example, I have seen suggestion systems and educational-assistance programs with standard procedures that actually discouraged, rather than promoted, employee initiative and imagination.

2. *You complicate jobs.*   Some organizations have thick standard-procedure manuals designed to cover almost every conceivable situation that an employee may face. Consequently, the employee's job is complicated by all the standard procedures that he is expected to follow. For example, I have seen situations where employees spend more time making out reports than in making the accomplishment that the reports describe. These situations often occur where the manager is defensive and is afraid that his people will make mistakes for which he will be held responsible.

3. *You will not attract and hold capable people.*   Of course it takes capable people to follow standard procedures. But your most capable people generally want to be held more accountable for achieving *results* than for performing their activities according to standard procedures or methods. They want the opportunity to develop new and better ways of doing things and to try out new solutions to the problems they face.

It is unlikely that they will accept or stay in positions where they feel they must function largely as automatons.

THE CASE FOR STANDARD PROCEDURES

There are at least three arguments for your use of standard procedures.

1. *You increase production.*   When left to their own devices, some employees will develop better work procedures or methods than other employees performing the same activities. By studying the best procedures or methods, you can generally develop the "one best way" to perform each activity. Then, by standardizing on the best way to perform each activity, you are generally able to increase production substantially. For example, many managers have increased production in the sales-service area by developing standardized ways to handle most correspondence with customers.

2. *You ensure quality of production.*   The lifeblood of any organization is usually its products or services. Internally, for example, a data-processing manager will be in trouble with those he serves if his reports are inaccurate. All employees make errors, so he needs to develop standard procedures to verify the accuracy of his data—especially input data on which an entire data-processing system is dependent.

3. *You reduce training costs.*   With standard procedures or methods, an employee can learn his job without having to waste time and money developing his own way of doing things. He is able to take advantage of what may be years of accumulated know-how for the job he now holds. He can be productive quickly because he doesn't have to "reinvent the wheel." Furthermore, he has the assurance that what he is doing is consistent with what the rest of the organization expects of him.

HOW TO DEVELOP YOUR PROCEDURES

The case for or against standard procedures is not entirely clear, is it? There are many variables for you to consider, including the size of your organization, the complexity of your products or services, the amount of creative responsibility that your people have, and the capability of your people. You have to decide about the kinds of procedures you need, but there are some guidelines.

1. *Develop standard procedures when significant gain or loss is at stake.*   If you have responsibility for repetitive operations such as routine sales or customer service, order processing, production of standardized products or services, or shipping, you probably need standard procedures or methods. Economically speaking, you have much to gain

or to lose depending upon the efficiency at which your people perform such operations. You also have much to gain or to lose where relatively large amounts of money are involved. Therefore, you should probably have the kinds of standard procedures shown in Figure 10-2.

FIGURE 10-2   Examples of Standard Procedures in Areas of Managerial Responsibility

Area of Responsibility	*Example of Standard Procedure*
Markets	Pricing of products or services
Men	Selection and hiring
Machines	Preventive maintenance
Materials	Inventory levels
Money	Buying
Methods	Forms control
Management	Salary administration
Facilities	Office furnishings

In the area of maintenance, employees can be injured or killed when working on equipment. Therefore, many maintenance managers have developed standard procedures such as that shown in Figure 10-3.

FIGURE 10-3   One Company's Tag-out Procedure

To prevent accidental injury to personnel and damage to equipment, this procedure for tagging equipment will be used.

1. Any employee working on equipment must first remove the source of energy and tag it out with a "Danger Tag" bearing his name and the date.
2. The employee must verify that the proper machine has been made safe.
3. Upon completion of the job, the "Danger Tag" must be removed promptly by the man whose name it bears.
4. The supervisor, in some cases, may remove an employee's tag if he is positive that the employee has gone home and all efforts have been exhausted to reach the employee. If the employee is reached by phone, he may be required to return to the mill, without pay, to remove his "Danger Tag."
5. Any of the following violations of the Tag-out Procedure will result in disciplinary action which may include discharge.
   a. Failure to tag out equipment when needed.
   b. Operating equipment that is tagged out.
   c. Removing someone else's "Danger Tag."
   d. Failure to remove one's own "Danger Tag" when job is completed.

2. *Make forms and instructions self-explanatory.*   Forms are a key element in the communications network of any organization. Often, however, the person who designs a form is the only one who understands it. You can help to streamline your organization's use of forms by making

sure that simple instructions are printed on your forms and by eliminating, or keeping to a minimum, any accompanying standard procedures.

3. *Get specialized assistance when an interdepartmental system may
be involved.*   As a manager, you are not expected to be a specialist in
the development of systems, procedures, and methods. Therefore you
should probably get specialized assistance whenever your system, procedure, or method has a direct effect upon the operation of more than
one department; you may also wish to get such assistance for just your
own department if there is much to be gained or lost. Get the help of
specialists such as systems and procedures analysts, methods engineers,
consultants, or suppliers in the development of systems for material
handling, data processing, accounting, purchasing, and other interdepartmental systems.

One critical interdepartmental system is your management control
reporting or management information system. You will be able to manage effectively only if you have a carefully designed system that tells
you at the right frequency how you're doing compared to planned performance in all your critical areas of responsibility. Many managers rely
too much on the reports designed by an accountant or a data-processing
specialist who often understands his own technology better than he does
the information requirements for a manager to manage. Consequently
managers often get information that

■ Shows performance compared to the past rather than compared
to objectives

■ Emphasizes performance for a current period (e.g., a week or a
month) rather than cumulative (e.g., year-to-date) performance

■ Provides the same amount of detail to managers at all levels of
responsibility

■ Overlooks important areas of managerial responsibility such as
staffing and personnel development

If your management control reports are to help you manage as much
as you should, you must accept personal responsibility for working
with your specialists; *you* must see that your management control system is properly designed and backed up with appropriate standard
procedures. It is likely that your management control reports will serve
you well if they meet the requirements shown in Figure 10-4.

4. *Give your key people as much freedom as possible to do their work
in their own way.*   In key positions most people have many variables
with which to contend and/or they have considerable creative responsibility. For such positions, you should probably rely more upon the
ability of your people than upon standard procedures or methods that

FIGURE 10-4   Requirements for Effective Management Control Reports

1. Show current and cumulative performance toward measurable goals

2. Show significant deviations—both positive and negative—from planned performance

3. Are integrated from first-line management through top management for timeliness and detail in relation to responsibility for action

4. Show performance in all critical areas of each manager's responsibility

5. Can be understood easily

6. Can be prepared and distributed economically

7. Stimulate action to correct unsatisfactory performance and to take advantage of unusually good performance

you expect them to follow. What you can do, however, is provide your key people with carefully developed training so they will at least have a knowledge of what appear to be sound ways for them to do their work. For example, many sales managers train their salesmen in suggested selling methods, but leave it up to the individual salesman to determine the specific selling methods that he will use.

To summarize this chapter, here is my key point: *Develop standard procedures or methods for repetitive operations with significant cost-profit impact.* These are operations you should scrutinize at least annually to see whether important improvements can be made.

Generally speaking, procedures or methods that have been in effect for three or more years are probably obsolete. So perhaps you should even have a standard procedure for improving your standard procedures.

HOW TO DEVELOP YOUR PROCEDURES

1. Develop standard procedures when significant gain or loss is at stake.

2. Make forms and instructions self-explanatory.

3. Get specialized assistance when an interdepartmental system may be involved.

4. Give your key people as much freedom as possible to do their work in their own way.

KEY POINT: *Develop standard procedures or methods for repetitive operations with significant cost-profit impact.*

11

DEVELOPING YOUR STANDARDS

STANDARD   *A level of individual or group performance defined as adequate or acceptable.*

How many of your people know whether or not they are doing a good job? Do you really know how well your people are performing? And how about you? How well are you performing as a manager?

Your answers to these questions depend on the kinds of performance standards that you and your people have. For your job, perhaps you would like to take the quiz shown in Figure 11-1.

At the end of the chapter, I'll comment about performance standards for managers. At this point, let's see whether you have any misconceptions about standards for your people.

MISCONCEPTIONS ABOUT STANDARDS

If you have one or more of the following misconceptions, you can probably do a better job of developing standards for your people.

Misconception No. 1: *Your day-to-day judgment is probably the best standard for evaluating the performance of your people.* Ultimately, you must rely upon your judgment to evaluate how well your people

FIGURE 11-1 Which of the Following Are Sound Standards for Measuring Managerial Performance?

(✔)

____ 1. Extent to which measurable objectives were achieved or exceeded
____ 2. Extent to which written program was implemented
____ 3. Extent to which schedules were met
____ 4. Extent to which forecasts were accurate
____ 5. Extent to which there was budget compliance
____ 6. Extent to which duties and responsibilities on job description were carried out
____ 7. Extent to which policies and standard procedures or methods were followed

are doing. However, if you rely primarily upon your judgment for this purpose, your people will be in doubt about what you expect from them. They are likely to feel that you evaluate individual and group performance based on how you happen to feel on a particular day. Unless your people have a clear concept of their performance standards, they may concentrate too much on trying to adapt themselves to you as a personality.

Misconception No. 2: *Your people don't like standards.* People don't like standards that are arbitrary, unfair, inconsistent, or unclear; however, people do like standards that are carefully developed, fair, consistent, and clear. Your people know that you cannot meet production schedules or determine how many employees you need without performance standards. But it is your obligation to see that your standards are properly developed.

Today, for example, most organizations that apply modern industrial engineering techniques have successful experience with work-measurement programs for production, maintenance, and office employees. Even where work measurement is not always feasible, many organizations have had successful experience with a Zero Defects program, a program designed to motivate employees to produce products or services without defects. As one executive with a defense contractor explained:

> Zero Defects is not a "speed-up" program. It is not a program to establish arbitrary work standards. It is simply a program to encourage each and every worker to set his own standard for quality, and achieve it. Its strength lies in the fact that the normal human being derives great satisfaction from his work, and if he is convinced that work is important, he will set for himself a standard of perfection. [1]

Contrary to the beliefs of some managers, many labor unions support work standards and even have their own work-measurement specialists to assist in preventing and resolving standards problems.

You can utilize work-measurement techniques to set standards for production-type positions where the quantity and quality of production can be fairly easily identified and where the individual controls his output. For engineers, salesmen, staff specialists, and other thinking-type positions, you probably can't utilize work-measurement techniques to develop performance standards. However, you can define specifically what you expect these persons to accomplish and the factors that you will use to evaluate their performance. With defined standards, your people will perform better and they will feel more secure because they can evaluate their own performance on the basis of the same factors that you utilize.

Misconception No. 3: *Past performance is generally a sound yardstick.* Almost any industrial engineer will tell you that when there are no work standards against which to measure productivity, the performance of production employees typically ranges from 50 to 60 percent of what it should be. Without standards, employees have no targets to shoot for and they tend to utilize inefficient methods without even being aware of it.

The value of having carefully developed standards was proved by Rockwell Manufacturing Company. The company tooled up two plants at the same time to make the same product. At one plant, the industrial engineering department assisted management in developing engineered standards and controls. In the other plant, the industrial engineering department was not involved until after the plant was in operation. The result was the plant with standards averaged 50 percent more production than the plant without standards.[2]

Misconception No. 4: *Standards should be unattainable.* Recently I talked to a sales manager whose quotas for his salesmen seemed high in relation to the previous year's performance. I asked him about it and he replied, "Most of my men probably won't reach their quotas but I want them to keep reaching."

This sales manager was misguided; I found that his salesmen did not take their quotas seriously. To be meaningful, performance standards must be realistic. Employees should be able to feel a sense of accomplishment when they achieve or exceed their performance standards.

HOW TO DEVELOP YOUR STANDARDS

There are five important actions for you to take in developing standards for your people.

1. *Prepare a brief job description for each of your positions.* If you developed your organization structure along the lines that I recommended in Chapter 8, you will already have job descriptions for each of your positions. In any event, you need them to develop your standards, because the job description is the fundamental document for out-

lining what you expect from your people in terms of their duties and responsibilities.

2. *Define measurable standards for each of your people in terms of quantity and quality of performance.*   Scientific management has been defined as measurement plus control. In commenting on this equation, William M. Aiken, management consultant and vice president of H. B. Maynard & Co., Inc., says:

> . . . measurement provides the means by which management can effectively control the elements of a business. In other words, before you can control something, you must first be able to measure it. This applies not only to production, but also to office work, sales, maintenance, engineering, and other functions of a business.[3]

For production-type work, the best standard is often the standard allowed hour. This is the amount of time that it should take an employee with average skill and average effort to perform an operation, with appropriate allowances for personal time, fatigue, and the like. To develop this kind of standard, you need specialized industrial engineering assistance.

There are many kinds of standards that you can develop to measure quantity or quality of performance, but they will be best understood if expressed in numbers. For example, a certain caterer has standards for every party that he caters. He subtracts points when the vegetables for the last ten guests don't arrive as crisp and green as they should. He subtracts 1 percent for each guest who has to ask for a second cup of coffee, a host who has to request another round of wine, and anytime there is a one-minute wait at the buffet table. He says that an excellent party gets a rating of 94 percent or higher. Examples of other kinds of measurable standards are shown in Figure 11-2.

3. *Make sure each measurable standard is meaningful enough to stimulate control action.*   There is little point in having standards unless somebody does something about them when performance is out of line. For example, many managers have found that it is cumbersome to try to keep every item in a large inventory within specified minimum and maximum quantity levels. Generally, only about 20 percent of the items in a large inventory are costly or critical to an organization, so many managers develop quantity standards for only those items. Inventory for the remaining items is controlled on a sight basis; i.e., the responsible person requisitions a new supply whenever he sees that a quantity of an item in inventory is getting low.

4. *Determine who will do what and when to measure performance effectively and economically.*   To determine whether your people are meeting quality standards in a production operation, you can rely on your

FIGURE 11-2   Examples of Measurable Standards

MARKETS

Specifications for key accounts
Credit ratings of accounts in relation to amounts purchased
Criteria for products that can be shipped together

MEN

Standard allowed hours by operation
Minimum and maximum qualifications required for each position holder
Percent of total employees from minority groups

MACHINES

Standard cost per machine-hour
Percent utilization of rated capacity
Percent of scheduled repair time to total repair time

MATERIALS

Minimum and maximum quality specifications for each item purchased or produced
Minimum and maximum quantities for each item in inventory
Standard cost per item produced

MONEY

Ratio of current assets to current liabilities
Minimum and maximum limits for invested cash
Average collection period

METHODS

Specifications for engineered work standards
Specifications for new forms
Criteria for entries in suggestion system

MANAGEMENT

Percent of managerial promotions made from within during past twelve months
Percent of managers who have completed this year's personnel appraisals for their people
Average age of managers by level of responsibility

FACILITIES

Specifications for insurance coverage
Specifications for housekeeping
Mimimum and maximum standards for new construction

---

people to inspect their own work or you can rely on quality-control specialists. Further, you can make 100 percent inspection or you can inspect only a representative sampling of the work produced. You must determine what is both effective and economical in your particular situation.

5. *Determine how your standards will be maintained.* Many wage-incentive programs have failed because the work standards became loose due, for example, to significant improvements in work methods. Many quality-control programs have been ineffective because quality

standards were not changed to reflect current customer requirements. If your standards are to have meaning over the course of time, you must see that they are kept up to date. One way to ensure this is to schedule an annual audit to determine the effectiveness of your various performance standards. Perhaps you or one of your people can conduct such an audit; otherwise, you might rely on specialized assistance.

The thread throughout this chapter can be expressed with this key point: *Develop performance standards that are measurable.* On this basis, you and your people are likely to have common understanding about the quantity and quality of performance that you expect. On this basis, I would also say that the items in Figure 11-1 are all sound standards for measuring managerial performance. However, I'd give most weight to those standards that are most measurable; viz., those standards expressed in numbers. And, if your objectives were well conceived, I'd give most weight to the extent to which you achieved or exceeded them.

HOW TO DEVELOP YOUR STANDARDS

1. Prepare a brief job description for each of your positions.
2. Define measurable standards for each of your people in terms of quantity and quality of performance.
3. Make sure each measurable standard is meaningful enough to stimulate control action.
4. Determine who will do what and when to measure performance effectively and economically.
5. Determine how your standards will be maintained.

KEY POINT: *Develop performance standards that are measurable.*

REFERENCES

1. "You Can Cut Your Reject Rate with a Zero Defects Program," *Pacific Factory*, January, 1965, p. 17.
2. Willard F. Rockwell, Jr., "Managing a Highly Decentralized Organization," in H. B. Maynard (ed.), *Top Management Handbook*, McGraw-Hill Book Company, New York, 1960, p. 930.
3. William A. Aiken, "Work Measurement and Incentives," in H. B. Maynard (ed.), *Handbook of Business Administration*, McGraw-Hill Book Company, New York, 1967, pp. 7–135.

Part **3**

DIRECTING

12

DIRECTING: AN OVERVIEW

DIRECTING *Implementing and carrying out approved plans through subordinates to achieve or exceed objectives*

If you like dealing with people, directing is probably the part of your managing job that you like best. Here is where you exercise your leadership and human relations skills for staffing, training, supervising, delegating, motivating, counseling, and coordinating.

Your leadership (human relations) methods can be described in various ways.

KINDS OF LEADERSHIP METHODS

In terms proposed by the late Douglas McGregor, you may utilize the methods of Theory X or the methods of Theory Y.[1] The Theory X manager utilizes methods based upon these assumptions:

1. The average human being has an inherent dislike for work and will avoid it if he can.

2. Because of this human characteristic of dislike for work, most people must be coerced, controlled, directed, and threatened with punishment to get them to put forth adequate effort toward the achievement of organizational objectives.

3. The average human being prefers to be directed, wishes to avoid responsibility, has relatively little ambition, and wants security above all.

The Theory Y manager utilizes methods based upon these assumptions:

1. The expenditure of physical and mental effort in work is as natural as play or rest.

2. External control and the threat of punishment are not the only means for bringing about effort toward organizational objectives. Man will exercise self-direction and self-control in the service of objectives to which he is committed.

3. Commitment to objectives is a function of the rewards associated with their achievement.

4. The average human being learns, under proper conditions, not only to accept but to seek responsibility.

5. The capacity to exercise a relatively high degree of imagination, ingenuity, and creativity in the solution of organizational problems is widely, not narrowly, distributed in the population.

6. Under the conditions of modern industrial life, the intellectual potentialities of the average human being are only partially utilized.

Or looking at your job from the viewpoint of Robert R. Blake and Jane S. Mouton, you may utilize methods described on a management tool called the "Managerial Grid."[2] The Grid measures a manager's concern for people on a vertical scale and his concern for production on a horizontal scale. The Grid has eighty-one possible categories (nine times nine) for measuring a manager's relative concerns for both people and production.

In terms more generally used, however, you may utilize the autocratic method, the democratic method, or the free-rein method. Characteristics of these methods are shown in Figure 12-1.

FIGURE 12-1   Characteristics of Three Leadership Methods

Autocratic Method

Leader-centered ("I decide.")
Few meetings
Tight control

Democratic Method

Group-centered ("We decide.")
Many meetings
Moderate control

Free-rein Method

Individual-centered ("You decide.")
Informal atmosphere
Loose control

In training his people, for example, the manager who utilizes the autocratic method might say, "Here's what you ought to know." Utilizing the democratic method, he might say, "What would you like to know?" Utilizing the free-rein method, he might say, "Please see me if there is something you would like to know."

What is your belief? Do you believe that one of the three methods is superior to the other two? What leadership method do you believe is appropriate for each of the situations shown in Figure 12-2?

FIGURE 12-2 What Leadership Method Should You Use?
(A — Autocratic, D — Democratic, F — Free-rein)

_____ 1. You are much more experienced, knowledgeable, and capable than any of your people.

_____ 2. Your people are highly educated and have staff assignments with relatively little overlapping of activity.

_____ 3. You must reduce costs within ninety days or face the likelihood of significant financial loss.

_____ 4. You and your people face a gradually developing operations problem; your people are capable and more knowledgeable than you are about certain phases of your operation.

I'll give you my answers later in the chapter. In the meantime, let's consider the impact of your own background upon the leadership methods that you utilize.

**YOUR PARENTAL GHOST: THE WAY YOU WERE
BROUGHT UP**

A psychiatrist friend of mine tells me that a man and a woman think differently about each other as soon as they are married. Subconsciously, the man expects his wife to act as his mother did and he takes on the identity of his father. Likewise, the wife expects her husband to act as her father did and she takes on the identity of her mother. In other words, people always have with them the "ghosts" of their backgrounds whether or not they are consciously aware of this.

In dealing with your people, it is likely that you utilize the same kinds of methods that your previous superiors utilized in dealing with you. Psychologists tell us that we are influenced most by our early environment, so you are probably affected most by the way your parents or guardians dealt with you.

If you were brought up in an optimistic environment, you may tend to believe that your people can solve their own problems without much help. For example, you may give inadequate training to your people or you may not take disciplinary action when you should. If you were brought up in a pessimistic or critical environment, you may tend to believe that your people see many problems and obstacles in doing their work. For example, you may feel that you have to check on your people frequently to help them keep things from going wrong. If you were brought up in a perfectionistic environment, you may tend to believe that your people are as interested in details as you are. For example, you may give instructions in too great detail, or you may be concerned with fine points that may not seem important to your people. If you were brought up in a strongly opinionated environment, you may tend to see your people as being stubborn and hard to change in opinions, ideas, and work habits. For example, you may pound the desk and speak loudly about how you won't settle for less than 100 percent results.

Depending upon how you were brought up, you may have natural tendencies toward one leadership method over another. To get an indication about whether you have traits of the autocratic, democratic, or free-rein manager, see Figure 12-3.

Even though you may have vowed never to deal with your people the way your parents or other superiors dealt with you, you may utilize such methods when under emotional pressure. For example, if your parents criticized you severely for making a mistake, you may be tempted to criticize your people severely when they do something that upsets you. On the other hand, if your parents became more determined to solve the problems they faced when under emotional pressure, you may react the same way when you are under emotional pressure.

Someone once said that an organization is the lengthened shadow of one man. In other words, there is a tendency for you to staff and develop your people into your own image. Your image is formulated in the minds of your people by the way in which you deal with them. The way you deal with your people is largely influenced by the way you were brought up; however, this doesn't mean that you need to be a victim of your upbringing. If you are aware of your tendencies, you can control the way that you deal with your people. Accordingly, you can take advantage of

FIGURE 12-3   Traits of Managers According to Their Leadership Methods

---

Traits of Autocratic Managers

  Action-oriented
  Competitive
  Opinionated

Traits of Democratic Managers

  People-oriented
  Cooperative
  Cautious

Traits of Free-rein Managers

  Technically oriented
  Independent
  Deliberate

---

your favorable tendencies and minimize the effect of your less favorable tendencies. To put it in another way, the mature manager acts; the less mature manager reacts.

HOW TO DIRECT YOUR PEOPLE

In general, I believe that the democratic method is the best one for directing the efforts of your people. Reason: You are able to tap the resources of your people individually and as a group. But I believe even more strongly that you make a serious mistake if you always rely on the same leadership method; there are too many variables involved. Therefore, my key point for this chapter is: *Tailor your leadership and human relations methods to your people and your objectives.*

Carl Heyel is one of the management authorities who has studied various human relations methods. Here is one of his conclusions:

> The concept of "democratic supervision" is sound—within limits. Yes, if it means careful indoctrination of the worker by the supervisor on what is expected of him, careful teaching of methods, solicitation of suggestions, voice for the employee *to the extent feasible* in work allocation, and then a minimum of "breathing down the employee's neck." Yes, *if by his experience in his own department* he knows that his people are ready for it. No, if he has "green" help, or if methods in his department have undergone a significant change, or if the quality record is poor, or if there has been a past record of poor management/employee relationships. Of course, the application of the principle depends upon the type of operation. Supervisors of highly creative departments (such as research and development) are the best candidates for the "linking pin" concept and are most effective when they consider themselves largely as representative of the employees to

higher management rather than as strict directors of their efforts. The same could be true in almost any highly skilled, low-turnover department.[3,*]

After studying leadership patterns, Robert Tannenbaum and Warren Schmidt concluded:

> The successful leader is one who is able to behave appropriately in the light of these perceptions. If direction is in order, he is able to direct; if considerable participative freedom is called for, he is able to provide such freedom. Thus, the successful manager of men can be primarily characterized neither as a strong leader nor as a permissive one. Rather, he is one who maintains a high batting average in accurately assessing the forces that determine what his most appropriate behavior at any time should be and in actually being able to behave accordingly.[4]

Robert Golembiewski has studied the autocratic, democratic, and free-rein styles of leadership and observes:

> Supporters of any all-or-nothing view have one thing in common: they will often be surprised to find that the research literature does not consistently support any one leadership style. The reason for this lies not in any failing of the research itself but in the simple fact there is no "best" style. Indeed, the question "Which kind of leadership should we use?" prevents any useful answer. The question should be, rather, "Which kind of leadership *when?*"[5,†]

To develop further the key point of this chapter, I have three recommendations.

1. *Use the autocratic method when you are the expert and/or when there is an emergency.*   If you happen to be the technical expert in addition to being a manager, you may have no choice but to use the autocratic method in dealing with your people. You should not allow that situation to exist indefinitely; however, in the meantime you cannot expect your people to make decisions in areas where they are unknowledgeable. Further, if you have a number of people with certain kinds of characteristics, you may have to rely on the autocratic method. For example, Prof. William Fox describes this situation:

> When a company is operating in a relatively stable environment with little competition (e.g., a railroad during the years before the advent of good roads, busses, trucks, and planes), centralized management can reduce its load to manageable proportions through the extensive use of rules, procedures, and standard practices. This is feasible because centralized man-

* Reprinted by permission of the publisher from *Management for Modern Supervisors*, by Carl Heyel © 1962 by The American Management Association, Inc.

† Reprinted by permission of the publisher from *Personnel*, July/August 1961 © 1961 by the American Management Association, Inc.

agement will be confronted for the most part with predictable situations. The security-minded, dependent-type employee can be attracted, held, and effectively used in this environment, because there is little need for fast, innovative local action to cope with unforeseen developments. In fact, given well-conceived goals by those at the top and a well-drilled and disciplined organization, centralized autocracy can spare top managers the problems of dealing with the centrifugal tendencies generated by decentralized, autonomous units staffed with creative and ambitious young men.[6]

Even when you have capable, self-reliant people, you may face an emergency. For example, some college and university heads have been successful in handling large numbers of dissidents by relying more on autocratic than on democratic or free-rein methods. One newly named chancellor turned down a faculty-student review board that favored probation for riot leaders; he insisted on expulsion with the stipulation that the students would not even be considered for readmission for a full year. This and other autocratic-type actions helped to restore peace to the campus.

All managers face emergency situations at one time or another. You may not face such situations as often as a manager of a law enforcement group or a military group, for example, but you should be prepared to use autocratic methods in emergency situations where quick and decisive action appears to be warranted in achieving whatever objectives you have.

2. *Use the democratic (participatory) method when your people are most capable as a group.*   Chances are your people have ideas, knowledge, and skills that you don't have. When you get the participation of your people, you are able to take advantage of their contributions and you are able to create a synergistic effect—i.e., where team effort and accomplishment is greater than that of individuals performing independently. If you depend on your people working together in a team effort to accomplish most of your objectives, you should probably rely upon the democratic method much more than on the autocratic or free-rein method.

The more you utilize the democratic method, the more you develop the capability of your people. They learn as they participate in helping solve mutual problems and they get a personal commitment that they might not otherwise have. However, there is a danger. You can become so concerned about getting favorable reactions and support from your people that you become a victim of "good guy" management. A "good guy" manager often has difficulty making tough but necessary decisions— e.g., to enforce, discipline, lay off, or terminate.

3. *Use the free-rein method when each of your people is capable of functioning independently.*   Professional and highly educated or trained

people are often able to function effectively with very little direction. In fact, they may not stay in an atmosphere where there is close direction and control. They are usually trained in and committed to generally accepted methods and standards of performance for their respective fields. If you have such people reporting to you, you should probably rely heavily on the free-rein method of directing their efforts. This means that you get agreement with them on the results that you expect; then you give them considerable freedom in the methods that they use to achieve the results.

The free-rein method is often the best way to deal with research and development people and with functional specialists in such areas as law, taxes, and economics. Most educational institutions use the free-rein method in directing the efforts of their faculty members. Also, firms that offer professional services in such areas as public accounting, psychology, and engineering often rely heavily upon the free-rein method.

Based upon the above discussion, my answers to the questions in Figure 12-2 are (1) autocratic; (2) free-rein; (3) autocratic; and (4) democratic. I believe the answers are fairly clear-cut for the situations described.

If it wasn't apparent to you before, I hope you now see the need for your being proficient in each of the three leadership methods that I have discussed. Each of these methods may be applicable at different times as you direct the activities of your people through staffing, training, supervising, delegating, motivating, counseling, and coordinating. We will go into each of these elements of managing in more depth in succeeding chapters.

HOW TO DIRECT YOUR PEOPLE

1. Use the autocratic method when you are the expert and/or when there is an emergency.

2. Use the democratic (participatory) method when your people are most capable as a group.

3. Use the free-rein method when each of your people is capable of functioning independently.

KEY POINT: *Tailor your leadership and human relations methods to your people and your objectives.*

REFERENCES

1. Douglas McGregor, *The Human Side of Enterprise,* McGraw-Hill Book Company, New York, 1960, chaps. 3 and 4.
2. "Grid Puts Executives on the Griddle," *Business Week,* Oct. 18, 1969, p. 158.
3. Carl Heyel, "Changing Concepts of Human Relations," *Management for Modern Supervisors,* American Management Association, New York, 1962, pp. 44–67.
4. Robert Tannenbaum and Warren H. Schmidt, "How to Choose a Leadership Pattern," *Harvard Business Review,* March-April, 1958.
5. Robert T. Golembiewski, "Three Styles of Leadership and Their Uses," *Personnel,* July-August, 1961, pp. 34–45.
6. William M. Fox, "When Human Relations May Succeed and the Company Fail," *California Management Review,* Spring, 1966.

13

STAFFING

STAFFING   *Seeing that a qualified person is selected for each position.*

A top executive of a very successful retailing organization was once asked how hard he worked. He replied, "I don't work very hard except when I select my key people. I give a great deal of time and attention to their selection; then, I find that they do most of my work for me."

No doubt this executive gave an oversimplified answer, but his remarks do highlight the importance of staffing. In financial terms, your people cost money, so it behooves you to get as high a return as you can on your investment. Generally speaking, the selection of the wrong person will cost you anywhere from several hundred dollars for lower-level positions to several tens of thousands of dollars for higher-level positions. The selection of the wrong $15,000-a-year man, for example, will cost you $30,000 in identifiable expenses by the time you realize your error and select and train someone else. Your much larger cost is the return you should have been making on a properly placed individual.

How good are you at selecting your people? For example, which of the two men described in Figure 13-1 would you hire—assuming there were no other pertinent factors involved?

**FIGURE 13-1 Which Man Would You Hire?
(Opening: Cost accountant for new
position)**

Final Candidate A has a good education, excellent psychological test results, ten years of experience with three employers in your industry, and a work record with average accomplishment in cost accounting and other activities.

Final Candidate B has a satisfactory education, fair psychological test results, six years of experience with two employers not in your industry, and an excellent record of accomplishment in cost accounting and other activities.

COMMON ERRORS IN STAFFING

There are several staffing fallacies that frequently lead managers off the track.

Fallacy No. 1: *Candidates need experience in your business.* Have you ever noticed the number of positions-available ads that make a certain kind of industry experience a requirement? Generally speaking, specific industry experience is not nearly as important as ability. A person with ability can generally learn what he needs to know about the technical aspects of your business within a few weeks or months and he will outperform less capable candidates who have experience in your kind of business. Too often the person with ten years of experience has had one year of experience ten times. Further, he often brings with him a fallacious attitude about what can't be done in your kind of business.

I recognize that technical knowledge of your business may be very important—especially at lower levels of responsibility where most technical decisions are made. I also recognize that a good candidate may have experience in your industry. But I hope that you do not make it an absolute requirement if there is a practical way for a new person to learn the technical aspects of your business. A capable salesman, accountant, or engineer, for example, can generally transfer effective use of his skills from one industry to another.

Fallacy No. 2: *Candidates aren't available internally.* I know a national sales manager who was once a production manager in another of the company's divisions. He would never have had the chance to prove the breadth of his ability if his management had not been open to the possibility that a man in one functional area might also be good in another. Likewise, you should consider whether you can fill your openings with internal candidates, whether or not they are currently in your particular department or division. Good people will be more likely to stay with an organization that promotes from within and seeks to uncover its talent wherever it may be within the organization.

Sometimes even the small organization overlooks internal candidates. I know of a small retailer who was considering going outside to hire an advertising and merchandising man. One of his salesmen indicated interest in the job, so the retailer decided to give him a chance. With some limited assistance from an advertising agency, the man has proved to be very effective in his new job.

Even though it is generally advisable to promote from within, there is a danger that your organization will become ingrown. Therefore, you might consider occasionally hiring someone from outside of your organization—especially if the outside candidate's qualifications are clearly better than those of any internal candidates.

Fallacy No. 3: *A good candidate must have a good appearance.* Remember the cartoon in which a manager was interviewing a candidate? Both men looked and were dressed exactly alike. In the caption, the manager was saying, "Mr. Smith, I think you'll be perfect for the job."

That cartoon typifies what to many managers is a good appearance in a candidate. How strongly are you influenced by a candidate's height, weight, complexion, color and style of hair, manner of dress, and mannerisms? Subconsciously, you may be influenced more by such factors—some of them correctable—than you realize; therefore, you may have to make a conscious effort to decide in favor of a candidate's ability and proved experience. You may also have to make a conscious effort not to be negatively influenced by a person's race, religion, nationality, past employers, and memberships. As a matter of fact, you may do well to give some preference to those candidates who are noticeably different from you and your other people. Such candidates may have insights and perspectives that could be very valuable in helping you achieve your objectives.

Fallacy No. 4: *Candidates must have management potential.* Perhaps you refer to some companies as "universities" simply because they hire and train more potential managers than they can realistically utilize in their operations. Generally, this is a costly error because good men will not stay with an organization where they cannot utilize their abilities adequately. You can avoid this kind of error by thinking through the number of potential managers that you need—with some provision for turnover—and then selecting your people accordingly. If you are a sales manager, for example, perhaps no more than a third of the salesmen you hire really need to have management potential.

Fallacy No. 5: *Candidates must sell you.* A good candidate will generally seek employment with a number of organizations. Therefore, he can have only a limited amount of knowledge about your organization and the opportunities that you may offer. Furthermore, if he is just entering the job market, he may have little knowledge of the working world and not really know what he wants to do. If you expect him to sell you on why he wants to come to work for your organization, you may be asking him a question for which he cannot realistically give you a good answer. By all means ask candidates what their ambitions are and what kinds of activities they think they might enjoy, but concentrate on what the candidate does know—viz., what he has done in the past and what he likes and dislikes. Then you can describe what you have to offer in terms of the candidate's interests, knowledge, and experience. His reactions should indicate his interest in what you have to offer.

Fallacy No. 6: *Candidates will reform.* If you have a favorable personal reaction to a candidate, you may be tempted to overlook the fact that he has a poor work record or family and financial problems or a poor school record. Furthermore, you may feel that you are uniquely qualified to help the candidate succeed even though his previous superiors have failed. The odds of your succeeding, however, are remote. What a person has done in the past is the best indicator of what he will do in the future—irrespective of what he says. The candidate may have what appear to be good reasons for his failures of the past; he may speak very convincingly about what he is going to do to change; and he may even have new family obligations to motivate him. You want to believe him and he himself may even believe what he is saying. However, if you hire him, it is likely that you will make a costly mistake.

There is an exception to this advice against hiring candidates with failure patterns. That is when you participate in programs to help the hard-core unemployed. Such programs are especially designed to help underprivileged individuals gain success experiences as a basis for their becoming productive members of our society.

Aside from the above common errors in staffing, I sometimes see managers who are afraid to hire people who may have greater ability or potential than they have. When this fear exists at all levels in an organization, we see at work what one psychologist calls "the Law of Diminishing Competence." If the manager at the top hires someone not quite as good as he is and the same thing happens all the way down the line, the competence of the entire organization will deteriorate. The folly of this is apparent. I hope that you have the confidence and conviction to feel that you will progress furthest by selecting people who are in the best interests of your organization.

HOW TO DO STAFFING

As a manager, you are not expected to be a personnel specialist. But there is certain staffing knowledge that you need to have, and there are certain actions that you should take.

Probably the most important staffing knowledge that you need is expressed in this chapter's key point: *Select each of your people on the basis of his past performance.* By doing so, you will avoid the kinds of staffing errors that we have just reviewed. You will also avoid reliance on the personal-preference method of personnel selection. In describing this method, industrial relations authorities George Odiorne and Edwin Miller say:

> This is still the most commonly-used method, even when disguised by the apparatus of science; the hunch of the manager, his own biases or his likes and dislikes determine the selection of employees.[1]

In Figure 13-1, did you select Candidate A or Candidate B? On the basis of my key point, I believe Candidate B is clearly the better candidate.

If you have a personnel department, you should utilize its assistance as much as possible to take advantage of its expertise and to avoid functioning as a doer—in this case, as an individual personnel specialist. If your personnel department's assistance is not readily available to you, you should at least delegate as much of the personnel selection routine as you can. Your managerial actions are as follows.

1. *Define your requirements.*   A job description shows what an individual is responsible for, but it does not tell you the qualifications that the individual needs. One way to define those qualifications is shown in Figure 13-2.

Note the distinction between essential and desirable qualifications. Also note the emphasis on past performance—e.g., it is essential that the candidate has excelled in at least one competitive activity. With a clear definition of your requirements, you will find it much easier for you and others who assist you to screen candidates.

If you give careful thought to your real requirements, you may find that you don't need the kinds of qualifications that may be generally demanded. For example, there was a time when hospital administrators were expected to be doctors. But finally there was recognition that medical training was not an essential for administrative work. In the insurance business, one firm has developed a large sales force consisting mostly of salesmen who have only a modest education and usually no previous selling experience—e.g., delivery truck drivers and soda jerks.[2] Other firms are utilizing women in outside selling and other positions that traditionally are filled by men.

2. *Have recruiting done internally and/or externally.*   Your personnel department should have methods for identifying internal candidates through such means as review of personnel records, publicity in internal publications, and solicitations of suggested candidates through appropriate members of management. Externally, present employees may be

able to suggest candidates; ads in newspapers or magazines may produce results; state and commercial employment agencies may be helpful; and executive recruiting firms can be effective in filling higher-level

FIGURE 13-2 Sample Qualifications for a Salesman of a Consumer Products Manufacturer

Qualifications	Essential	Desirable
1. Education	Two years of college or equivalent; at least average grades	Bachelor's or master's degree; above-average grades
2. Ability to persuade	Must demonstrate present and/or past effectiveness in selling himself and/or his ideas	Has experience and/or education in salesmanship
3. Temperament	Willing to work hard with limited day-to-day supervision; willing to work under pressure of firm deadlines; willing to do accurate detail work	Has successful experience in proving he can handle essentials
4. Competitiveness	Has excelled in at least one competitive activity; e.g., sports, grades, offices, or working way through school	Has excelled in several competitive activities
5. Management ambitions	Must indicate desire to achieve management responsibility	Has degree in business or management and/or has successful experience in directing others; e.g., officer in extracurricular activity, supervisor in part-time work
6. Experience		At least one year of full-time business or sales experience
7. Health	Able to pass company physical examination	No physical or mental handicaps
8. Draft classification		Any classification except 1A or 2S

positions. Whatever recruiting means you use, try to make it easy for candidates to express preliminary interest. The well-qualified candidate whose current job is satisfactory may make a phone call outside of regular working hours to inquire about an opportunity whereas he would not take the time to write a letter or send a résumé.

3. *Have candidates screened through review of applications, short personal or phone interviews, and/or psychological testing.*   To save time for both you and the candidate, try to avoid interviewing candidates until after they have gone through your screening process. You may want to meet briefly with higher-level candidates to answer any questions they may have; but save your in-depth interviewing for final candidates.

Psychological testing can be very helpful providing there is professional interpretation of results. Psychological tests can help you identify candidate's ability, aptitude, interests, knowledge, skills, and temperament. Generally speaking, however, they should never be used as the sole basis for accepting or rejecting a candidate. Normally, test data should be validated through such means as reference checking, comparison with work and personal history data, and interviewing.

4. *Have phone reference checks conducted to find out whether each final candidate's previous superiors would rehire him.*   The value of phone reference checks was dramatized to me a few years ago. I was very impressed with a man who appeared to have all the qualifications to head up manufacturing for a client organization. He was very personable, had excellent psychological test results, and his résumé showed that he had excelled in his previous positions. I made a phone reference check with his most recent superior, who did not give him a favorable recommendation. I decided that there must have been a personality clash and went to the next phone reference check. To my disillusionment, the results of this reference were also unfavorable. I checked further and did not get a single favorable recommendation for the man. I even went back to his college and I found that he had not completed his work for the degree he claimed he had received.

Whether or not you personally conduct them, phone reference checks are probably your best single means for evaluating the past performance of a candidate. Most previous superiors won't put it in writing but they will give phone information about the candidate's positions held, accomplishments, how well he did his work technically, how well he got along, his main assets and liabilities, his personal habits and problems that may have affected his work, why he left, and whether or not they would rehire him. Most previous superiors do not want to hurt a person when he is down, so they tend to withhold any damaging information. They will speak well of a candidate until they are asked whether they would rehire him. That is the point at which they may provide the most significant reference-check information.

5. *Conduct final interviewing to hire successful candidate.* Generally, you should interview the one to three final candidates who appear best qualified. You can afford to spend time with a final candidate to discuss his personal goals or ambitions, to review job responsibilities and opportunities, to explain any disadvantages of your position, to evaluate and answer his questions, to get clarification of points raised in testing or reference checks, and to obtain further evidence or explanation about his ability to excel. When you have made up your mind that you have the best candidate and that he meets your requirements, make your offer immediately and try to finalize arrangements. Otherwise, you may lose a good candidate to another organization that is more decisive in making an offer.

With capable people, you can get whatever other resources you need to achieve or exceed your objectives. Make sure you are skilled at staffing so you can get the quantity and quality of capable people that you want.

HOW TO DO STAFFING

1. Define your requirements.
2. Have recruiting done internally and/or externally.
3. Have candidates screened through review of applications, short personal or phone interviews, and/or psychological testing.
4. Have phone reference checks conducted to find out whether each final candidate's previous superiors would rehire him.
5. Conduct final interviewing to hire successful candidate.

KEY POINT: *Select each of your people on the basis of his past performance.*

REFERENCES

1. George S. Odiorne and Edwin L. Miller, "Selection by Objectives: A New Approach to Managerial Selection," *Management of Personnel Quarterly,* Fall, 1966.
2. "How to Grow Wealthy with Positive Thought," *Business Week,* July 13, 1968, p. 82.

14

TRAINING

TRAINING *Teaching individuals or groups how to fulfill their duties and responsibilities.*

A few years ago Charles Brower, chairman of the board of Batten, Barton, Durstine & Osborn, Inc., stated in a widely publicized talk:

> Here in America we have reached the high tide of mediocrity, the era of the great goof-off, the age of the half-done job. The land from coast to coast has been enjoying a stampede away from responsibility. It is populated with laundry men who won't iron shirts, with waiters who won't serve, with carpenters who will come around some day maybe, with executives whose mind is on the golf course, with teachers who demand a single salary schedule so that achievement cannot be rewarded, nor poor work punished, with students who take cinch courses because the hard ones make them think, with spiritual delinquents of all kinds who have been triumphantly determined to enjoy what was known until the present crises as "the new leisure."[1,*]

Many managers would say that this quotation describes today's environment in which they are expected to get results. Whether or not

* Charles H. Brower, Address before the National Sales Executives Convention, May 20, 1958, *Speeches and Articles by BBDOers*, Gen. 1202.

you feel this way, your training activities determine to a large extent what your people think and how they perform.

DO YOU TRAIN AS YOU WERE TRAINED?

If you have received effective training in the course of your development, you probably realize what training can accomplish and you probably do a better-than-average job in training your people. On the other hand, if you have had to rely mostly on yourself to learn your jobs and to grow and develop, you probably have a tendency to expect your people to do likewise. Certainly your people have responsibility for learning and for developing themselves, but, as a manager, you also have responsibility to train them. How effective are your training activities? Do they suffer from one or more of the defects shown in Figure 14-1?

FIGURE 14-1 Do Your Training Activities Have These Defects?

($\checkmark$)

——— 1. Hazy performance objectives
——— 2. Overreliance on buddy system
——— 3. Training oriented more toward employer than employee
——— 4. Overbalance of technical training versus skill training
——— 5. Too much telling
——— 6. Little or no follow-up to ensure application of the training
——— 7. Overreliance on "cream will rise to the top" philosophy

Defect No. 1: I find that most training has hazy performance objectives. Reason: It is left up to each individual to determine from among the hundreds of ideas presented what, if anything, he will apply on his job. Training that imparts knowledge or develops skills can be valuable, but you will get a far greater return on your training investment if you *train to do*. This means that you see that each of your people has a specific program of *actions* that he will take as a direct result of his training.

If, for example, you have your supervisors take a supervisory training program, have each of them prepare a one-page program of actions that he will take within ninety days to apply what he has learned in solving his one or two most important supervisory problems. If you train your salesmen in creative selling techniques, ask each of them to submit within sixty days at least one case history describing his experience in applying the creative selling techniques. If you train your production and office employees in work-simplification methods, ask each person to submit to his immediate superior within thirty days one or more suggestions for simplifying work in his own job. If you send someone to an outside program, have him prepare and submit his recommendations for program ideas that might have application within your organization.

Defect No. 2: You are using the buddy system when you use an experienced employee to train another employee. You are relying too much on this system when you have not taught your experienced employee how to train and when you expect him to do training while still getting out his regular work.

Defect No. 3: Training that stresses how great your organization is or the rules and regulations that employees are to follow may be oriented more toward the employer than the employee. Your people are most interested in how they benefit as a result of your organization's past accomplishments and as a result of their following the rules and regulations that affect them. By the same token, avoid any tendency to decry your competitors. Your people know or will find out that your competitors also do good work. You'd do better to stress how heavily you depend on your people to help you keep on competing successfully against capable competitors.

Defect No. 4: If you are like most managers, you do a better job of providing your people with technical training than with skill training. If so, your people probably get better training in your products, processes, technology, industry, markets, policies, and procedures than they do in problem solving, planning, salesmanship, effective presentation, report and letter writing, reading, questioning and listening, conference leading, supervising, managing, and so on. Perhaps you feel skills are universal in nature and should be the responsibility of the individual employee. There is merit to that point of view, but I doubt very much whether you are satisfied with the various skill levels that your people have. Unless you take steps to see that your people get the skill training that they need, the cost of substandard performance among your people may be far greater than the cost of the skill training.

Defect No. 5: Learning-retention studies show that most people remember no more than 10 to 20 percent of what they hear. Yet telling or lecturing is probably the most common method used to train individuals and groups. My associate, Steven Brandt, describes telling this way:

> It is a one-way operation: source to receiver.
> Training, when effective, causes measurable sought-after changes in individual performances. It is a two-way operation in that it requires specific feedback from the receiver.[2]

Your training activities are more effective when you get your learners actively involved through such means as discussions, exercises, role playing, and tryouts.

Defect No. 6: A good portion of the time and money that you invest in training will be wasted if there is little or no follow-up to ensure application of the training. Even with performance objectives for their training, your people are likely to become engrossed when they get back on the job. Unless you or someone else follows up, most of your people will not do what they planned to do as a result of their training. Furthermore, the learning reinforcement that comes from applying training is lost.

Defect No. 7: Professor Lawrence Peter has humorously identified "the Peter Principle," which is:

> In a hierarchy, each employee tends to rise to his level of incompetence. Every post tends to be occupied by an employee incompetent to execute its duties.[3]

Less humorously, each of your people will reach "his level of incompetence" sooner than he should if you leave his training and development largely up to him—i.e., if you rely too much on a "cream will rise to the top" philosophy.

You probably see the need for training more clearly at lower levels of responsibility than you do at higher levels of responsibility. At lower levels, it is generally easier to identify how each person is to do his job and there are often several people that need similar training at about the same time. At higher levels, fewer people are involved and it is less clear how each person is to do his job. Furthermore, at higher levels, it is logical to assume that your people have already proved themselves and are motivated to continue to grow and develop on their own. However, at any level, there are training actions that you can take to help your people grow and develop and that are largely outside of their control. For example, it is unlikely that your people can make training decisions about their own job rotation, special assignments, and participation in outside programs that require more than a week away from the job.

HOW TO TRAIN YOUR PEOPLE

If you have access to specialized training assistance either within or outside of your organization, you should probably take advantage of it. In any event, there are certain actions that you should take to fulfill your training responsibility.

Probably your most important guideline for all your training actions is covered in this key point: *Have scheduled training for your people based upon what they can apply.*

Unless you *schedule* your training activities, it is unlikely that they will get their proper place in relation to the other activities that you and your people have. Unless your people can *apply* what they learn, you are probably wasting your training investment—except where your organization has an educational-assistance program and employees must take certain courses to fulfill their academic requirements.

Here are four training actions you should take.

1. *Orient all new employees.* Your new people begin forming their attitudes toward you and your organization as soon as they report for work. When you have an organized orientation program, you make your new people feel that they are important and you provide them with factual information about which they might otherwise get misconceptions. For example, do you know that many hourly employees equate sales with profits?

Employee orientation is especially important in a start-up operation when most employees are new to the organization. Recognizing this, the management of a new pulp and paper mill developed and conducted the twenty-hour orientation summarized in Figure 14-2.

FIGURE 14-2   Summary of Twenty-hour Orientation Program Used by a Pulp and Paper Mill

Orientation Subject	*Main Point*
1. OUR OBJECTIVES AND PLANS	Recognize that our real boss is the customer.
2. OUR MANUFACTURING PROCESS AND LAYOUT	View your job as an important link in a chain of operations.
3. OUR PRODUCTS AND THEIR ADVANTAGES	Take pride in the products you help produce.
4. OUR SAFETY PROGRAM	Memorize your safety rules to think or react safely in a danger situation.
5. OUR LANGUAGE AND TERMS	Ask your supervisor about the meanings of terms that are unclear to you.
6. OUR WORK RULES	Support our work rules for the mutual benefit of all employees.
7. WHO'S WHO IN OUR MILL	Ask your supervisor about what his management expects of him.
8. YOUR EMPLOYEE BENEFITS	Keep yourself and your dependents informed about your employee benefits.
9. HOW TO FIGURE YOUR PAY	See your supervisor if you have a question about your pay.
10. OUR PARENT ORGANIZATION	Develop and maintain interest in the company with family and friends.
SUMMARY:	*Achieve your objectives by helping to achieve mill objectives.*

Key members of management presented the various orientation subjects so new employees could get to know their management. The program was presented over the course of five consecutive half-days. Oral quizzes were conducted every day to review and get feedback on what had been communicated the previous day. As shown in Figure 14-2, every subject had a main point that suggested what each employee was to *do* as a result of his orientation. The orientation program was instrumental in helping the mill achieve one of the best start-ups in the industry.

The orientation program must be economical. When you have only one or two new employees, you can't afford to tie up key people very long. One consumer products company has solved this problem by developing a self-instructional, twelve-hour orientation program that utilizes tape-slide and programmed instruction presentations. Other organizations rely on their training departments to orient new employees. Regardless of the method utilized, you should take steps to identify the information that all new employees should have and then develop some economical means of providing them with this information.

An orientation program will not guarantee that your employees will always have the attitudes that you think they should have, but it will help ensure that new employees form beginning attitudes on the basis of correct information.

2. Plan and conduct scheduled training to teach your people how to do their jobs.   Every manager has some means of teaching his people how to do their jobs. However, not every manager has an efficient and economical means for training his people to perform as effectively as they should. For example, with carefully developed training, you can generally teach your people how to perform effectively within one-third or less of the time normally required with informal on-the-job training.

To train your people how to do their jobs takes just three steps. First, analyze what each of your people needs to know to perform his job. Second, estimate the amount of time it will take each of your people to learn his job and to get adequate practice. Third, schedule and conduct the training in some logical order. Generally, a person's immediate superior should be actively involved in his training; but experienced employees can also be used to assist in the training.

Training your people how to do their jobs generally takes somewhere between a week and six months. In the production area, for example, I have found that most employees can learn how to perform effectively within a month—assuming that they have the necessary qualifications to fill their jobs. An example of the kinds of subjects for training production employees in their jobs is shown in Figure 14-3.

FIGURE 14-3 Subjects for Training Production Employees in Their Jobs

Your Job Description
Department Functions and Objectives
Department Organization and People
Your Performance Standards

Equipment You Should Know
Materials You'll Work With
J.I.T. (Job Instruction Training) Breakdowns for Job Method
Quality Requirements for Your Job

Department Language and Terms
Department Health and Safety Protection
Housekeeping Requirements
Your Paper-work Requirements

Department Policies and Procedures
How to Handle Abnormal Situations
How to Handle Suggestions
Qualifications Review for Job Knowledge

3. *Plan and conduct replacement and upgrading training.* Even though your people know how to do their present jobs, you still need to train replacements to take care of attrition and to meet your expansion requirements; and you need to upgrade your people by providing them with important new knowledge and techniques.

Generally, you should make sure that you have a trained replacement for each of your key positions. You can accomplish replacement training by having replacement candidates take whatever formal instruction you have and by having them substitute in the positions that they are learning—perhaps on an overtime basis. You can also rotate your people in the jobs you want them to learn. The value of job rotation at higher levels of responsibility is described by the president of one manufacturing company as follows:

> Like many companies, we place a high value on job rotation in addition to outside schooling, temporary assignments and other accepted development techniques. At the executive level, a manufacturing vice president will soon switch jobs with the top sales executive in his division for a month. In one of our plants, the manufacturing engineer has become superintendent, while the superintendent is doing the job of industrial relations manager for the next three months. These men will all go back to their original jobs— but not their original perspective.[4]

To upgrade your people, you can provide them with courses conducted internally or externally; you can assign them methods-improvement or other kinds of special projects; and you can assign them to standing or ad hoc committees. You can also have them assist in developing and conducting training wherein they exchange ideas and experiences about the best ways to perform their jobs. A consumer foods company has done this for its salesmen around the subjects shown in Figure 14-4.

FIGURE 14-4 Subjects in a Forty-hour Program to Train Field Sales Personnel

Consumer Foods Field Selling Today
Your Customers for Consumer Foods
How Your Retailers Merchandise
Selling Your Promotions at Retail

What You Should Know about Your Products
Selling Distribution on New and Established Products
Economics of the Grocery Business
Suggested Order Selling

Our Consumer Foods Marketing Philosophy
The Marketing Director and You
Setting and Achieving Your Retail Call Objectives
Overcoming Objections and Handling Special Situations
 at Retail

Handling Your Direct and Headquarter Account Responsibility
Implementing Your Retail Coverage Plan
Developing Your Competitive Strategy
Practice in Analyzing Retail Sales Calls

Your Relationship with the Distribution Department
Planning Your Time to Sell by Objectives
Realizing Your Potential

This same company also did what few companies have done: it developed its own program to help its district sales managers distinguish managing from doing. Every subject covers an important facet about how a manager can accomplish planned results through his people. Subjects in the program are shown in Figure 14-5.

4. *Encourage your people to develop themselves.* Your good people will take the initiative to develop themselves whether or not you help them. However, they can be much more effective in their self-development efforts if you do help them.

Many people, disappointed when an expected promotion fails to come through, never understood the qualifications needed for promotion. This is a prevalent problem among people who aspire to supervisory and managerial positions. They assume that by performing well as individual doers, they are qualifying themselves for positions in which they are

FIGURE 14-5   Subjects in a Thirty-hour Program to Train District Sales Managers

Your Job as a District Manager
Our Managing Philosophy
Supervising Your People as Individuals
How to Plan Account Assignments and Retail Coverage

How to Set Objectives for Your People
Giving Instructions to Your People
Your Part in Selecting Your People
How to Do Field Training

How to Hold Sales Meetings
Disciplining Your People
Motivating Your People
Counseling Your People

Evaluating Progress toward Your Objectives
When and How to Take Control Action
How to Plan Your Time
How to Progress on the Managerial Ladder

expected to get results through others. You can help such persons by making sure they understand the qualifications required to fill the positions to which they aspire. If necessary, get the assistance of your personnel manager.

Other ways to encourage and help your people develop themselves are:

a. Let your people know that you are available to counsel them about their self-development efforts.
b. Recommend to your people the names of specific courses and reading materials that may be available inside or outside of your organization.
c. Recommend to your people that they become active members in professional and community organizations in which they may be able to provide useful service while helping to develop their personal skills.
d. Support your organization's management development program, if you have one, by fulfilling whatever managerial responsibilities you have in it.

Whatever you do to encourage your people to develop themselves need not be time-consuming. But your actions can be very significant, for they show you care and are interested in helping each person realize his potential.

I once heard a training authority say in jest: "When you know what you are doing, it's training. When you don't know what you are doing, it's education."

In this context, I hope you devote more time to training than to education. It will pay off for both you and your people.

HOW TO TRAIN YOUR PEOPLE

1. Orient all new employees.
2. Plan and conduct scheduled training to teach your people how to do their jobs.
3. Plan and conduct replacement and upgrading training.
4. Encourage your people to develop themselves.

KEY POINT: *Have scheduled training for your people based upon what they can apply.*

REFERENCES

1. Charles H. Brower, address before the National Sales Executives Convention, May 20, 1958, *Speeches and Articles By BBDOers*, Gen. 1202.
2. Steven C. Brandt, "Are They Really Learning the Ropes?" *Nation's Business*, August, 1967, p. 77.
3. Lawrence J. Peter, "When You Reach Your Level of Incompetence," *Think*, March–April, 1968, p. 8.
4. A. C. Daugherty, "Rockwell Report," *Business Week*, May 20, 1967.

15

SUPERVISING

SUPERVISING   *Giving subordinates day-to-day instruction, guidance, and discipline as required for them to fulfill their duties and responsibilities*

A few years ago, a friend of mine told me in a letter that he was in a management training program. With tongue in cheek, he wrote:

> At the present, I am studying the humanistic approach to superior-subordinate relations. I am amazed to see how much time and money is spent by large businesses trying to teach Christianity to the straw bosses. I can't help but wonder if the whole message couldn't be taught better by the big boss acting like a Christian instead of a successful savage. Of course someone would have to teach him how to act like a human being, which would be a rather lengthy teaching process.

My friend verbalized what many people probably feel about their bosses. How do your people feel about you? In large measure, their feelings are based on the way you supervise them day to day.

PROBLEMS YOU FACE IN SUPERVISING

You probably spend more time supervising than in performing any other element of managing. If so, it is likely that you have developed your methods of supervising to the point where you feel quite confident about how to supervise. In any event, you might like to ask yourself the questions in Figure 15-1.

**FIGURE 15-1   Questions to Ask Yourself about Your Supervising
(Am I sure . . . ?)**

Yes	*No*	
___	___	1. About how direct I should be with each of my people?
___	___	2. About how much detail to give each of my people when I explain what I want done?
___	___	3. About whether or not to give each of my people approximately the same amount of supervision?
___	___	4. About how to supervise my people when one or more of them is under pressure?
___	___	5. About when and how to discipline each of my people?
___	___	6. About how to get group approval when there are opinion leaders in the group?

I'd be surprised if you could answer yes to each of the six questions. But even if you could do so now, I doubt whether you could tomorrow if you had personnel changes. The way you supervise depends on the make-up of each person who reports to you. Individually and as a group, your people may be experienced or inexperienced, interested or indifferent, aggressive or timid, cooperative or uncooperative, and so on. Every personnel change means a new supervisory problem. Furthermore, this kind of supervisory problem is complicated by changes in your work environment. There are changes in objectives, programs, schedules, budgets, products, processes, policies, procedures, and so on.

GENERAL RULES FOR SUPERVISING

Every manager relies upon a number of general rules for supervising. Examples of such rules are given in Figure 15-2.

FIGURE 15-2   Some Do's and Don'ts of Supervising

A. *Do:*

1. Give directions in the form of questions or requests.
2. Tell your people in advance about changes that will affect them.

    3. Listen attentively to the views of your people.
    4. Praise promptly and in public.
    5. Treat your people fairly.

B. *Don't:*

    1. Show that you like or dislike a person based upon your emotional reaction to his physical appearance, politics, nationality, race, religion, geographical upbringing, education, memberships, or the like.
    2. Criticize in public.
    3. Bribe your people with special favors or privileges—e.g., time off or choice of assignment.
    4. Use threats—e.g., threaten to withhold a pay increase.
    5. Put off necessary discipline.

A training manager once explained supervising to me this way:

The five most important words: "I am proud of you."
The four most important words: "What is your opinion?"
The three most important words: "Will you please?"
The two most important words: "Thank you."
The one most important word: "You."

There are many general rules for supervising. Most of them have value—especially when things are going well for you and your people. However, they don't always work! This is because all your people differ from you and from each other; further, pressure situations stir emotions.

HOW TO SUPERVISE

There are many factors for you to take into account when you supervise, but I believe it's most important that you *supervise your people according to their individual differences.* Implementation of this key point involves the following actions.

    1. *Supervise each of your people on the basis of what he can do, likes to do, and will do.* What a person *can do* is reflected in his intelligence or problem-solving ability and aptitudes. People vary in their ability to think, speak, read, write, memorize, and create. Some people are better at performing mental tasks; others, at performing physical tasks.

What a person *likes to do* is reflected in his interests. He may have many different interests; but you can generally say that his main interests are in people, things, or ideas. He may not necessarily have much ability in the area in which he has a high level of interest. For example, I know several people who have a high interest in music but who can't even carry a tune. Likewise, just because a person has a high interest in persuading people does not mean that he has the aptitude to be very successful at it.

What a person *will do* is reflected in his temperament or personality. Generally, what a person *will do* has a greater effect on job performance than what he can do or likes to do. A person with the will to do a good job will generally exert extra effort to compensate for less ability or aptitude, and by doing so, will often develop his interest in what needs to be done. You will be more effective in supervising if you supervise your people according to their "will do" or temperament characteristics. How to do this is suggested in Figure 15-3.

FIGURE 15-3 How to Supervise Individuals According to Their Temperaments

Temperamental Type	*How to Supervise*
1. *The Good Guy:* Outgoing, friendly, sociable, optimistic, energetic, industrious, emotional, excitable, nervous, distractible, talkative, adaptable, versatile, alert, cooperative	1*a.* Be enthusiastic and optimistic. *b.* Appeal to teamwork and group spirit. *c.* Avoid giving excessive details. *d.* When necessary, counteract optimism with negative facts. *e.* Ask him to repeat important instructions. *f.* Praise or criticize directly.
2. *The Worry Wart:* Pessimistic, cautious, conscientious, indecisive, procrastinating, inactive, unalert	2*a.* Encourage and show confidence in him. *b.* Offset pessimism with optimism. *c.* Help him take first step. *d.* Give assignments in small batches. *e.* Supervise closely. *f.* Praise directly; be mild in criticism.
3. *The Shy Guy:* Sensitive, bashful, blushing, imaginative, dreaming, impractical, unapproachable, seclusive	3*a.* Express confidence in his ability. *b.* Ask for his ideas. *c.* Explain background of new job but let him work out details. *d.* Appeal to his imagination. *e.* Insist on his being concrete. *f.* Praise his work, not him. *g.* Criticize mildly by stressing his good intentions, giving him an "out," and asking for his suggestions.

4. *The Know-it-all:* Aggressive, driving, argumentive, intolerant, conceited, suspicious, prejudiced, close-minded, stubborn, defensive, revengeful, rationalizing

4a. Ask for his ideas and opinions.
  b. Show him credit and recognition he will get.
  c. Appeal to his desire for power, prestige, and position.
  d. Avoid kidding; praise directly.
  e. Criticize directly but give an "out."

5. *The Self-centered:* Ambitious, materialistic, selfish, gambling, buck-passing, scheming, disloyal, untrustworthy, credit taking

5a. Stress immediate gains or financial reward.
  b. Show long-range benefit.
  c. Show what he stands to lose.
  d. Enforce standards of performance.
  e. Praise or criticize directly.

6. *The Plodder:* Project-oriented, single-minded, detail-minded, deliberate, slow, persistent, matter-of-fact, monotonous, planner

6a. Appeal to his desire to accomplish.
  b. Give him sufficient details.
  c. Ask him to set own deadlines.
  d. Avoid interrupting his work.
  e. Praise accomplishments and importance of his undertakings.
  f. Criticize in unemotional, friendly way with emphasis on overall objectives.

7. *The Conservative:* Dependable, reserved, controlled, inhibited, perfectionistic, and conforming

7a. Be objective, logical, specific, matter-of-fact, and impersonal.
  b. Give only required level of supervision.
  c. Encourage initiative.
  d. Be mild in criticism.

The temperament types listed in Figure 15-3 are those generally recognized by psychologists, although the psychologist would probably use terms such as "manic" for good guy, "depressive" for worry wart, "autistic" for shy guy, and "paranoid" for know-it-all.

No one is a pure temperament type. But for supervising purposes, you can generally type a person as a combination of two or three of the types described. One common combination is the good guy and the worry wart. This person may be optimistic sometimes and pessimistic at other times. This means that you should supervise him according to the temperament type he is *currently displaying.* Another common combination is the shy guy and the know-it-all. This person may tend to be quiet and retiring sometimes and aggressive and argumentative at other times.

Again, supervise such a person according to the temperament type he is currently displaying.

Perhaps most important, you should recognize that people really do have different temperaments and you should supervise them according to their individual differences. For example:

a. Give close supervision to the worry wart because he needs help and encouragement, and to the self-centered because he is likely to take advantage of any laxness in supervision. Avoid giving close supervision to the conservative because he feels he is dependable and will probably resent close supervision even if he doesn't show it outwardly.

b. Give detailed instructions to the plodder because he is interested in details. Avoid giving unnecessary details to the good guy because he is not interested in excessive detail.

c. Criticize mildly the conservative, worry wart, shy guy, and plodder because a little criticism will go a long way with these temperament types. Criticize directly the self-centered, good guy, and know-it-all so they will take the criticism seriously.

Here is a summary showing how to supervise each temperament type:

The good guy: Appeal to his interest in pleasing others.
The worry wart: Help him get started.
The shy guy: Talk impersonally about what needs to be done.
The know-it-all: Get his ideas.
The self-centered: Appeal to his desire to get ahead.
The plodder: Give him project-type assignments with details.
The conservative: Explain your logic to him.

2. *Recognize when each of your people is under pressure.*   Everyone has a different tolerance for pressure. Some persons seem to thrive under pressure; in fact, they need pressure such as tight deadlines to do their best work. Other persons seem to fall apart; they either perform poorly or react emotionally by exhibiting some of their less desirable temperamental tendencies. Situations that may put your people under pressure are listed in Figure 15-4.

A pressure situation may last anywhere from a few minutes to several months. In any event, you should try to be sensitive to when each of your people is under pressure, and you should try to avoid upsetting anyone unnecessarily when he is near his tolerance point for pressure.

If one of your people reacts emotionally to a pressure situation by losing his temper, for example, you may be tempted to react emotionally yourself. However, this may be the time to listen or to talk calmly or to take some other rational course of action. When *either* you or one of your people is under pressure, act as if you see a *yellow* light. Slow down and proceed cautiously until you are in control of the situation. When *both*

FIGURE 15-4   Situations That May Put Your People under Pressure

1. Need to meet deadlines and other performance standards
2. Necessity for performing activities that are routine or distasteful
3. Work-load adjustments due to changes in organization or staffing
4. Failure to get along with others
5. Direct or implied criticism from you or others
6. Rejection of request and/or recommendation
7. Receipt, or administration, of disciplinary action
8. Direct challenge of position and/or opinion by one or more individuals in a meeting
9. Failure to get anticipated promotion, transfer, or salary increase
10. Misinterpretation of words or events
11. Serious personal problem
12. Unusual opportunity to benefit financially or in some other way

you and a subordinate are under pressure, act as if you see a *red* light. Stop and assess the situation; don't proceed until the green light of self-control and good judgment appears. As one sales manager told me: "When either I or my people are under pressure, I have found that it pays to avoid jumping to conclusions. I try to take the necessary time to evaluate rationally the situation and the people involved before I act."

3. *Be sure to take any necessary disciplinary action.*   Disciplining is taking action to enforce compliance with instructions or rules whenever there is serious and/or repeated offense. It begins where normal coaching and training leave off.

Most managers are uncomfortable when they have to take disciplinary action. If you feel this way, it is probably because you do not have a clear concept of what constitutes effective discipline. The best concept of discipline I ever heard was described in a talk given by Dr. Oliver Byrd of the Stanford University School of Education. The concept of discipline that he described was based upon the principles given in Figure 15-5.

Regardless of your level of responsibility, you may have to take disciplinary action for serious and/or repeated offenses such as these:

Failure to comply with important policies or procedures
Lack of cooperation—e.g., failure to follow instructions, lethargy
Poor work habits—e.g., poor attendance, short day, inefficient use of time
Undermining company policies, programs, or organization
Disclosure of confidential information to customers or competitors
Excessive drinking or other personal habits that have a detrimental effect on job performance
Insubordination

FIGURE 15-5   Principles Underlying Effective Discipline[1]

1. *The reason for discipline must be clearly understood by the person being disciplined.* All discipline must be explained in advance.

2. *The severity of the discipline should fit the severity of the misbehavior.* Serious misbehavior will not be changed effectively by innocuous discipline. Severe discipline for a mild infraction is unfair and will be recognized as such.

3. *The person should know that he is still liked even though he has been disciplined.* Affection is one of the basic emotional needs of all ages. The supervisor should take pains to show that he likes the person before and after discipline. This is an effective way of getting the person to adapt behavior and accept discipline as just.

4. *Discipline should be consistently applied.* The *certainty* of the discipline is greater as a deterrent to misbehavior than the *severity* of the penalty. Misbehavior that does *not* result in discipline is temptation for repetition.

5. *Misbehavior must be recognized* as such by the person being disciplined. Also, it must appear reasonable that the undesirable conduct is undesired.

6. *The type of discipline must be a reasonable one* to the person being disciplined. If it seems unreasonable, then there will be rejection of the corrective efforts rather than acceptance of them.

7. *There must be a sense of power and authority associated with the person who applies the discipline.* Discipline should *not* be given in an indecisive, ineffectual manner for this weakens its effects.

8. *Discipline must be accepted by the group* of which the person is a member. The power of the group is indicated in the effective use of group discipline as a means of disciplining an individual.

Before you decide on any disciplinary action, it is important that you get the offender's version of what happened. Perhaps he didn't really understand what was expected of him even though you may have thought you made it clear in written instructions and/or in normal coaching and training. If you decide that there was a deliberate offense, you may wish to take one or more of the following disciplinary actions:

Give constructive counsel—orally and/or in writing.
Have individual correct unsatisfactory work.
Give oral and/or written warning.
Withhold or delay recommendation for pay increase.
Withhold or delay recommendation for transfer or promotion.
Change individual's responsibilities.
Recommend that individual be put on probation for a specific period of time.
Recommend termination.

Do not look upon disciplinary action as punishment—as a means to get even. Rather, use disciplinary action as a constructive means for getting satisfactory job performance. Take only the amount of disciplinary action required to achieve desired results. Use termination as a last resort; however, you may have to terminate someone for a first offense if it is serious enough. Examples of serious offenses are gross insubordination, theft, and deliberate violation of a safety rule that could cause serious injury or loss of life.

Except in instances of termination, it is desirable that you try to re-establish an effective working relationship with a person after you have disciplined him. You are more likely to be able to do so if the discipline is imposed early in the day or week in which you will have several contacts with the individual.

4. *Give special attention to opinion leaders when you need group approval.*   In every group, there are one or more opinion leaders. An opinion leader is not necessarily the person with the most responsibility; he may be influential by virtue of his personality, his experience, or his informal status with the group. You shouldn't show him any favoritism, but you are foolish if you do not recognize that he may be able to help or hinder you more than other members of the group.

When you want to get approval for a program, for example, you will generally be wise to get preliminary individual reactions from some or all of your people before you have a group meeting. Probably the best way to get individual reactions is to meet with each of your people personally; then you can also appeal to each of them in terms of his particular interests. You can use preliminary reactions as a basis for modifying your program or for planning the strategy for presenting your program to the group. During your group meeting, make clear whom you have contacted for preliminary reactions so the group will know who has participated in the formulation of your program. Then give everyone in the meeting the same opportunity to express himself; however, if you did a good job of identifying your opinion leaders before the meeting, it is likely that those you contacted will be most influential with the group during the meeting.

In the event that you cannot, or do not wish to, use a group meeting to announce a program, you can still get preliminary reactions from a sampling of your people—including your opinion leaders. If you take their views into account, your opinion leaders can be expected to support your program and to set the example during its implementation.

If you feel your people are complicated, you are right. You would make a serious mistake if you felt that you understood all there is to know about anyone—including yourself. I hope I have made clear how important it is that you try to *supervise your people according to their individual differences.* You will never size up your people correctly at all times. But the more you try to be sensitive to their differences, the more you are likely to improve your supervising.

HOW TO SUPERVISE

1. Supervise each of your people on the basis of what he can do, likes to do, and will do.
2. Recognize when each of your people is under pressure.
3. Be sure to take any necessary disciplinary action.
4. Give special attention to opinion leaders when you need group approval.

KEY POINT: *Supervise your people according to
their individual differences.*

REFERENCE

1. Adapted from content in article by R. L. Jenkins, "The Constructive Use of Punishment," *Mental Hygiene,* 29:(4)561–574, October, 1945.

16

DELEGATING

DELEGATING *Assigning work, responsibility, and authority so subordinates can make maximum use of their abilities.*

Recently, a manager of a retail-wholesale operation asked me, "Do you remember that management seminar we had a couple of years ago?" "Of course," I replied, "why?" "Well," he explained, "you made a statement that has had a major impact on me and my operation. You told us, 'Your people have more ability than you think!' That challenged me and I decided to see if you were right. So I gradually began to assign to my people tasks that had been the cause of my overworking. To my amazement, my people responded and almost all of my people have more responsibility now than they used to have." "I'm pleased to hear that," I said. "Does that mean you solved your problem of overworking?" "No," he admitted, "but now I'm working on other problems I could never get to before."

I'd say that manager has further to go yet in his delegation efforts, but he's making progress. Unfortunately, delegation isn't something a manager achieves once and for all. Because of changing objectives, programs, policies, people, and so on, it's a continuing problem—one that many managers don't know they have.

DO YOU REALLY DELEGATE?

As a manager, you know you should delegate. And no doubt you do a certain amount of delegating. But how good a job are you doing? You can get an indication by answering the questions in Figure 16-1.

FIGURE 16-1   Questions to Check How Well You Delegate

Yes	No	
——	——	1. Do you allow your people to make mistakes?
——	——	2. Do your people make most of your day-to-day expenditures without your approval?
——	——	3. Do your people get promotions at least as frequently as other persons with equivalent responsibility in your organization?
——	——	4. Do you take several planned actions in the course of a year to train your replacement?
——	——	5. Does your operation function smoothly when you're absent.

If you answered yes to each of the five questions, you probably do a good job of delegating. On the other hand, if you answered no to one or more of the questions, you probably need to improve your delegating. Here's why:

1. If you don't allow your people to make mistakes, you may have defined what your people can and can't do to the point where they might just as well be in straitjackets. You may give your people so little freedom to develop their own methods of doing things that they have lost the initiative that they might have had. Of course, you shouldn't delegate to the point where your people can make *serious* mistakes—those that can have a major effect on whether or not you achieve your objectives. But your people should certainly venture out of the straight and narrow often enough to make a number of minor mistakes—many of which may not really be mistakes but merely deviations from *your* way of doing things.

2. Most decisions of consequence have cost implications. So unless your people can make day-to-day decisions about such things as what to purchase, how to sell, when to hire, and whom to give wage and salary increases, you aren't really delegating. This isn't to say that you shouldn't have control of major decisions that involve a lot of money or that could breach important company policy, but most day-to-day decisions should be made by your people if you delegate.

3. If your people don't progress as fast as or faster than others in comparable positions in your organization, it may be because you haven't developed them so they *qualify* for promotions—either within or outside of your area of responsibility. The best way to develop people is to give them responsibility. That you do by delegating so they can make maximum use of their abilities in whatever positions they hold. Generally, this doesn't mean that you give your people more work to do; it means you give them *more responsible* work to do whenever it is feasible.

4. Although you have selected your replacement, he may never qualify if he basks in the limelight of your shadow. The time to train your replacement is *before* he's put in your position. There are numerous planned assignments that you can give your replacement so he gets the "feel" of the responsibility you have. One of the best assignments is to have him substitute for you when you are absent or out of town—instead of letting your work pile up or obliging your people to track you down.

5. If your operation doesn't function smoothly when you're absent, you are probably holding the reins too tightly. You ought to be able to leave your job unexpectedly for two weeks, for example, and come back to a clean desk—at least insofar as day-to-day activities are concerned. Further, you ought to be able to take your earned vacation in time instead of in cash as some managers do.

Many managers delude themselves about how well they delegate. One more way that you can check on yourself is to get occasional opinions from your subordinates, associates, and superiors. For example, you might ask them to describe what they consider to be good delegating—in the abstract. Then, if you get a meaningful response, you might ask them to suggest one or two ideas for you to consider to help you improve your delegating.

WHY YOU MAY NOT DELEGATE

If you are basically a doer, it is likely that you don't delegate as well as you might; doers don't delegate. However, there are other reasons why you may not delegate.

1. *You are autocratic or perfectionistic.* Professor Earl Brooks of Cornell University found that executives give these reasons for not delegating:

> Subordinates lack experience.
> It takes more time to explain than to do the job myself.
> Experimentation and mistakes can be too costly.
> My position enables me to get quicker action.

There are some actions for which I'm responsible that I can't delegate to anyone.

Most of my subordinates are specialists without the over-all knowledge many decisions require.

My people are already too busy.

Many of my people just aren't willing to accept responsibility.

We lack adequate controls and performance measurements.

I like keeping busy and making my own decisions.[1]

If you find yourself thinking along these lines, recognize that you may have autocratic or perfectionistic tendencies and that you may be rationalizing for not delegating. Consequently, your delegating problem may be more in you than in your people; likewise, the solution.

2. *You are understaffed.* This may be a legitimate reason for not delegating—providing you are not *permanently* understaffed. Like every manager, you must fill in and pitch in; e.g., when there's personnel turnover, loss of people to other parts of the organization, unexpected increases in the work load, or rapid expansion. But if your main responsibility is to manage, you must take corrective action so you can delegate most of your doing tasks.

Your temptation will be to continue performing doing tasks because you like them or because you used to do them before you achieved managing responsibility. So, for example, you may delay recruiting or put off the realignment of duties and responsibilities among your people. You may even tell yourself that you are keeping costs down by understaffing; however, that's a poor long-term solution if you are to realize your potential as a manager—a manager who delegates.

3. *Your boss wants details.* In discussing delegation, management consultant Marvin Bower describes the typical complaint of the high-level manager whose boss wants details:

> I cringe whenever I hear the president wants to see me. I know he is going to ask me things about my operations that I don't know. He doesn't discuss plans and results—just operating details that are so inconsequential that I don't know them or *want* to know them. But I try to keep informed on minutiae so he won't think I'm stupid. As a matter of fact, I waste so much time and get into so many details with my subordinates that they must think I don't have confidence in them. So the disease spreads down the line.[2]

Mr. Bower goes on to say:

> Many otherwise able chief executives have the strange belief that asking high-level managers questions about details will "keep them on their toes." Actually, it keeps them back on their heels. Certainly the practice does nothing to develop them or the managers below them, each of whom must keep his superior informed.[3]

Admittedly, you face a difficult situation if your boss wants details. But you're more likely to satisfy him and avoid delegating problems with your people if you're secure in your knowledge about what is sound delegating. You may decide, for example, to resign yourself to a certain amount of criticism for not knowing details and to take the initiative whenever you can report progress toward your primary objectives. Probably your worst cause of action is to get defensive and to disturb your people every time you are put on the spot.

HOW TO DELEGATE

Perhaps the best single way for you to make sure you delegate well is to *stress results more than methods.*

It is only natural for you to want your people to emulate your methods — methods that enabled you to get where you are. But your people aren't like you — in ability, knowledge, experience, ambition, and so on. They want to do what you have done — develop their own methods when there are alternative ways of doing things. They want to develop their own methods of designing, selling, producing, delivering, and accounting, providing you prove to them that *you want* them to. However, you must distinguish and make clear the results you want.

Stress with your research and development people the characteristics of the product you want, rather than how to design it. Stress with your marketing people how much you wish to sell or to whom you wish to sell, rather than how to sell. Stress with your production people what needs to be produced, rather than how to produce it. Stress with your physical distribution people when deliveries must be made rather than how to make the deliveries. Stress with your accounting people what you want the figures to accomplish, rather than how to do the accounting. In other words, *hold your people more accountable for results than for methods* — assuming their methods are ethical and don't violate company policy.

Here are five other guidelines you can follow to help you do a good job of delegating.

1. *Implement your organization plan.*   If you have developed your organization structure as I suggested in Chapter 8, you have conceptualized how to delegate in terms of duties, responsibility, and authority for each of your positions. However, you must make assignments and put yourself on record through meetings with your people about how your organization plan is supposed to work — so you get committed and so your people understand. Then you have the foundation for the effec-

tive assignment of work on a day-to-day basis with mutual understanding by all concerned.

2. *Avoid making routine decisions.*   It's one thing to say you won't make routine decisions and another thing not to make them. That's because it's probably natural and easy for you to make decisions on routine problems that your people find difficult to handle—especially if your people are less experienced than you. Perhaps the best way for you to avoid this problem is through defined policies and procedures (see Chapters 9 and 10). As with your organization plan, however, you must *implement* your policies and procedures by announcing them to your people and by making sure that everyone understands.

3. *Get your subordinates' recommendations.*   I believe every manager who wants to do a better job of delegating should frame and hang in his office these words: "What do you recommend?" Time after time I have observed managers forget to ask this question—in a few instances immediately after discussion of the subject. If you are like most managers, you enjoy solving the problems your people face and you like to feel needed. But it's poor practice to give your solution without at least getting a recommendation, assuming your employee is past the training phase of his job. To delegate, you must make your people self-reliant— even though they may lean on you if you let them.

4. *Have your key people participate in meetings that you have with your boss.*   This is one of the best planned actions that you can take to develop your replacement and to give your key people perspective about what your boss expects from you. Whenever practical, delegate to your people the responsibility for reporting progress on your behalf to your boss. Also, try to bring them into the act whenever your boss wants detailed information in their areas of concern.

5. *Avoid overdelegating.*   I know an entrepreneur who built a very successful business largely around himself and his own ability. When it came time for him to retire, he removed himself from the scene entirely. Within a few months, the business floundered and he had to come back to rescue it. In effect, he had overdelegated and his delegating efforts were not successful until those in top management had time to adjust to their new responsibilities.

Many managers abdicate when they mean to delegate. They put their people in a sink-or-swim situation and then complain when only a few survive.

If you're going to delegate, you must educate. Train each person in his new responsibilities and give him a few weeks or months in the job before you leave him on his own. Even then, you should have adequate reports and controls so nothing critical can happen without your being aware of any negative trends.

Based on the ideas covered in this chapter, I hope you will evaluate at least annually how well you are delegating. By doing so, you help ensure that you can concentrate on other challenging, and perhaps more interesting, parts of your job.

HOW TO DELEGATE

1. Implement your organization plan.
2. Avoid making routine decisions.
3. Get your subordinates' recommendations.
4. Have your key people participate in meetings that you have with your boss.
5. Avoid overdelegating.

KEY POINT: *Hold your people more accountable for results than for methods.*

REFERENCES

1. Earl Brooks, "Get More Done—Easier," *Nation's Business,* July, 1962, p. 56.
2. Marvin Bower, *The Will to Manage,* McGraw-Hill Book Company, New York, 1966, p. 176–177.
3. *Ibid.*

17

MOTIVATING

MOTIVATING *Encouraging subordinates to perform
by fulfilling or appealing to their needs.*

Industrial psychologist Harry Levinson says:

> A steam engine operates at about 35 percent efficiency. People probably
> operate at about 10 percent of their potential. Most organizations construc-
> tively utilize even less of their potential power.[1]

How true do you feel that observation is of you and your organization? The extent to which you are utilizing the potential of your people
depends in large measure on how well your people are motivated. If you
feel that you must exert considerable pressure on your people to get them
to perform, you are probably realizing a relatively low percentage of their
potential. If, on the other hand, your people are largely self-generated,
it is likely that you are realizing a better-than-average percentage of their
potential. In this context, motivation isn't something that you do *to your
people;* it is something that they do *to themselves.* What you must do is
provide the work environment or climate that encourages your people to
start and maintain their own generators.

So far, the task of motivation probably doesn't sound too complicated.

However, you will be successful in motivating your people only if you acknowledge the reality of the motivation problems you face. That reality is not the same as it was a few years ago—perhaps before you became a manager. So you may be out of step without even realizing it.

MOTIVATION PROBLEMS YOU MAY FACE

Some of the motivation problems that confront managers today are indicated in Figure 17-1. Which of them do you face?

FIGURE 17-1   Which of These Motivation Problems Do You Face?

(✔)

—— 1. Your people want to get ahead much faster than you did.

—— 2. Your people expect higher earnings than you had at the same experience level.

—— 3. Some of your people may feel that you have a tendency to resent them because they are better educated than you.

—— 4. Your recent college graduates may know more about modern management concepts than you do.

—— 5. Your people may not respect authority the way you do.

—— 6. Your people may not feel that loyalty to one's employer is a virtue.

—— 7. Your people may feel they can advance faster by job hopping from one organization to another.

—— 8. Your people may be unimpressed with the fringe benefits your organization offers.

—— 9. Your people may want to give more time and consideration to their families than you give yours.

—— 10. Your older people want promotions ahead of your younger people.

Problem No. 1: If it took you ten or fifteen or twenty years to achieve your current level of responsibility, you may tend to expect that it should take your people about as long. However, your people may feel that they have the right to get where you are in less than half that time.

Problem No. 2: Today's graduates from our colleges and universities often *start* at salary levels that may have taken you five or ten years to reach. Naturally, with a higher starting base, they also expect to be paid more than you were paid for equivalent experience and responsibility.

Problem No. 3: Today grade schools offer subjects that used to be offered only at the high school level; high schools offer subjects that used to be offered only at the college and university levels; and colleges and universities offer more subjects in greater depth than ever before. Furthermore, more students are going to school longer. For example, graduate degrees are nearly as commonplace today as bachelor's degrees used to be. Therefore, it is likely that some of your people have a better formal education than you. They may feel that you have a tendency to resent them—especially if they have keen interest in nonbusiness subjects and your main interest in life has been your business.

Problem No. 4: It is your job to practice management; yet your recent college graduates may know more than you do about current management theories, mathematical models, computer technology, and so on. Will your people be less motivated to perform for you if they find that they know more than you do about what they feel are important management subjects?

Problem No. 5: Today, traditional values in the areas of right, wrong, respect, love, law, order, and so on are being challenged at all levels in our society—from the home to the school to the church to business and to government. If your people were brought up in this kind of environment, they may question authority wherever they face it. Consequently, they may not do what you want them to do just because you ask or tell them to do it.

Problem No. 6: I still talk to managers who feel that loyalty—like truth and honesty—is a virtue unto itself. They believe that they are supposed to instill in their people that their organization *is* the best in its field and that employees are to think and speak no evil about their employer. Further, these managers tend to feel that an employee should be grateful for whatever his employer does for him. Today, however, employees are better educated and more independent than in the past. They are unlikely to accept the concept of loyalty that may have been effective in an earlier day. Many technical and professional employees are much more loyal to their profession than to the employer they happen to be working for.

Problem No. 7: Good people have confidence in themselves and recognize that they will limit their potential if they stay too long in low-level positions. So, if they do not see themselves progressing steadily with their present employers, they will look for greener pastures. The activities of executive recruiters and employment agencies also promote movement of people from one organization to another. Where a person used to move three or four times in the course of his career, he can now move five to ten times without suffering the stigma of a job hopper.

Problem No. 8: Most organizations offer their employees fringe benefits such as vacations, medical and disability programs, group life insurance, and retirement plans. Consequently, employees, especially younger employees, tend to feel that one organization is about the same as another as far as fringe benefits are concerned. Further, competitive pressures force employers to make steady improvements in the fringe benefits they offer.

Problem No. 9: Many a manager appears married to his employer. He works long hours and his business is his life. If this describes you, you may have the tendency to feel that your people should follow your model. Today, however, people are being educated about the responsibilities that they have to their families and to the larger community. So, for example, a man must spend the time and energy to fulfill his role as a husband and a father as well as his role as a breadwinner.

Problem No. 10: It is likely that your older people resent the progress that they see your younger people make. Older people tend to feel that they know more about your business and that they deserve the promotions. Even so, they are less likely to change employers because of their vested interest in your pension plan or because they feel age is against them. Unless they resign themselves to their situations, they may complain to you or they may complain to others, thereby hurting the morale in your organization.

You will be better prepared to handle these kinds of motivation problems if you have an understanding of some of the modern concepts of motivation. Later in the chapter, I'll also describe the approach that you might use to handle each of the above motivation problems.

CONCEPTS OF MOTIVATION

Many managers tend to oversimplify motivation. They see it primarily in terms of reward or punishment as indicated in Figure 17-2.

FIGURE 17-2 Reward and Punishment Systems in Our Society[2]

Reward	Punishment
Business	
A job	Termination
Advancement	No promotion
Salary increases	No raises
Prestige	Nonrecognition
Security	Insecurity
Religious Order	
Acceptance	Nonacceptance
Participation	Excommunication
Salvation	Damnation
Heaven	Hell

Educational Institutions	
Acceptance	Nonacceptance
Advancement	Nonadvancement
Graduation	Expulsion
Higher degrees	No degrees
Chance for a better job	Poorer job

Political Institutions	
Participation	Ineligibility
Appointment	Being passed over
Election	Defeat
Deification	Obscurity

Military	
Acceptance	Rejection
Promotion	Being passed over
Permanent rank	Temporary rank
Medals and honors	Court martial
Retirement at rank	Dishonorable discharge

Social and Fraternal	
Acceptance	Being blackballed
Exposure to others	Exclusion
Committee work	Being passed over
Officer position	Rank-and-file status
Retirement banquet	Expulsion

There is some validity to the reward and punishment concept, but behavioral scientists have shown us that there is more to motivation than that. Professor Abraham Maslow of Brandeis University has described man's needs in terms of a hierarchy. First, there are physiological needs for food, water, air, shelter, and sex. Second, there are needs for safety, protection, and care. Third, there are needs for companionship, affection, and love relationships in the family, work group, and community. Fourth, there are needs for respect, standing, and esteem as gained through achievement and through recognition by others. Fifth, there are needs for self-actualization which is the fulfillment of one's potentialities. More simply stated, man has needs according to the levels shown in Figure 17-3. When man gratifies the first level of needs, the second level becomes most important to him. When he gratifies the second level of needs, the third level becomes most important to him; and so on.

FIGURE 17-3   Levels of Human Needs

5. Use of ability
4. Respect
3. Belonging
2. Security
1. Physical needs

Professor Frederick Herzberg of Case Western Reserve University describes motivation in terms of motivators and dissatisfiers. He says:

> The growth or *motivator* factors that are intrinsic to the job are: achievement, recognition for achievement, the work itself, responsibility, and growth or advancement. The dissatisfaction-avoidance or *hygiene* factors that are extrinsic to the job include: company policy and administration, supervision, interpersonal relationships, working conditions, salary, status, and security.[3]

In other words, Dr. Herzberg has found that employees will be motivated based upon job content and what they *do*. Employees may be unhappy—and perhaps even seek other employment—if there are significant dissatisfiers (i.e., dissatisfaction-avoidance or hygiene factors) in the job environment. However, correcting such dissatisfiers will not make employees happy; rather, such action will merely serve to keep employees from being unhappy. Dr. Herzberg says that a dissatisfier is a hygiene factor in the sense, for example, that a sanitary system keeps a person from being unhealthy but won't make him healthy.

Perhaps you noted in the quotation that Dr. Herzberg includes salary as a dissatisfier. Professor Edward Lawler, III, of Yale University has analyzed Dr. Herzberg's findings and says:

> The results of Herzberg's study of motivation have been frequently cited as evidence that pay cannot be an effective motivator of good job performance. According to this view, pay operates only as a maintenance factor and, as such, has no power to motivate job performance beyond some neutral point. However, this interpretation is not in accord with results of the study. The study, in fact, found pay may or may not be a motivator, depending upon how it is administered. A careful reading of Herzberg shows that where pay was geared to achievement and seen as a form of recognition by the managers, it was a potent motivator of good job performance. It was only where organizations had abandoned pay as an incentive and where organizations were unsuccessful in fairly relating pay and performance that pay ceased to be a motivator and became a maintenance factor.[4]

On this basis, you can see that you can still use pay as a motivator if it serves as recognition for specific job performance. Otherwise, pay is a dissatisfier if your compensation policies and procedures are not competitive for your industry and your geographical location.

Dr. Herzberg's motivators are encompassed in the upper levels of Dr. Maslow's hierarchy of needs, and I have found these motivators to be meaningful in suggesting to managers how they can motivate their people.

HOW TO MOTIVATE

There are several actions that you can take to motivate your people.

1. *Help your people achieve more.* Most people like to excel in both quality and quantity of effort; however, they often need help to do so. You can help a salesman achieve higher sales by showing him how to select and concentrate on key accounts. You can help an engineer produce more by training him in design short-cuts. You can help a supervisor accomplish more by teaching him how to do a better job of delegating. Generally the key to higher achievement is improved methods rather than greater effort.

2. *Give your people personal recognition.* Giving an employee a routine increase in pay does little to give him personal recognition. However, if the pay increase is based on specific performance, then it can be a motivator. Accordingly, some organizations provide employees with the opportunity to achieve increases over and above those associated with regular salary reviews.

If you are to use recognition as a motivator, you must also use non-monetary means. Managers know that they are supposed to compliment an employee for good work—either orally or in writing—but they often just don't get around to doing it. This kind of recognition often means much more to the employee than the manager realizes. Many employees have told me that their bosses operate on the assumption that, "If you weren't doing a good job, I'd tell you so."

When I was employed by one company, I once received the President's Award for a piece of work that I did. This meant more to me than a pay increase. If you don't already offer this kind of recognition, you may want to consider doing so. I know the head of an insurance brokerage firm who offers annual awards in the areas of field services, personal services, administrative services, and policyholders' services. In addition, he offers a special award to the employee who does the best overall job in relation to assigned responsibility.

3. *Help make your people's work interesting.* People will give their hearts and souls to an endeavor that they find interesting and that they feel has meaning. That is one reason why young people today are at-

tracted to positions in government and education even though they might be able to do better economically in business or the professions. The success of the Peace Corps is an outstanding example of what people can do when they are committed. When people are interested in what they are doing, there is vibrancy and excitement in the air. You can help create and maintain such an atmosphere by helping your people identify with your goals and the worthwhileness of your operation. Your people are most likely to identify this way if they have positions that are structured so they can make good use of their ability. Telling a person who is performing a routine task repetitively that he is building a machine or helping feed the hungry people in the world will not do the trick. People find work interesting when they have some responsibility for independent decision making and for suggesting ways to help accomplish the goals of your operation.

4. *Give your people responsibility.*   This does not mean to give your people more work to do; rather it means to assign to your people tasks that have greater importance and require a higher level of knowledge or skill. In Dr. Herzberg's terms, provide job enrichment, not job enlargement. Delegation is the means by which you give your people responsibility. Wherever there are highly repetitive tasks, you should try either to eliminate them or to automate them. For example, many organizations send monthly statements to customers when it would be relatively simple to educate most customers to pay from the original invoices or bills.

5. *Help your people grow and advance.*   The rule in some organizations is to grow or go—in other words, become promotable or get out. That's a fairly hard-nosed attitude, but it does tend to suggest that many people don't gain new knowledge and skills without help and direction. You can provide such help and direction by performing and promoting training activities within your organization and by seeing that each of your key people has an annual program for individual growth.

6. *Try to eliminate dissatisfiers in such areas as pay or working conditions.*   Elimination of dissatisfiers in the job environment will not motivate your people, but dissatisfiers can prevent your people from being motivated. Therefore, you must take steps to solve any significant problems relative to pay, working conditions, policies and procedures, and interpersonal relationships. You need not be better than other employers in these areas, but you should at least see that you offer a comparable job environment.

Now perhaps you'd like to ask yourself how you would handle the

FIGURE 17-4 What to Do about Motivation Problems That You Face

---

Problem No.

1. Help each person achieve the highest job level he can as soon as he can.
2. Give careful attention to providing compensation plans that are up to date and competitive for your industry and geographical locations.
3. Help your people build upon their formal education with the practical guidance you can give them.
4. Invite and use their ideas wherever practical.
5. Encourage them to question you when they believe they have good reason to do so.
6. Let them know that you expect only as much loyalty as you deserve.
7. Show them how they can get diversified experience and responsibility within your organization.
8. Make sure your people know what their fringe benefits are, but stress the job content and opportunity they have.
9. Help them balance the needs and opportunities of the business against their family obligations and interests.
10. Counsel each of them about the results they are to achieve and the qualifications they need if they are to be promoted.

---

specific motivation problems given in Figure 17-1. The approaches that I would use in handling each of these problems are described in Figure 17-4. The assumption underlying what to do about motivation problems that you face is that you try to understand each problem. You should be aware that you may find it hard to be sympathetic to the views of today's employees if you have not held similar views yourself.

If you want to motivate your people, you can't get so wrapped up in yourself and your problems that you treat your people as inanimate vehicles for getting work done. Probably the best single way for you to motivate your people is covered in this key point: *Help each of your people define and attain what he wants from his job.* At least annually, find out from each of your people the responsibility he is seeking within the next one to five years, what he'd like to learn, and how he thinks the content of his job can be improved. At the same time, help each of your people develop an annual program for personal growth through such activities as reading, courses, and planned experience. This way you'll help your people run their own generators to accomplish the objectives of your operation while at the same time accomplishing their own personal objectives.

HOW TO MOTIVATE

1. Help your people achieve more.
2. Give your people personal recognition.
3. Help make your people's work interesting.
4. Give your people responsibility.
5. Help your people grow and advance.
6. Try to eliminate dissatisfiers in such areas as pay or working conditions.

KEY POINT: *Help each of your people define and attain what he wants from his job.*

REFERENCES

1. Harry Levinson, *The Exceptional Executive: A Psychological Conception*, Harvard University Press, Cambridge, Mass., 1968, p. 7.
2. Adapted from "On Motivation," *Kaiser Aluminum News*, September, 1968, p. 25.
3. Frederick Herzberg, "One More Time: How Do You Motivate Employees?" *Harvard Business Review*, January-February, 1968, p. 57.
4. Edward E. Lawler, III, "The Mythology of Management Compensation," *California Management Review*, Fall, 1966.

18

COUNSELING

COUNSELING *Holding private discussion with a subordinate about how he might do better work, solve a personal problem, or realize his ambitions.*

Counseling is one of your most important responsibilities—not because you counsel frequently, but because of the seriousness of the problem that requires counseling. It differs from the normal day-to-day supervising or training that you provide your people for the performance of their jobs; it is private and covers a work or personal problem that can seriously impede the progress of an individual—from the point of view of the manager or the individual.

Many managers do a good job of supervising or training; but surprisingly few are good at counseling. Their biggest handicap, I find, is that they tend to feel that they are expected to "play God" when they counsel.

MUST YOU "PLAY GOD" TO COUNSEL?

Your effectiveness in counseling is dependent upon your beliefs. Do you have any of the beliefs shown in Figure 18-1?

FIGURE 18-1   Are These Your Beliefs about Counseling?

(✔)

____   1. You don't have the moral right to counsel your people about matters that can have lasting effects on their lives.

____   2. Counseling should be done only by professionals such as doctors, lawyers, clergymen, marriage counselors, psychologists, and financial advisors.

____   3. Your people will solve any serious problems they face if you avoid hand-holding and treat them as adults.

____   4. A person's personal values and behavior are strictly his own business.

Managers who believe that they must "play God" to counsel tend to have these kinds of beliefs. Consequently, they are not psychologically attuned to their roles as counselors and they don't really do a good job—even though they may be forced to go through the motions when employees come to them or when their personnel managers tell them that they must do certain counseling.

Unless you do a reasonably good job of counseling, you are letting your people down. You may be the most important part of the problem that your subordinate faces—e.g., when your subordinate needs your recommendation to get the position he wants. In any event, he will tend to look to you for help whenever he faces a serious problem because he knows that you will be affected if he does not perform satisfactorily on his job. Even when he is unaware that his job performance is being hurt by a problem he faces, you may cause permanent damage to his career if you do not act early to counsel him about your observations and try to help him develop a solution to a problem while it is still manageable.

The need for counseling is brought out in an observation made by Charles W. Coker, president of Sonoco Products Company:

> Always there is a conflict between the way individuals see themselves or appraise their abilities against the cruel facts of appraisal by their superiors. These men must appraise on the hard facts of performance, ability to accept responsibility and courage to face issues intelligently and realistically. This is, of course, absolutely necessary for them because they, in turn, are being judged by their superiors on exactly the same basis—and primarily on the ability of themselves and their associates to produce a profit.[1]

In his book, *The Exceptional Executive,* Dr. Harry Levinson says that psychological injuries need attention just as physical injuries do. He describes the need for counseling by suggesting, for example, that a person should have the opportunity to discuss with his superior any important change before it occurs. This makes it possible for the person to deal with the change and his feelings more reasonably.[2]

WHEN DO YOUR PEOPLE NEED COUNSELING?

You should consider counseling an employee whenever you observe that he has a serious work or personal problem. Such problems are listed in Figure 18-2.

FIGURE 18-2   Problems That May Require Counseling

A. *Work Problems*
1. Poor performance against objectives for quality and/or quantity of work
2. Poor record of controlling waste, equipment, or other costs
3. Unsatisfactory attendance, disciplinary, or safety record
4. Unsatisfactory relations with you, other employees, and/or outside personnel
5. Desire for promotion, transfer, and/or increased compensation
6. Other (e.g., better job opportunity elsewhere, poor demeanor or appearance)

B. *Personal Problems*
1. Financial
2. Domestic
3. Legal
4. Personal or family illness: physical and/or mental disorder including alcoholism
5. Family attitude toward the job and/or personal progress
6. Other (e.g., negative attitude, promotion of political or religious beliefs)

Often your employee will come to you for help when he feels he faces a serious problem; however, you must take the initiative whenever you observe that his performance on the job has either declined markedly or has declined gradually over a period of a month or more.

It may not be difficult for you to take the initiative where you are quite sure your employee has problems that have their roots at work, but you may be reluctant to get involved when you know or suspect your employee has personal problems. Normally, an employee's personal problems are his own business; however, they are your business if they begin to have a significant detrimental effect on his job performance. At this point, personal problems *are* work problems as far as you are concerned. It is not your responsibility to develop solutions for your employee's personal problems, but it is your responsibility to see that he gets satisfactory solutions.

You can generally be confident that your employee faces a serious work or personal problem by the time there has been a measurable decline in job performance. However, you may wish to initiate counseling before that time if you observe indications such as those listed in Figure 18-3.

FIGURE 18-3   Some Indications That Your Employee May Have a Serious Problem

1. He exhibits marked reduction in interest or effort.

2. He becomes unusually critical of others or of himself.

3. He becomes overly sensitive or defensive.

4. He becomes ill-tempered.

5. He becomes inattentive.

6. He begins to have difficulty in expressing his thoughts.

7. He becomes unusually quiet or reclusive.

8. He begins to drink excessively.

9. He gets hurt on the job, fails to appear for work, or calls in sick with undue frequency.

The indications to observe are those that are *clear deviations* from the normal behavior pattern of your employee. Some people, for example, are *usually* quiet and reclusive. Relative to the last item, you should consider having a counseling meeting with an employee who becomes injured or ill, because he may have secret concerns about how things will work out on the job or at home.

Managers who do a good job of counseling generally do so as *corrective* action for serious problems that their employees already face. However, these managers do not always look at counseling as a *preventive* action. You should consider counseling an employee whenever you plan to make a change that you feel may upset him seriously—e.g., when you make a personnel move that may cause him keen disappointment or shock.

HOW TO COUNSEL A SUBORDINATE

My key point for this chapter is: *Help each of your people solve his own problems*. The underlying assumption is that you cannot solve a person's problems *for* him; rather, any real solutions must be self-directed. You can suggest alternative courses of action within the realm of your competence, but any decisions must be made by the individual himself. In other words, a person's solutions must come from the inside—not from the outside.

There are six steps that I suggest you follow when you counsel a subordinate.

1. *Initiate and/or welcome the counseling meeting.* When you initiate the counseling meeting, do some planning. Try to think through

what you want to discuss. For example, pinpoint your recommendations when you want to help an individual develop his personal growth program for the next year or so. Set up an appointment with him if you also want him to do some planning. Always tell him what the reason for your meeting is; otherwise, he may imagine all kinds of consequences. When your employee asks for the counseling meeting, try to see him the same day if practical. In any case, time and hold your meeting in quiet and privacy where you will both be unhurried and free from interruptions. In this way, you communicate your desire to give full attention to your employee and his problem.

2. *Present and/or invite facts and opinions to define his problem.* If you initiated the counseling meeting, you are obligated to present facts and opinions which indicate that your employee has a problem. Then draw him out to try to get common agreement about what the problem is. If he merely nods his head and agrees with you, you may find yourself trying to help him develop a solution for a problem that he doesn't really feel exists. Recognize that he may be reluctant to admit that he has a serious problem, although he is more apt to admit it if he initiated the meeting.

3. *Repeat your understanding of what he thinks and feels.* This is the essence of nondirective counseling, where the individual develops his own solutions, as compared to directive counseling, where the counselor advises the individual what to do. Even if you are skilled in the technique, you probably do not have the time to do nondirective counseling in the same way that a psychologist might. But you should certainly apply the technique sufficiently to prove to your employee that you are really listening to him. In the process, you are also more likely to draw him out so he will express what he really thinks and feels. This is information that you must have if you are to help him develop solutions to his real concerns.

4. *Ask him what he feels are alternative courses of action and then probable results.* I once heard a minister say that the worst thing one person can do to talk another out of a threatened suicide is to stress all the things he has to live for. Rather, the approach should be to ask the person to express how he feels and then get him to try to see the consequences of the alternative courses of action that he has—starting with the suicide alternative. I cite this example to try to dramatize the importance of your helping your employee think through the consequences or results of the alternative courses of action that he has to solve the problem he faces. For example, it may be clear to you why an employee will be hurt by continuing to perform poorly, but it may not be clear to him

that his job is at stake or that he causes problems for other employees.

5. *Help him decide what he will do, by when, to resolve the problem.* An employee's resolve to do better on the job is probably meaningless unless he has one or more specific actions that he will take by a certain time. With a personal problem, for example, the action may be as simple as seeing his family doctor by next Friday. Where work problems are concerned, you are probably qualified to help your employee decide whatever he needs to do to resolve his problem. When your employee faces a serious personal problem, however, recognize that about the only thing you should do is to help him decide to put himself in the hands of a professional such as a doctor, lawyer, or marriage counselor.

6. *Follow up with him after he was to take action.*   Just because your employee says he will take action by a certain time doesn't mean that he actually will. A person who suspects that he has a serious illness, for example, may have great difficulty bringing himself to see his doctor because he is afraid to find out that he actually has the illness. Likewise, an employee who has difficulty in his relationships with other employees may delay contacting them in connection with work on a certain project. When your employee knows that you are going to follow up with him, he is much more inclined to take the action that he agreed to take. If it turns out that he doesn't, you may need to have another counseling meeting with him or at least set a new deadline.

SAMPLE COUNSELING INTERVIEW

Now perhaps you'd like to see the application of some of the counseling suggestions just described. In the dialog that follows, John is going to have a counseling meeting with Carl, who has shown much less interest in his work during recent weeks. The meeting is in John's office and is timed to enable both John and Carl to give full attention to their discussion.

J: Have a chair, Carl.
C: Thanks, John.
J: Here's an ashtray, if you care to smoke.
C: O.K.
J: Carl, I have the feeling that something is bothering you. If this is so, I thought there might be something I could do to help.
C: Why do you say that?
J: Well, over the past month or so, I've noticed that you seem to have less interest in your work. For example, you used to keep me posted on the progress you're making on that special project you're working on. Is something wrong, Carl, here or at home?

C: Oh, we all have our ups and downs.

J: That's true. Tell me, is there something specific that's bothering you here at work? How about the number of customer complaints we've been having?

C: I don't care for them but I understand why we've had them.

J: What else has been on your mind? How are things at home?

C: Things are a little tight financially but I guess we'll manage.

J: You're having some trouble making ends meet.

C: Doesn't everybody?

J: Yes, I suppose so. Have you any pressing obligations?

C: Our main obligation is the mortgage payment on our home.

J: The reason I ask is that professional help, such as from your bank, can often suggest solutions which you or I wouldn't know about.

C: I'm not really concerned about our current obligations but we will be having higher expenses as the kids get older.

J: You're concerned more about the future.

C: Right.

J: Has your future been of special concern to you during the past month or so?

C: Oh, I wouldn't say that.

J: You feel you're making satisfactory progress on the job.

C: Well (pause), I was counting on being further along by now.

J: You feel that your progress has been a little slow.

C: (Pause) As a matter of fact, I've been wondering why I didn't get the manager's spot that Joe got last month.

J: You feel you should be a manager by now.

C: Joe is younger than I am and he doesn't have as much experience here as I do. Tell me, why did Joe get the job over me?

J: That's a natural question, Carl, but is that really the issue? Isn't the issue what *you* need to do to qualify for the responsibility you want?

C: No, John. I thought I was next in line for manager.

J: You feel you are qualified now to be a manager.

C: Ah (pause), I have reason to believe that I can get a manager's position at another company nearby.

J: That's certainly an alternative. Are you saying that you believe you might be able to progress faster in another company than you can here?

C: I've been thinking about it.

J: What other alternatives have you been thinking about?

C: Another possibility is to transfer to another department or division. Perhaps I can get ahead faster with a fresh start somewhere else.

J: That's also another alternative for you. Other departments and divisions need good people also.

C: Say, are you discouraging me from becoming a manager in this department?

J: Not at all. I'm merely trying to help you evaluate the various alternatives you have for getting ahead.

C: I really *do* think I am better qualified to be a manager than Joe.

J: I appreciate your being so frank with me, Carl. And it's part of my responsibility to help you define and attain what you want from your work. I feel you do have many of the qualifications you need to be a manager here.

C: You mean I don't meet all of the qualifications?

J: You have enough experience; you know the work; and your performance in your present job has been good. But there's more to being a manager than being able to *perform* the various activities.

C: I want to be able to do whatever I ask my men to do. I can do most of the jobs in this department now.

J: But is that the job of the manager? Are you supposed to duplicate the efforts of your people?

C: Don't you have to know the jobs to train people in them?

J: A manager should understand what is involved in each job; but why can't he rely on his experienced people to help him train new employees?

C: I suppose he can. I know you've had me assist you in training new people. But hasn't anyone ever accused you of not knowing how to perform the various activities?

J: Obviously you've had some questions—which I can well understand. However, it's more important that I be skilled in managing than in doing. It's more important that I be skilled in setting objectives, giving instructions, dealing with people, checking progress, motivating, training, developing, disciplining, improving, and even counseling.

C: (Pause) I guess I thought I could learn about those things, *after* I became a manager.

J: If there aren't better-qualified candidates available, it's *possible* to get promoted with excellent performance in one's present job.

C: But, you're suggesting I stand a better chance for promotion if I prepare for the specific qualifications of the job I want.

J: Absolutely.

C: Is that why Joe got the job over me?

J: Well, he did study managing.

C: Have you any suggestions for what I might do?

J: As a start I'd suggest you read and take notes on this book. It describes the job of today's manager. I'll be glad to lend you my copy for a month or two.

C: I haven't done much studying lately but I guess it wouldn't hurt me. Have you any other ideas?

J: In addition to the reading, I suggest that you take the company's new supervising by objectives program. It can be taken by individuals and covers various supervisory techniques, an important part of every manager's job. I suggest you complete it within the next four months.

C: How do I make arrangements?

J: Just see our training manager.

C: Maybe I can see him this week.

J: Good. Have *you* any ideas about how you can prepare yourself for management responsibility?

C: After I've completed the supervising by objectives course, I'd like to do something on the job. Are there any special projects that would give me management experience?

J: How about preparing an outline for training someone in your job? Here is a sample write-up.

C: I see that it covers both knowledge and job skills.

J: When do you feel you could have a draft of your outline prepared?

C: How about November? I'd like to get the reading and supervising by objectives course behind me first.

J: That sounds reasonable. I'll mark my calendar for follow-up on November 15.

C: All right.

J: Why don't you let me know every month or so how you're coming?

C: Fine. Well, I'd better get back to work, John.

J: O.K., Carl. Let me know if there's anything else I can do.

In real life, John and Carl would probably use many more words to cover the same ground. The purpose of this dialog has been to provide one example of how a manager can help one of his people identify and solve his own problem. In this case, Carl's original concern was that Joe got promoted ahead of him. His real concern should have been about the specific actions he could take to qualify himself for managerial responsibility. Note also that this was a corrective counseling situation; earlier preventive counseling might have made clear to Carl what he needed to do to qualify himself for the manager's position that Joe actually filled.

The best way for you to improve your counseling skills is through practice. If in the past you have avoided counseling situations except when absolutely necessary, perhaps you will now seek out additional counseling opportunities with your people. It's not only sound managing but it proves to your people that you care about them as individuals.

HOW TO COUNSEL A SUBORDINATE

1. Initiate and/or welcome the counseling meeting.
2. Present and/or invite facts and opinions to define his problem.
3. Repeat your understanding of what he thinks and feels.
4. Ask him what he feels are alternative courses of action and then probable results.
5. Help him decide what he will do, by when, to resolve the problem.
6. Follow up with him after he was to take action.

KEY POINT: *Help each of your people solve his own problems.*

REFERENCES

1. Charles W. Coker, "Business Leadership," *Business and Economic Review,* Bureau of Business and Economic Research, The University of South Carolina Press, Columbia, October, 1964, p. 1.
2. Harry Levinson, *The Exceptional Executive: A Psychological Conception,* Harvard University Press, Cambridge, Mass., 1968, pp. 247–248.

19

COORDINATING

COORDINATING *Seeing that activities are carried out in relation to their importance and with a minimum of conflict.*

The eunuch in many organizations is the person with the title of "co-ordinator"; often he has no authority to function as anything except a communications bottleneck. Yet, coordinating is an important respon-sibility of every manager—providing he has the authority to do some-thing about the things he coordinates. Unless the manager does a good job of coordinating, he may have a number of individual efforts that compete keenly and selfishly with each other or that function loosely and obliviously to the efforts of others. In short, the manager may have star players but he may not have a team.

ARE YOU A STAR OR A TEAM PLAYER?

Whether or not your people tend to be stars or team players largely depends on whether you are a star or a team player. You can get an idea of where you stand by answering the questions in Figure 19-1.

FIGURE 19-1 Questions That Indicate Whether You Are a Star or a Team Player

Yes	No	
___	___	1. Have you always been strongly competitive—as a doer and as a manager?
___	___	2. Do you have a tendency to make unrealistic commitments to people inside or outside your organization to get them "on the hook"?
___	___	3. Do you feel strongly that reliance on staff or other help reflects on your ability to solve your own problems?
___	___	4. Do you tend to be close-mouthed about any methods or ideas that you believe give you advantage over other managers in your organization?
___	___	5. Are you openly critical of other managers in your organization?

If you answered yes to one or more of the five questions, you probably are not as much of a team player as you ought to be.

If you have always been strongly competitive, you may develop for yourself the kinds of problems that a certain production superintendent had. He encouraged each of his shift foremen to compete with each other for the best weekly production record. On the surface, this sounded like a good idea; but it developed that each foreman would neglect to pass on to the next shift important operating instructions or he would change the settings on the equipment at the end of his shift—thereby causing the next shift quality difficulties that took an hour or more to locate and correct. When the production superintendent became aware of what was happening, he was able to take corrective action to coordinate the foremen's efforts so they functioned cooperatively as a team rather than as individuals out to cut each other's throat.

If you have a tendency to make unrealistic commitments to others to get them "on the hook," you may face the problems of a certain sales manager. He is so intent upon building sales that he accepts customer orders that cause havoc with the production department. In effect, the sales manager is scheduling the production department; consequently, he and his people spend a high proportion of their time expediting orders and explaining away delivery delays to disappointed customers.

If you resist the efforts of staff people or others to help you, you may face the problems of a certain plant manager. He feels so completely responsible for his own efforts and those of his people that he deludes himself into believing that he doesn't need outside help. For example, his operation is located in a high-employment area and the turnover of his people is excessive. He resists help from the corporate personnel department because he feels that he and his people are better equipped to understand and solve their own problems. In reality, he is so defensive about an outsider finding something wrong with his operation that his turnover problem goes unsolved. His rationale is, "I was hired to do a job. I have no intention of adding to the overhead of our operation by bringing in someone who takes up the time of my people and becomes a part of the problem rather than solving it."

If you tend to be close-mouthed about your methods or ideas, you may encourage other managers to treat you likewise. For example, the *Wall Street Journal* reports that one major corporation had several instances where "one division made technical breakthroughs that it couldn't take advantage of immediately and kept them secret rather than let sister divisions use them."[1] This did little to encourage reciprocal cooperation.

If you are openly critical of other managers in your organization, you may find yourself in the position of one vice president. Along with excellent capability, he had a great personal ambition to head his organization. Rather than propose to the president how the entire organization might do better planning, for example, he would criticize openly the planning efforts of two vice presidents whom he considered to be his rivals. The end result was that he found himself on the outside looking in because he was forced to leave the organization.

EFFECTS OF POOR COORDINATION

Considering the organization as a whole, there are at least four effects of poor coordination.

1. *Parts hurt the whole.*   An organization would be more likely to realize its potential if there were fewer destructive efforts among its parts. The organizational development unit of Union Carbide puts it this way:

> . . . employees often expend more energy in destructive struggles — between line and staff groups, between departments, between division and corporation — than they channel toward achieving corporate goals. Even top-flight executives often feel they must focus their attention on getting to the president's ear before the vice president for sales does, or on maneuvers to extend their span of authority in order to insure their job security. Two divisions may come into conflict because each is concerned with forwarding its own area of interest, rather than the best interests of the company as a whole.[2,*]

2. *Few improvements are made by internal and external specialists.* There are so many specialties in the field of management today that it is impossible for any manager to recognize all the problems and opportunities he has in each specialty. An organization that has a prepon-

* Reprinted with permission of *News Front*, Management's News Magazine, Copyright 1969.

derance of go-it-alone managers will suffer competitively if it does not take advantage of the assistance the specialists can offer in such areas as personnel selection, personnel development, compensation, organization planning, management information systems, labor relations, tax planning, law, public relations, insurance, international operations, industrial psychology, and operations research.

3. *Short-range activities hurt long-range results.*   Many organizations are so intent upon performing well for each financial period that they cripple the results they could otherwise attain next year and the year after. To get current results, these organizations go after high-volume, low-profit sales; they disregard production schedules to get easy shipments made; they make imprudent decisions to reduce inventory or to reduce other large costs such as direct and indirect labor; or they skimp on their investment in research and development. Often these organizations do a fairly good job of planning but their plans fall by the wayside under pressure of current conditions.

4. *There is excessive disruption due to change.*   Even with contingency plans, an organization cannot plan for everything that will happen. Yet it should have the coordination required to handle unforeseen competitive activity, strikes, deaths or disabilities of key people, delays by important customers or suppliers, peaks or valleys of activity, reorganization, merger or acquisition opportunities, significant actions by other departments or divisions, and so on. An organization is bound to suffer some disruption when these kinds of changes occur, but excessive disruption may cripple part or all of the organization.

Regardless of your level of responsibility, there are several coordinating actions that you can take.

HOW TO COORDINATE

The essence of coordinating is expressed in this chapter's key point: *Help your people integrate their activities with those of others affected.* This has implications in your organization up, down, sideways, now, and in the future—as indicated in the following coordinating actions.

1. *Encourage your people to cooperate with other individuals and groups in your organization.*   Of course you want your people to be determined and competitive and to achieve or exceed objectives. But you should make clear to your people that these attributes are destructive when carried too far. The sole purpose of an organization is to achieve synergistic results. When there is destructive criticism or lack of cooperation between the parts, the organization becomes crippled.

Encourage your people to support the objectives and plans of others in your organization with whom they work or have contact. Ask your people to suggest to you corrective action when there appear to be conflicts. A sales manager in an electronics company, for example, proposed a revised sales-compensation plan rather than put unrealistic pressure on production to get out shipments on which sales-incentive payments were based.

I like the way one president of a manufacturing company describes the need for coordination. He says:

> As a business organization grows, there is a tendency for "paper curtains" to build up between groups within it. The organization chart becomes larger and it becomes sharply divided vertically; often, the only sharing of ideas and interaction between groups in the company is at the very top. Sometimes field managers in large companies don't really know their counterparts from a different division, even though they work in the same city.
>
> Finding ways to overcome this is one of management's biggest jobs. We work hard to teach our managers the concept of a "third eye"; two for their specific responsibilities and one for the rest of the corporation's business. And not just at the "general" manager level, but including second and third level "specialist" managers. We're also continually trying to create the means by which ideas can be shared and communicated *across* the organization between managers at these levels.
>
> . . . We've found there's a direct correlation between a manager's horizontal communications ability and his potential for advancement.[3]

2. *Encourage your people to work with qualified specialists.* I am not proposing that you and your people should be easy prey for every internal staff man or external consultant. What I am proposing is that you and your people listen open-mindedly and nondefensively to what such specialists propose. Then if you decide a certain specialist may be able to help, ask your people to cooperate fully. A specialist will do the best job where he feels his chances of success are best. That's generally where he gets honest cooperation and where there is some evidence that his efforts will be followed up by those he is trying to serve.

One plant manager in a farm equipment manufacturing company goes a step further. He takes the initiative to contact corporate staff departments once or twice a year to get their suggestions about how he and his people might do a better job—in the accounting area, for example. He would rather not rely upon the staff departments for always taking the initiative to come to him when they have something important to contribute to his operation.

3. *Hold your people accountable for both short- and long-range results.* What do you do when your people want to compromise on the quality of your product or service? What do you do when your people want to

disregard commitments to customers or to others that you serve within your organization? What do you do when your people "can't find time" to train and develop replacements for key positions? What you do in these kinds of situations will have significant effects on the results that you will be able to achieve one or two years from now—unless you are gambling on your being promoted and having a replacement who will have to pick up the pieces. Of course you and your people must succeed in the present if you are going to have a future. But you must let your people know that your mutual success in the future will be seriously hampered if you have to drag along ill will, a blemished reputation, or problems that should have been resolved much earlier.

4. *Make sure your people know what they are to do when likely and unforeseen changes occur.*   If it is likely that you will have peaks and valleys of activity, your people should know how they will be affected should it become necessary to increase or reduce the number of employees. If it is likely that there will be unplanned absences or quits, your people should know how duties and responsibilities are to be reassigned. Identifying and deciding what you want to do about the kinds of likely and unforeseen changes that might occur is an important part of your coordinating responsibility. One of the most dramatic examples of how to handle the unforeseen is the major fire that Neiman-Marcus had in its Dallas store during the height of its Christmas season a few years ago. The store was able to live up to most of its Christmas commitments because employees at all levels were able to take prompt remedial action in a coordinated fashion.[4]

Many managers do not view coordinating as a separate and distinct part of their day-to-day managing responsibility; however, I believe there is much opportunity for them to improve their coordinating. One important result will be that each manager will help his organization to function more as an organization rather than as a number of individual parts.

HOW TO COORDINATE

1. Encourage your people to cooperate with other individuals and groups in your organization.
2. Encourage your people to work with qualified specialists.
3. Hold your people accountable for both short- and long-range results.
4. Make sure your people know what they are to do when likely and unforeseen changes occur.

KEY POINT: *Help your people integrate their activities with those of others affected.*

REFERENCES

1. "The 'Enemy' Within," *Wall Street Journal,* Jan. 16, 1968, p. 1.
2. "The Inner Force That Gets Results," *News Front,* June, 1966, p. 15.
3. A. C. Daugherty, "Rockwell Report," *Business Week,* Dec. 17, 1966.
4. "But They Came Back Same Day," *Business Week,* Dec. 26, 1964, p. 15.

Part 4

CONTROLLING

20

CONTROLLING: AN OVERVIEW

CONTROLLING *Measuring progress toward objectives, evaluating what needs to be done, and then taking corrective action to achieve or exceed objectives.*

Suppose you have responsibility for an inventory consisting of 2,000 items. What would be the best way for you and your people to control this inventory if it could be described according to the graph shown in Figure 20-1?

The graph shows that you could control 80 percent of the annual dollar value of your inventory by controlling only 20 percent of the items. In other words, you and your people should give much more attention to the 400 items that make up most of the annual dollar value of your inventory than you should to the remaining 1,600 items.

The essence of controlling is to spend your time where the dollars are —or on whatever else has the greatest effect on what you are trying to achieve. This sounds simple enough, but in practice, it is often difficult to do.

FIGURE 20-1   What Are the Control Implications Shown in This Graph?

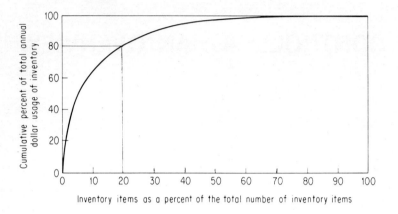

Inventory items as a percent of the total number of inventory items

(y-axis: Cumulative percent of total annual dollar usage of inventory)

DO YOU CONTROL THE WAY YOU'RE CONTROLLED?

The biggest single factor in the way you control is the way you are controlled by your boss. You will tend to use the same control methods that your boss uses with you —especially if you emulate him. If he uses sound control methods, the chances are good that you do also. If he does not use sound control methods, you may be influenced by his methods and follow his example. It is likely that your control methods are not what they should be if your boss:

- Expects you to have on-the-spot detailed information about your entire operation.
- Is more concerned with whether or not you comply with budgets, policies, and procedures than with the achievement of your primary objectives for output or other results.
- Gives you so much freedom that he relies almost entirely on whatever progress reports you decide to give him; or checks your progress more on a spasmodic, emotional basis than on a regular, objective basis.
- Relies mostly on your organization's controller to provide him with control reports and recommendations affecting your area of responsibility.
- Grabs the ball from you to solve most of the important problems that you report to him—because he is more of a doer than a manager.

Perhaps you can influence your boss to improve on such control methods; in any event, you can improve on the control methods that you use with your people if you have a clear concept of what constitutes sound controlling.

MISCONCEPTIONS ABOUT CONTROLLING

Here are five misconceptions about controlling.

Misconception No. 1: *If you watch the pennies, the dollars will take care of themselves.*   Managers who are detail-oriented — perhaps because they have been trained as accountants or engineers where attention to detail is critical — often have this misconception. If the operation is small enough, a manager can stay on top of the details. However, he will not develop responsible subordinates and his operation will not grow as much as it should if he tries to keep track of everything that each of his people does. He cannot expect to see that every order is produced without waste, that each employee is busy 100 percent of the time, that each item is purchased at the lowest price, or that every piece of correspondence is clear and concise. If he functions in this way, he is like the rancher who tries to count his sheep by counting their legs and dividing by four — a feat that was possible only when he had a small flock.

Misconception No. 2: *The main purpose of control is to check compliance.*   Refer to almost any dictionary and you will find that most of the meanings of the word "control" have a restraining or curbing connotation. Perhaps this explains why many managers — especially defensive ones — appear to devote most of their control efforts toward seeing that their people comply with appropriate budgets, policies, and procedures. I have seen several sales managers, for example, spend more time criticizing their salesmen for exceeding the telephone or entertainment budget than for missing sales objectives. Certainly a manager has control responsibilities to see that there are appropriate compliances, but he has much more important control responsibilities to see that his people achieve or exceed their primary objectives for sales, production, profit contribution, or whatever.

Misconception No. 3: *The best control is the least control.*   Recently a teacher in a local high school read to her students a poem which, subsequently, was judged by a number of parents to be pornographic. Parents who complained found that the administration "did not wish to interfere with the professional prerogatives of its staff."

This is an example of what can happen when an organization has little or no control over the results that it is trying to achieve. It's one thing for an organization to give its people as much freedom as possible for independent thought and action, but it's another thing to give them so much freedom that it abdicates its responsibility for seeing that there is enough control so planned results are achieved.

Misconception No. 4: *It's the controller's job to control.*   The controller in many organizations has the authority to authorize or veto new positions, salary increases, capital expenditures, and so on. When he has such authority, he is generally assuming authority that line managers should have. He does not have responsibility for line results, and incidentally, probably does not have sufficient understanding of the problems and opportunities involved. Of course he should have functional responsibility to see that accounting and other procedures are followed; but his main role should be to supply the line with information, to analyze that information, and to advise the line on what action might be taken. If he is to serve his organization best, he should not make line managers' decisions. Management consultant Marvin Bower puts it this way:

> When a controller over-reaches the information function and actually exercises control—as some do—it is neither good for the company nor good for the controller himself in his relations with the line. Perhaps his title subtly encourages the controller to over-reach his authority. That may be the reason why a few companies (General Motors among them) still use the former title "comptroller."[1]

Another reason that the controller should not make line managers' decisions is that he often relies primarily upon accounting reports for his information. It is impossible for him to stay abreast of the kinds of control information that each line manager gets through personal observation and through nonaccounting oral and written reports.

Misconception No. 5: *Reporting absolves you of responsibility.* Recently a data-processing manager showed me a letter that he had written to his superior some months back and in which he described the problems he faced. He used this letter as "evidence" that he had put himself on record about what would happen if he did not get the budget approval that he believed he required. Almost everything that he said would happen did happen—not because he didn't get as large a budget as he believed he needed but because he had resigned himself to the belief that there was little he could do to correct the problems he faced.

I find that many managers have the viewpoint that if they report their problems to their superiors, they shouldn't be held accountable for what happens. They are particularly prone to this viewpoint if they have bosses who grab the ball and try to solve the problems that their subordinate managers are supposed to solve.

HOW TO CONTROL THE PERFORMANCE OF YOUR PEOPLE

Earlier I suggested that the essence of control is to concentrate on whatever has the greatest effect on what you are trying to achieve. I believe this can be stated more meaningfully in terms of this chapter's key point: *Control through management by exception.*

Management by exception is a concept of management control wherein you concentrate on important exceptions from planned performance rather than on performance in those areas where progress is satisfactory. Some of the elements and advantages of using management by exception are given in Figure 20-2.

FIGURE 20-2   Why Use Management by Exception?

1. You concentrate on major opportunities and/or problems rather than on minor ones.

2. You avoid worry about minor deviations from planned performance.

3. You avoid wasting time in areas where progress is satisfactory.

4. You rely on your people to evaluate their own problems and to take their own control action; you get involved only if there is a clear need to do so.

5. You are able to evaluate results before you evaluate methods for accomplishing results.

6. You are able to highlight the need for accomplishing long-term objectives in addition to short-term objectives.

7. You are able to evaluate crisis-type problems in relation to your overall objectives.

8. You are able to increase your scope of responsibility in terms of people, products, and markets.

What management by exception can accomplish is indicated by the experience of Teledyne, Inc., which carried out a growth program involving over 100 acquisitions and mergers within a period of seven years. Describing Teledyne's control methods, *Business Week* reported:

> Through the traditional route of financial reporting, each company is measured weekly by performance against plan. Any deviation over $20,000 in cash flow gets circled in red on the reports to [the president]. It is a system of "management by exception reporting" that does not require computers.[2]

The assumption, of course, underlying management by exception is that you have a system of control reports or management information that will tell you periodically how you are doing in relation to planned performance in each of your critical areas of responsibility. The requirements for such a system were covered in Chapter 10.

Here are four suggestions that will help you control through management by exception.

1. *Keep your eye on the ball—your primary objectives.*   The sales manager of one organization established a primary objective to achieve

a certain volume of sales for newly developed standard products. As time went on, he found he had the opportunity to accept business for products that were custom-designed for each customer. He and his people became so involved with this kind of business that he missed his primary objective, which would have made a much larger contribution to profit and which would have laid the foundation for much larger sales and profits in the future.

Many managers get sidetracked because they allow themselves to become controlled by the forces around them. Often they spend their time on doing activities they prefer or on doer-type problems that could be delegated. The result is that they tend to forget to spend their time on those activities that are really most important to their success— especially their success in the long range. One way to remind yourself what your primary objectives are is to post them on your office wall or to keep them in plain view on your desk. Also, your people will be reminded about their part in helping you achieve your objectives whenever they spend time with you in your office. A manager of an engineering group told me that he and his people accomplished 50 percent more than they had in a previous six-month period simply by posting their primary objectives.

2. *Give special attention to key problems and opportunities.*   As a manager, you should know about Pareto's Law. This law, named after an Italian engineer of the late nineteenth century, states that the significant items in a given group normally constitute a relatively small portion of the total items in the group. Conversely, a majority of the items in the total will, even in the aggregate, be of relatively minor significance.[3] In other words, your most important problems and opportunities are concentrated. As indicated at the beginning of the chapter, this is why you can often control 80 percent of the annual dollar value of your inventory by controlling 20 percent of the items. Likewise, you can apply Pareto's Law to any area of responsibility that you have. Eight more examples are shown in Figure 20-3.

If you have a primary objective to achieve a certain level of sales, you can rank your customers and prospects according to their anticipated sales and you will find that you can get 70 or 80 percent of your sales by concentrating on 10 or 20 percent of your accounts. By the same token, if you are not realizing anticipated sales, your major problems are likely to be with a relatively few accounts. This same kind of thinking will help you achieve any objective that you have and helps explain why management by exception works so effectively.

3. *Have a regular meeting with your key people to measure, evaluate, and correct the performance of your people.*   Your control efforts will

FIGURE 20-3 Some Applications of Pareto's Law

Markets:	Determine which customers and prospects on which to concentrate attention.
Men:	Determine which causes of attendance problems should get the most attention.
Machines:	Determine which machines to replace.
Materials:	Determine which products to redesign.
Money:	Determine which capital expenditures require approval by the board of directors.
Methods:	Determine which tasks should have engineered work standards.
Management:	Determine which are critical qualifications for the selection of future managers.
Facilities:	Determine the amount of warehouse space required for each size of product.

be more effective if you rely upon your key people to help you. In turn, their control efforts will be most effective if they meet regularly with you to get a current picture of each others' progress and plans—at least insofar as their efforts affect each other. The frequency with which you and your key people should meet depends on the dynamics of your situation and the extent to which control actions can be taken as a result of the meeting. A production superintendent may meet with his foreman daily for thirty or sixty minutes if the daily influx of orders causes significant adjustments in assignments and schedules. A plant manager may need to meet with his department heads on a weekly basis. A regional sales manager may need to meet with his district managers no more frequently than monthly. A board chairman, on the other hand, may not need to hold a meeting of the board of directors any more frequently than quarterly.

4. *Use a control method that has minimum dependence on you.* Controlling is one of your major responsibilities, but this does not mean that you should devote a high percentage of your time to this activity. If you apply management by exception and rely upon your key people as much as possible. you may find that the activity may not take up more than 10 or 15 percent of your time.

One of the best managers I have ever met took over the reins of a small manufacturing company and turned it into a highly profitable operation within about a year and a half. He credited his success largely to the management-by-exception methods of control that he used. In all likelihood, this also explained why he had the reputation of having his feet on his desk most of the time.

In this chapter I have presented an overview of what each manager should know about controlling. I hope you will keep this overview in mind as you read each chapter covering the controlling elements: measuring, evaluating, and correcting.

HOW TO CONTROL THE PERFORMANCE OF YOUR PEOPLE

1. Keep your eye on the ball—your primary objectives.
2. Give special attention to key problems and opportunities.
3. Have a regular meeting with your key people to measure, evaluate, and correct the performance of your people.
4. Use a control method that has minimum dependence on you.

KEY POINT: *Control through management by exception.*

REFERENCES

1. Marvin Bower, *"The Will to Manage,"* McGraw-Hill Book Company, New York, 1966, p. 218.
2. "Making Big Waves with Small Fish," *Business Week,* Dec. 30, 1967, p. 39.
3. C. J. Slaybaugh, "Pareto's Law and Modern Management," *The Price Waterhouse Review,* 11(4):27, Winter 1966.

21

MEASURING

MEASURING *Determining through formal and informal reports the degree to which progress toward objectives is being made.*

Probably the biggest single problem that managers face in measuring progress toward their objectives is that they rely too much on their accounting reports. More often than not, accounting reports are designed more for financial and accounting purposes than for operational purposes. They show historical data that tend to show more where you've been than where you're going. If you rely on them too much, you may be like the driver who concentrates on his rearview mirror while traveling on a winding mountain road.

DO YOUR ACCOUNTING REPORTS HELP OR HINDER YOU?

If the accounting reports you receive have been designed specifically for operational purposes, you may have no complaints about them. On the other hand, perhaps you have one or more of the complaints in Figure 21-1.

187

FIGURE 21-1   Do You Have Any of These Complaints about the Accounting Reports You Receive?

Yes	No	
____	____	1. They're late. I receive them several days or weeks beyond the point when I can act effectively on them.
____	____	2. They're inaccurate. They don't reflect current assignments of my people.
____	____	3. They have irrelevant information. They show overhead costs that are allocated to my area of responsibility and over which I have no control.
____	____	4. They're incomplete. They show cost variances but neglect variances in sales volume, sales mix, and sales price.
____	____	5. They show unfair comparisons. I get charged for all the advertising costs before there are any results from the advertising.
____	____	6. They don't pinpoint responsibility. They show costs of claims and makeovers but neglect to pinpoint who was responsible.

If you have such complaints, you may be tempted to pass the buck to your controller's department about what you can't do because you don't have the right information in the right form when you need it. In time, your controller's department may be able to provide you with the reports you need; but in the meantime, what do you do? It's *your* job to manage, so it's up to *you* to develop and get whatever information you need to control your operation.

The head of operations of a fast-growing electronics firm has the right idea—at least for the short range. He recently told me that he expects his key people to develop their own methods of getting the information they need to control their operations. He doesn't give his people an out just because there may be a temporary bottleneck in the data-processing department.

Whether or not your accounting reports provide you with the information you need to manage, there are some things not to measure.

WHAT NOT TO MEASURE

Here are four ways to measure progress that will make you *less* effective than you should be.

1. *The way "you used to do it."*   Because of your previous success in performing the tasks that your people now perform, you may subconsciously measure the performance of your people in terms of the methods that you used to use. If, for example, you used to clean up your paper work each day before you went home, you may expect your people to do likewise even though there is no clear need to do so. If you see your people frequently, you probably observe their methods much

more often than you measure the results that they are achieving. But don't let such observations mislead you so you take unnecessary and perhaps detrimental corrective action to try to get your people to perform exactly as you performed.

2. *Personality characteristics of your people.*   Chances are that you have more in common with some of your people than with others; you probably prefer the personalities of some of your people over the personalities of others. Therefore, you may have a tendency to measure the performance of your people in terms of how well you like them. This is a sure road to managerial ignominy (and explains why some organizations suffer from nepotism). You need to be on your guard so you don't overlook, or let slide, potential problems with those individuals whom you especially like. You must also guard against being overcritical in evaluating the performance of those individuals whom you don't like too well; otherwise, subsequent corrective actions that you take with such individuals may dampen their will to perform.

3. *Results that would make your measuring late.*   Suppose it is the first of the month and you suspect that you are significantly behind your year-to-date target for sales, shipments, purchases, inventory levels, collections, or whatever. What should you do if it will be a couple of weeks yet before you receive your regular monthly report describing exactly where you stand as of the end of last month? What you may overlook in this kind of situation is that estimates may serve your needs almost as well as accurate information. To estimate where you stand, you may have to compile some incomplete data, make a few phone calls, make some visits, or apply some rules of thumb; but your estimates are likely to be accurate within plus or minus 5 percent. Such estimates are far more valuable to you—providing they serve as the basis for prompt corrective action—than accurate data that you receive two weeks later.

4. *Detailed results for which your key people are responsible.*   I know a regional sales manager who tries to keep track of the sales to every account in his region. He has district sales managers who in turn have salesmen, yet he just can't seem to convince himself that progress in his region is satisfactory if each of his district managers is achieving his sales objectives. His district managers complain that he is duplicating their efforts to measure performance, but he continues to do so under the guise of trying to stay abreast of everything that happens in his region.

It is perfectly appropriate for a manager to get involved with the details of performance in an area where there is significant deviation from planned performance. However, he will bog down if he tries to keep track of detailed performance in those areas where overall performance is satisfactory. It is the job of the doer to keep abreast of detailed results; it is the job of the manager to keep abreast of overall results.

HOW TO MEASURE THE PERFORMANCE OF YOUR PEOPLE

The key point of this chapter is: *Check regularly to determine cumulative progress toward planned results.* You can implement this key point in five ways.

1. *Get written progress reports in time to take desirable control action.* Most managers are able to rely upon the services of staff departments such as the controller's department to provide them and their people with written reports that document progress in relation to planned results—i.e., in relation to measurable objectives. In any event, you must see that you and your people have whatever information is required to measure such progress even if you and your people must prepare the information or adapt information that is not in the form that you need it. The frequency with which you measure progress in each of your major areas of responsibility depends on the kinds of control action that you and your people are able to take. You should check progress frequently enough so nothing critical is likely to happen that would prevent you from achieving your objectives. A field sales manager, for example, might measure progress as shown in Figure 21-2.

FIGURE 21-2   Sample Checklist for Field Sales Manager to Measure Cumulative Progress toward Planned Results

1. *Weekly*

   a. Measure year-to-date progress toward volume objectives—overall and for each salesman, each major product line, each major market, and total target business. (Target business may be sales to key accounts, sales of new products or services, and/or sales to new types of accounts.)

2. *Monthly or by Four-week Period*

   a. Measure year-to-date progress toward sales coverage objectives (sales calls)—broken down as in Item 1*a* above.
   b. Measure year-to-date expense budget compliance—overall and in total for each salesman.
   c. Measure year-to-date progress toward personnel objectives for staffing, training and development, and compensation.
   d. Measure year-to-date progress toward innovation objectives—i.e., to improve methods or procedures for selling or sales management.

2. *Record key performance figures on five to ten simple charts.* Nothing shows a picture as clearly and as meaningfully as a well-prepared, simple chart. Yet, I have found that relatively few managers use charts to show key performance figures for them and their people. Suppose you wanted to review the sales of product line A for the past several months. Which would give you a clearer picture: your sales-volume reports or the chart shown in Figure 21-3?

FIGURE 21-3 Line Chart Showing Current Perfor-mance by Month and by Moving Annual Total

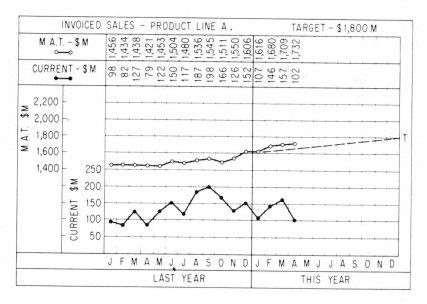

And now suppose you wish to review the year-to-date performance of each of your salesmen compared to his annual goals. Which would give you a clearer picture: your sales-volume reports or the chart shown in Figure 21-4?

Once you know what charts you want and develop the format for each of them, your secretary can keep them up to date—usually by spending no more than an hour or two a month to chart the information from your regular progress reports.

3. *Plot trends in relation to your objectives.* Current performance often varies so much from period to period that it is difficult to know what the trend is. Furthermore, some periods have more working days in them than others and there is always the possibility that you will react too strongly when current performance is exceptionally high or low. You can avoid these kinds of problems by plotting trends that show cumulative performance—e.g., year-to-date figures or moving annual

FIGURE 21-4   Bar Chart Showing Year-to-date Performance by Salesman

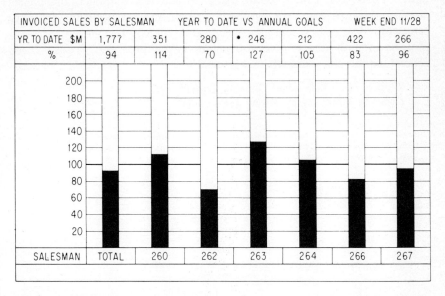

INVOICED SALES BY SALESMAN		YEAR TO DATE VS ANNUAL GOALS				WEEK END 11/28	
YR. TO DATE $M	1,777	351	280	• 246	212	422	266
%	94	114	70	127	105	83	96
SALESMAN	TOTAL	260	262	263	264	266	267

totals. In Figure 21-4, year-to-date performance is indicated in relation to the dark 100 percent line. In Figure 21-3, the upper line shows moving annual totals. A moving annual total shows performance for the current twelve months; each month you add the performance of the current month and subtract the performance of the same month last year. A moving annual total eliminates all seasonal fluctuations and shows current performance in terms of an *annual* figure for which most organizations are accountable to stockholders, members, or citizens.

4. *Make sure each of your key people gets his performance reports as soon as you do.*   Many organizations distribute reports at the same frequency and in the same detail to all levels of affected management. However, first-line managers with responsibility for relatively narrow results should receive detailed information frequently, as they are closest to the point where most corrective action should be taken; higher-level managers are responsible for broader results and generally need only summary information on a less frequent basis. Accordingly, even if you and your key people receive performance reports at about the same time, you should give them the opportunity to see where they stand and to take corrective action that they can report to you. It is even more desirable that they have some means of knowing where they stand — perhaps through estimates — *before* their performance is reported to you and to others affected.

5. *Make periodic personal visits to "measure" other factors not covered in formal reports.*   There has never been a reporting system designed that reports all pertinent performance information. Therefore, you must get out and meet with your people so you can make first-hand observations about what is going on. For example, I know of one organization with a compensation problem that is going to cause significant turnover of good people unless it is recognized and corrected. I know of another instance where large customers are dissatisfied with the delivery service they are getting and are planning to give their business to other suppliers if the service does not improve.

Have you ever attended a baseball game where the scoreboard was not used? If so, you probably found it a frustrating experience because you lost track of runs, strikes, balls, outs, and innings. Some managers try to run their operations with little regard to where they stand. Sometimes they succeed, but I wouldn't bet my money on a team that didn't maintain and pay close attention to its scoreboard. Would you?

HOW TO MEASURE THE PERFORMANCE OF YOUR PEOPLE

1. Get written progress reports in time to take desirable control action.
2. Record key performance figures on five to ten simple charts.
3. Plot trends in relation to your objectives.
4. Make sure each of your key people gets his performance reports as soon as you do.
5. Make periodic personal visits to "measure" other factors not covered in formal reports.

KEY POINT: *Check regularly to determine cumulative progress toward planned results.*

22

EVALUATING

EVALUATING *Determining causes of and possible
ways to act upon significant deviations from
planned performance.*

"Get the facts before they get you!"

This is the advice I once heard the executive vice president of a very
successful manufacturing company give to a group of managers. He
was giving a talk on the subject of management control and he was
explaining the kinds of facts that a manager needs to achieve his profit
objectives. Analysis of historical data, he said, can be helpful, but if
carried too far it's like giving a man an autopsy to bring him back to life.

Of course you must deal in facts of an historical nature when you
measure progress toward your objectives. But such facts generally
don't give you answers to these questions:

1. What deviations from planned performance are significant?
2. What caused such deviations?
3. What actions might you take?
4. What are likely results of each action?

That's the purpose of evaluating—to help you answer these questions.

THERE'S DANGER IN HAVING TOO FEW FACTS

Managers who take control actions based upon a "gut feel" often do not really realize the implications of their actions. One of the most common areas where this is done is in price cutting. Many managers reduce the prices of their products or services with inadequate facts. For example, what are the facts that you should know if you have the problem described in Figure 22-1?

FIGURE 22-1 An Evaluation Problem

Suppose you have a year-end profit contribution objective of $25,000 on a product that sells for $1,000 per unit and has a profit contribution margin of 25 percent. Your year-to-date sales are behind projection and two of your people have suggested that you reduce the price. To achieve your profit contribution objective, what dollar volume of sales do you need and how many more units must you handle if you reduce the price by:
a. 5 percent?
b. 10 percent?

The facts are that if you were to reduce the price by 5 percent, you would have to increase dollar sales by almost 19 percent and you would have to handle 25 percent more units. If you were to reduce the price by 10 percent, you would have to increase dollar sales by 50 percent and handle 66⅔ percent more units. You may also like to know that if you were to reduce the price by 20 percent, you would have to increase dollar sales by 300 percent and handle 400 percent more units; your profit contribution margin would be only $50 per unit and you would have to sell 500 units at a sales price of $800 per unit. Perhaps you should reduce the price, but you should do so only with a full knowledge of the facts that evaluating can provide you.

Another area where managers often get in trouble is in making decisions where allocated overhead (i.e., fixed expenses for management salaries, rent, depreciation, and so on) is involved. For example, they may not realize that any income over direct cost (i.e., material, direct labor, sales commissions, and other costs that vary directly with volume) makes some contribution toward overhead and profit even though the income may not be as much as the accounting department allocated to cover overhead expense. Consequently, it may be wise to keep selling a certain product or to keep open a certain office even though it may not pay for its full share of allocated overhead (which, incidentally, is always over- or underabsorbed because the overhead allocation is based on a certain projected volume). In an article describing how to use fixed and variable costs in decision making, management consultant Robert C. Trundle says:

> The problem with decision making is that the same facts don't always show the same picture. On face value a set of facts may show one thing. Examine them closer, put them together more wisely, and they may show exactly the opposite. The manager who uses a simple decision-making method for a complex decision problem may be like a man trying to sink a putt with a broomstick.[1,*]

Human behavior is another area in which managers often have inadequate facts to deal with. Industrial psychologist Harry Levinson says:

> The most important causes of human behavior are people's feelings, some so subtle that individuals, themselves, are unaware of them. Feelings of anger, which are hardest to deal with, are those which people hide from themselves as well as from others. To make things more complicated, people sometimes have so much difficulty in dealing with the unconscious feeling of anger that the only way they can get rid of it is to hurt themselves in some manner.
>
> . . . When a manager finds a situation in which people are hurting themselves, either physically or psychologically, in ways which cost them money or status—and hurting the organization at the same time—this is a strong indication that he needs to look further.
>
> "What's making this person or these people angry?"
>
> "Why do they have to express their anger this way?"
>
> The answers may not be readily apparent, and they will not be apparent at all unless he looks for them.[2]

Facts about human behavior are frequently difficult to get because they are subjective in nature. Nevertheless, you need such facts—particularly those relating to your direct subordinates—to evaluate any kinds of control actions that you can take through your people.

There's only one thing worse than having too few facts for evaluating purposes and that's having too many facts. With too many facts, you may suffer from "paralysis by analysis."

YOU WILL NEVER HAVE ENOUGH FACTS

Several college administrators have been criticized recently because they haven't acted decisively enough in handling student disorders. A key reason, it appears, is that they have tried to apply the same slow fact-gathering and analysis methods that are appropriate for academic pursuits. Such methods may be required for developing long-range solutions, but they do little to help you handle current eruptions that require short-range solutions. Furthermore, comprehensive studies are never entirely complete because they cannot take into account and stay abreast of all the changing psychological, sociological, economic, political, and other factors that affect the lives of all of us every day. In this context, semanticists remind us about the danger of the word *is;* nothing ever remains the same. Consequently, each manager must make his own judgment about when he has sufficient facts on which to base whatever control action he decides to take.

HOW TO EVALUATE THE PERFORMANCE OF YOUR PEOPLE

When progress toward your objectives appears to be significantly less or significantly more than you planned, *obtain additional facts and opinions before deciding upon corrective action.* In this way, you can avoid jumping to conclusions about what your problems and opportunities are and about corrective actions that you might take. Here are six guidelines.

1. *Look for relationships between results.* There are many reasons why you achieve or don't achieve sales, production, quality, profit, or whatever other objectives you may have. For example, your production may be less than planned because you have inadequate direct-material inventory or you are behind in your staffing program or equipment utilization has been poor or orders booked have been spasmodic. By the same token, it would be wrong for you to get excited about poor utilization of equipment when another of your reports may suggest that your order backlog has prevented effective scheduling of equipment.

2. *Consider whether sufficient time has elapsed for results to be meaningful.* Perhaps you can rely on a rule of thumb to determine what is a significant deviation in each area of planned performance. In a low-volume item, a deviation in excess of plus or minus 10 percent may be significant. For a high-volume item, a deviation of plus or minus 3 percent may be significant. However, you must consider elapsed time in determining whether a deviation is really significant. A 20 percent deviation in year-to-date planned performance during the first month of the year will generally not be as significant as a 5 percent deviation in year-to-date planned performance during the last month of the year.

Be especially wary of evaluating the sales of new products until sufficient time has elapsed so you can evaluate the extent to which there are repeat sales. Many companies have made the mistake of building expensive new plants to produce products with high initial sales in test markets only to find that repeat sales did not materialize.

3. *Meet with one or more of your key people to confirm reported data and to try to define any problems involved.* If you rely upon your key

people to achieve *their* objectives (which in turn enables you to achieve *your* objectives), you should not get excited when there are minor deviations in planned performance. However, when deviations appear significant, your key people should have a much better idea than you about possible causes and solutions. The way to find out is to meet with them and determine whether they need the help that you can provide. You may find, for example, that they do not know how to handle some of the human behavior problems that they face. In this respect, make sure you do not put too high a premium upon how well your people please you personally. In his book *The Effective Executive*, Peter Drucker says:

> Effective executives know that their subordinates are paid to perform and not to please their superiors. They know that it does not matter how many tantrums a prima donna throws as long as she brings in the customers. The opera manager is paid after all for putting up with the prima donna's tantrums if that is her way to achieve excellence in performance. It does not matter whether a first-rate teacher or a brilliant scholar is pleasant to the dean or amiable in the faculty meeting. The dean is paid for enabling the first-rate teacher or the first-rate scholar to do his work effectively— and if this involves unpleasantness in the administrative routine, it is still cheap at the price. [3]

In keeping with this advice, I hope you do not have appraisal forms that require you to evaluate your people in terms of their personality characteristics. Progressive managers gave up these kinds of appraisals years ago.

4. *Consider having one or more studies made to get detailed facts and opinions.* Suppose you are significantly behind in achieving your year-end profit goal of 10 percent on sales of $3 million. What you might do is indicated in Figure 22-2.

This analysis shows that a 10 percent reduction in fixed expenses will enable you to achieve your $300,000 profit objective with sales of $2,820,000. With a 10 percent price increase, you could achieve your profit goal with sales of $2,358,000. With a 10 percent reduction in variable expenses, you could achieve your profit goal with sales of $2,310,000. With this kind of analysis, you could go to your people to determine the feasibility of each alternative course of action. Perhaps you would decide on a combination of actions. You may even decide to increase either fixed or variable costs—e.g., by increasing advertising or by increasing the quality of the product—if you feel that such action will enable you to achieve your profit goal at a sales volume in excess of $3 million.

Any manager with profit responsibility should understand profit-volume relationship formulas on which the above analysis is based. Such formulas are shown in Figure 22-3.[4]

FIGURE 22-2 Sample Analysis to Increase Profits
(All figures are in thousands of dollars)

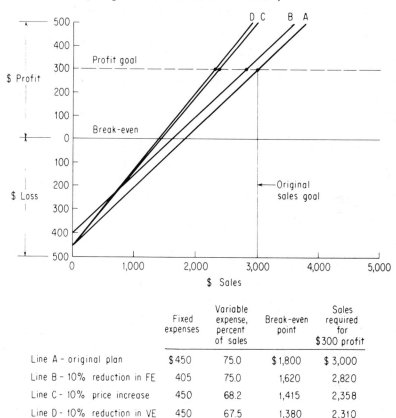

	Fixed expenses	Variable expense, percent of sales	Break-even point	Sales required for $300 profit
Line A - original plan	$450	75.0	$1,800	$3,000
Line B - 10% reduction in FE	405	75.0	1,620	2,820
Line C - 10% price increase	450	68.2	1,415	2,358
Line D - 10% reduction in VE	450	67.5	1,380	2,310

FIGURE 22-3 Profit-Volume Relationship Formulas

1. Sales minus variable expense equals marginal income. $S - VE = MI$

2. Sales minus the sum of variable expense and fixed expense equals profit. $S - (VE + FE) = P$

3. Marginal income equals fixed expense plus profit. $MI = FE + P$

4. Dollars of marginal income divided by dollars of sales equals percent of marginal income. $\dfrac{\$MI}{\$S} = \%MI$

5. Dollars of fixed expense divided by marginal income percentage expressed decimally equals breakeven point. $\dfrac{\$FE}{\%MI} = BE$

6. Percent marginal income times the difference between sales and breakeven equals profit. $\%MI \times (S - BE) = P$

From *Marketing for Profit* by Douglas P. Gould, Copyright © 1961 by Reinhold Publishing Corporation, by permission of Van Nostrand Reinhold Company.

The author of these formulas is management consultant Douglas P. Gould; he uses the term "marginal income," but it is synonymous with "profit contribution," and in some cases, "gross profit."

5. *Consider getting the ideas of associates, superiors, and/or outsiders.*   Some managers are so doer-oriented or defensive that they don't like to let the rest of the world know that they have problems. Consequently, they try to reinvent the wheel or do everything themselves to identify and solve the problems they face. Why not at least get the ideas of those inside or outside of your organization who have developed improved layouts, designed cost-accounting systems, conducted sales-promotion programs, administered profit-improvement programs, and so on? Don't overlook what your major suppliers may be able to do for you. Many suppliers offer services at little or no cost on the premise that they will get more business if you are more successful.

6. *Expend only an economical amount of time and effort before deciding upon appropriate action.*   If you are trying to achieve only a one-thousand-dollar result, it stands to reason that you cannot spend very much time and effort evaluating what you should do to achieve that result. On the other hand, if you are trying to achieve a million-dollar objective, you can probably afford to spend several hundred or several thousand dollars getting and evaluating facts and opinions as a basis for corrective action. If you or your organization tends to suffer from "meetingitis," don't overlook the cost of holding meetings that are too long or too frequent. It's one thing to get facts and opinions from your people, for example, but it's another thing to take up so much of their time that they are hindered from what they are trying to accomplish.

If you've seen the play depicting the life of George M. Cohan, perhaps you remember the scene where he is asked how he can tell whether a new Broadway production is really good. His reply indicated that it's the way you feel—e.g., the theater lights seem brighter. So it is with evaluating. You will never know for sure that you have obtained the right facts and that you have evaluated them properly in terms of the actions that you might take. However, if you have made a sincere effort and you feel that you have done a good job, chances are that you have.

HOW TO EVALUATE THE PERFORMANCE OF YOUR PEOPLE

1.   Look for relationships between results.
2.   Consider whether sufficient time has elapsed for results to be meaningful.

3.   Meet with one or more of your key people to confirm reported data and to try to define any problems involved.

4.   Consider having one or more studies made to get detailed facts and opinions.

5. Consider getting the ideas of associates, superiors, and/or outsiders.

6. Expend only an economical amount of time and effort before deciding upon appropriate action.

KEY POINT: *Obtain additional facts and opinions before deciding upon corrective action.*

REFERENCES

1. Robert C. Trundle, "How to Sharpen Profits with Decision Evaluation and Logic," *Business Management,* October, 1962, p. 71.
2. Harry Levinson, "Do You Look for Culprits—or Causes?" *Hydrocarbon Processing,* August, 1965, p. 165.
3. Peter F. Drucker, *The Effective Executive,* Harper & Row, Publishers, Incorporated, New York, 1966, p. 73.
4. Douglas P. Gould, *Marketing for Profit,* Reinhold Publishing Corporation, New York, 1961, p. 56.

23

CORRECTING

CORRECTING *Taking control action to correct an unfavorable trend or to take advantage of an unusually favorable ' trend.*

Just as an idea has no value unless somebody does something about it, your measuring and evaluating activities have no value unless you take appropriate corrective action. Being able to explain to your boss why your performance is not as planned may be satisfying to your ego, but you'll contribute little or nothing toward the achievement of your objectives. The past is passed and there is nothing you can do about it; the only thing you can control is the future. However, not all actions that you can take are sound.

HOW NOT TO TAKE CORRECTIVE ACTION

You can get an indication about how well you take corrective action by answering the questions in Figure 23-1.

202

FIGURE 23-1 Do You Make These Mistakes in Taking Corrective Action?

Yes	No	
____	____	1. Are you arbitrary in deciding what your people should do?
____	____	2. Do you tell your people what corrective action to take without getting their recommendations about the problems they bring to you?
____	____	3. Do you use hackneyed expressions with your people under the guise of taking corrective action?
____	____	4. Do you keep so much pressure on your people that they haven't distinguished which actions are most important?
____	____	5. Are you unduly influenced by individuals who do not have total perspective in your area of responsibility?
____	____	6. Do you procrastinate in taking corrective actions that may not be popular or that make you uncomfortable?
____	____	7. Do you time your corrective actions without adequate regard to the "business climate" and possible emotional reactions?
____	____	8. Do you neglect to improve your own managing methods?

Mistake No. 1: Many presidents are arbitrary when they order 10 percent across-the-board cost reductions. This kind of action is grossly unfair to the managers who have been doing a good job of controlling costs. As a matter of fact, many managers have learned that the way to prepare for inevitable cost reductions is to add fat when times are good. If a president wants to reduce costs by 10 percent, he should do so by giving his division heads some flexibility in determining which departments have the most fat and can make the most cost reductions without crippling vital operations.

If you have done a good job of evaluating, you probably won't take arbitrary corrective actions. However, you may be tempted to do so if the problem you face is complicated and if there are many corrective actions that you can take.

Mistake No. 2: You will probably be tempted to tell your people what corrective action to take without getting their recommendations when you have considerably more knowledge and experience than they or when you are under pressure and feel that quick action is required. Yielding to such temptation, however, is a poor way to develop your people and to make them self-reliant—but it's an excellent way to function as a doer and nondelegator.

Mistake No. 3: "You guys better get on the ball." "You can't work harder, but you can work smarter." "You'd better burn a little midnight oil." "I want everyone to do his part to increase our profits." These and other hackneyed expressions do little to encourage your people to take any meaningful corrective action. I'll wager, though, that as a subordinate, you've heard such expressions many times in the course of your career.

Mistake No. 4: A certain sales manager was assigned to beef up sales in a district that had only four salesmen. He wanted to do a good job, so he decided to work closely with each of his people. Each time he spent a day in the field with a man, he left a list of things for the man to accomplish. The result was that each man tried to do what the sales manager requested and lost perspective about other important activities that he was also supposed to accomplish. The problem wasn't resolved until the sales manager was given additional responsibility and was no longer able to spend so much time with each man.

When you face a performance problem, you may also have a tendency to give your people too many instructions. This is also a time when your people may have a tendency to rely too much on you because they may have lost some confidence in their own ability to take their own corrective action.

Mistake No. 5: You probably have reporting to you one or more people on whom you are particularly dependent. They are persons who control your largest accounts or have special knowledge and skills or are very influential with others in your group. Therefore, you may have a tendency to rely too heavily upon their views when you take corrective action. This is a sure way to abdicate your responsibility to improve systems, make capital expenditures, make changes in assignments, and take other corrective actions in areas where your people do not have perspective beyond their assigned areas of responsibility. I know one president, for example, who relied too much on the views of his dollar-conscious vice-president of finance. Consequently, when new competitors entered the market his company served, he went on a cost-reduction program to improve profits instead of making capital expenditures that would have improved customer service and discouraged competition.

Mistake No. 6: Unless you are sadistically inclined, it is unlikely that you enjoy terminating an employee, reducing a person's responsibility, curtailing costs that affect your people, and so on. Many managers delay for weeks, months, and sometimes years before taking such kinds of corrective action. Some managers never take certain kinds of corrective action. For example, many employees who perform poorly get bounced around in their organizations from one position to another over the course of 10 or 20 years; then no one wants to fire them because they have "put in so many years of loyal service." I am not suggesting that you be unkind or inconsiderate, but keeping such employees is often a disservice to them (because they know deep down inside themselves that they are misplaced) and a costly burden to your organization.

Mistake No. 7: Perhaps you've seen managers terminate employees just before Christmas simply to reduce costs, make significant increases in prices shortly after government requests to hold the line, and so on. The negative effect of such corrective actions generally far offsets any positive effect due to the emotional reactions of employees, customers, and others. In each instance, the action would probably have been sound had the timing been better.

If you have ever had negative emotional reactions to the corrective actions you have taken, chances are a major reason was your timing.

Mistake No. 8: Probably your most difficult realization is that you may be the main cause of your performance problems. It's unlikely that you will recommend to your superior that you be replaced, but this is the kind of corrective action that a manager's superior sometimes has to take—especially when the manager does little to improve his managing methods. If you are mature enough to point the finger at yourself, then you will seek ways to improve your own performance. And the way to do this is to improve your own managing methods. In the long run, this is the most important corrective action that you can take.

CORRECTIVE ACTIONS YOU CAN TAKE

Many organizations spend much time and money to develop computerized data-processing systems to provide managers with voluminous kinds of information, but they spend little or nothing to define the kinds of corrective actions that managers can take as a result of the information. Yet this is what control is all about—action. An information factory has weak underpinnings if its end products are bought by managers who use seat-of-the-pants methods to decide what to do about the information. It's hard enough for a manager to decide what to do when he has a range of choices before him, but his situation is unduly complicated when he doesn't even know his choices. Do you know what corrective actions you can take—either to correct an unfavorable trend or to take advantage of an unusually favorable trend?

With respect to unusually favorable trends, many managers overlook their opportunities. In many instances, all they do is tell their excellent performers to "keep up the good work" or tell their superiors things are going much better than expected in anticipation of a "that's nice" commendation.

I recall talking to one production employee who said, "I have often wondered why our management doesn't question how the department I'm in always manages to achieve maximum incentive. Actually, we have improved the methods on which our performance standards were based and could double our production if we felt we'd get a fair shake."

In the same light, a salesman once told me, "My boss praises me for the sales job I am doing but he has never expressed more than superficial interest in the selling methods that I use. I'd be willing to explain what I do to our other salesmen if I were asked to do so but I'm not going to take the initiative if it could be interpreted as grandstanding."

I believe that every manager should prepare for himself a list of the kinds of corrective actions that he can take to achieve his particular objectives. This effort will help him to do a better job of evaluating and finally selecting the corrective action that he does take. Examples of corrective action that any manager can take are shown in Figure 23-2.

FIGURE 23-2 Examples of Corrective Action for Any Manager

1. Provide your people with more day-to-day supervision—to give them more help and direction.
2. Provide your people with training in the knowledge and skills they need.
3. Improve your methods of delegating, motivating, or coordinating.
4. Counsel one or more of your people.
5. Add, move, or terminate one or more people.
6. Add, delete, or improve objectives, programs, schedules, budgets, forecasts, organization structures, policies, procedures, or standards.
7. Improve your methods of deciding, communicating, or improving.
8. Improve your methods of measuring, evaluating, or correcting.
9. Add, delete, or improve physical resources such as products, equipment, facilities, and capital.
10. Obtain specialized internal or external assistance.

Note that the first eight items cover the various managing elements that are described in this book. Improving your performance in these areas will help you improve your managing methods. Your listing of corrective actions will be more meaningful, however, if it is also tailored to your functional responsibility—as illustrated in Figures 23-3 and 23-4.

FIGURE 23-3 Examples of Corrective Action for Sales Managers

1. Increase or decrease field training with each of your people according to individual needs.
2. Teach each of your people why and how to deal with all influential persons in their accounts.
3. Increase or decrease interim objectives for volume or profit contribution.
4. Teach your people how to identify competitive programs, estimate effects, and recommend counteraction.
5. Teach each of your people how to use written proposals.
6. Teach your people how to establish with their accounts proper inventory levels for new and established products.

7. Check condition and proper use of sales equipment such as automobile, sales portfolio, and promotional materials.

8. Hold special progress reviews with those men who need them; counsel them about what they need to do to achieve maximum incentive.

9. Help each of your people plan and implement individual development programs covering, e.g., skills, reading, and courses.

10. Teach your people how to make more effective use of their time; e.g., in handling complaints, delivering samples or requested information, and reducing waiting time on all sales calls.

11. Reassign accounts to increase volume and/or to develop your people.

12. Hold sales meetings on selling methods and other subjects that your people or you want covered.

13. Recommend salary increases.

14. Make recommendations to increase or decrease number of positions reporting to you.

15. Recommend hiring additional and/or replacement personnel to upgrade your organization.

16. Publicize individual "How I Did It" success stories to stimulate action by others in your group.

17. Recommend specifically how to improve policies, procedures, or selling methods.

FIGURE 23-4 Examples of Corrective Action for Production Managers

1. Improve methods and layouts that currently result in expensive hand labor.

2. Add or replace equipment that will reduce labor or increase production.

3. Develop and train employees in standardized work methods.

4. Develop and conduct program for training supervisors in how to improve their effectiveness in getting results through their people.

5. Reduce overtime by adding a shift or by developing more clearly defined overtime policy.

6. Meet with key customers to determine their actual delivery requirements so additional time can be made available to produce their orders.

7. Encourage certain customers to place their orders at times that will eliminate some of the production peaks and valleys.

8. Develop program to eliminate certain causes of customer claims and complaints.

9. Develop program to reduce waste of expensive materials.

10. Determine optimum inventory levels for items of major cost.

11. Act upon cost-reduction ideas suggested by key suppliers.

12. Define and train production personnel in acceptable product-quality requirements to eliminate any instances where unnecessary quality is put into the product.

13. Eliminate from the product line any products that make an inadequate contribution toward fixed expenses and profit.

14. Develop reciprocal program with one or more competitors to produce orders for certain products during peak periods.
15. Develop new products or new applications of present products to increase utilization of production facilities.
16. Lay off employees in excess of minimum requirements when forecast indicates that there will be extended slack period.
17. Terminate employees whose performance is consistently below standard.

HOW TO TAKE CORRECTIVE ACTION

There are many corrective actions that only you can take — e.g., reassigning your key people, resolving interdepartmental problems, establishing new policies, and so on. However, the key point of this chapter is: *Let your people take the corrective action whenever possible.* This may seem very logical but does not always work out in practice. Consider what one management consultant says:

> Control is exercised by taking action, and action must be taken within the authority delegated. And just as no person can be said to control directly the activities assigned to another's jurisdiction, so the only person who can directly control activities is the one directly responsible for them. This is fundamental to the healthy and successful operation of any enterprise; at the same time it is probably one of the least observed principles of management. There are a great many more instances of its violation than there are of its wholehearted acceptance and practice.[1]

This observation was made in 1954, but I believe it is as valid today as it was then. Many managers make assignments to their people on the assumption that they are to get results *through* them, but they take over the reins of control long before there are significant deviations from planned performance. Of course, there are times when a manager should step in to take the corrective action that he should be able to rely upon his people to take; if he finds he must do so frequently, however, he needs to take other corrective action — perhaps by making some changes in staffing.

As far as the corrective action that you should take is concerned, I have four recommendations.

1. *Decide on action that will contribute toward achievement of your objectives.*   Many managers inadvertently take corrective actions that tend to hinder what they are trying to achieve. A purchasing manager may cause costly production delays when he tells his buyers to reduce the cost of items purchased, thereby increasing supplier lead times for many items. An engineering manager may cause construction delays when he decides to make in-house designs that were previously subcon-

tracted. A sales manager may increase unprofitable business when he installs a sales-incentive plan based only on volume—especially if the unprofitable products are easiest to sell. A production manager may increase indirect costs when he reduces the number of first-level supervisors. In this respect, management consultant Edward Schleh observes:

> Saving money on first-level supervision almost always leads to extra costs. If supervisors at the bottom are beyond their span of control, problems occur and more staff is set up to solve each one, a primary reason for excessive staff costs. Inadequate first-level supervision is almost universal in large companies.[2],*

At the general-management level, you may wish to improve your own performance by doing what the operating head of one management services company does. He meets periodically with an advisory board whose members have been carefully selected to provide him with advice and direction in major areas of management. He pays each board member normal fees for directors, but the board has no legal responsibility and he is free to accept or reject their recommendations. As a matter of fact, the board members do not even receive minutes of board meetings.

2. *Decide how you will get support for your action.* Even though your corrective action may be theoretically sound, you will not get the results you seek unless you get support for your action. You must decide whether you are going to tell or sell. If you decide that you are going to tell one of your people that you are terminating him, you need to have the support of your immediate superior and possibly that of your personnel director. If you decide that you want all your supervisors to use the accident-prevention methods that one of your supervisors has found unusually effective, you will need to develop some kind of selling strategy. For example, you may wish to sell your supervisors one at a time or in a group meeting; or perhaps you will decide to propose a pilot program to evaluate the general applicability of the accident-prevention methods you believe should be adopted.

One major consideration that will determine in large measure the kind of support you get for your corrective action is timing. Before you burden your people with additional assignments, for example, you should consider how busy they currently are and the extent to which they have completed other recent assignments that you have given them. If your action involves customers or others outside of your organization, you might wish to get a sampling of opinion from your salesmen or others about the timing of the action you are going to take.

---

* Reprinted by special permission from *Dun's Review*, April, 1967. Copyright, 1967, Dun & Bradstreet Publications Corporation.

3. *Take action.*   Most managers make clear who is to do what when they take corrective action, but they do not always make clear when the action is to be started and completed. Consequently, new employees don't get hired and trained in time to take advantage of a short-range expansion opportunity; new systems do not get developed in time to give suppliers the lead times they require; and so on. Unless you make clear when a corrective action is to be started and completed, you may get the reaction of one foreman who told me, "I have found that the way to get along with my boss is to agree with everything that he wants done because I find that over the course of time he tends to forget his instructions. Furthermore he always wants us to concentrate on the last thing he told us to do with the result that many earlier actions never get completed."

4. *Follow up to see that action is taken as planned and to evaluate results.*   I once worked with a manager who had recently entered industry from the military. I found that he had the naive assumption that something would be done all the way down the line just because he put out a directive. I don't know whether he made this assumption because of his particular experience in the military or because of his temperamental makeup; in any event, it took him some time to realize that the only way to find out whether an action is actually taken is to follow up. You can follow up by checking with your people personally, by making personal observations, by holding progress meetings, by reviewing performance reports, or by taking any other appropriate action to keep abreast of the results of your corrective action. The need for such follow-up is humorously illustrated by the story told by a certain naval officer. He reported:

> The new executive officer on our destroyer had completed a course in management just prior to reporting aboard. He immediately instituted a complicated system for man-hour accounting, which he called the Man-Hour Data Reporting System. A young ensign was detailed as the Man-Hour Data Reporting Officer for his division. At the end of the first week his report showed:
>
> Man-hours in repair of malfunctioning equipment   840
> Man-hours in preventive maintenance checks   762
> Man-hours in housekeeping duties   758
> Man-hours on watch stations   624
> Man-hours in Man-Hour Data Reporting 1,025
>
> The Man-Hour Data Reporting System was discontinued shortly afterward.[3,*]

If through your follow-up you find that you are achieving the results you expected, you may wish to take action to achieve further benefits—

* Lt. (JG) J. D. Ritchie, "Humor in Uniform," *Reader's Digest*, p. 205, November, 1964.

e.g., when the results of a pilot program are good. On the other hand, if results are not as you expected, you may wish to cancel, modify, or develop new corrective action—e.g., when a new system becomes burdensome.

The corrective action you take to achieve your objectives need not be perfect. There are generally a number of corrective actions that you can take to achieve a desired result. However, when you decide, take action with confidence. Your own confidence—and perhaps even enthusiasm—may communicate more than the action itself. I believe this is part of what Ralph Waldo Emerson had in mind when he said, "Self-trust is the first secret of success."

HOW TO TAKE CORRECTIVE ACTION

1. Decide on action that will contribute toward achievement of your objectives.
2. Decide how you will get support for your action.
3. Take action.
4. Follow up to see that action is taken as planned and to evaluate results.

KEY POINT: *Let your people take the corrective action whenever possible.*

REFERENCES

1. Arnold F. Emch, "Control Means Action," *Harvard Business Review,* July-August, 1954, p. 97.
2. Edward C. Schleh, "Cost Controls That Cost Money," *Dun's Review,* April, 1967, p. 49.
3. Lt. (JG) J. D. Ritchie, "Humor in Uniform," *Reader's Digest,* November, 1964, p. 205.

Part 5

INTEGRATIVE ELEMENTS OF MANAGING

24

DECIDING

DECIDING *Making a judgment about a course of
action to be taken.*

Your mind operates like a servomechanism in an inertial guidance system.

A servomechanism makes self-correcting changes in the direction of a rocket toward a target on the basis of electronic feedback that it receives continually. Likewise, you make self-correcting decisions toward what you are trying to accomplish on the basis of the feedback you receive from your accumulated up-to-the-minute knowledge and experience — both rational and emotional.

Sound complicated? It is. No one really understands how the mind works or how decisions are made, although cyberneticists are studying the problem. However, you should be aware of this: If you have pertinent up-to-the-minute knowledge and experience, you will probably make good decisions; if you do not have pertinent up-to-the-minute knowledge and experience, you will probably make bad decisions. In short, you are a victim of your own background.

HOW SOUND IS YOUR JUDGMENT?

Pragmatically speaking, there is method to decision making. You can improve your ability to make decisions in all your planning, directing, and controlling activities—providing you feel there is a clear need to do so. You can get an indication about whether you need to improve your ability to make decisions by deciding what you would do if you faced the situation described in Figure 24-1.

FIGURE 24-1   What Would You Decide?

Suppose that John Stanton, one of your key people, has just turned in a letter of resignation in which he says he has accepted a better job with another organization. Assuming that John has had duties and responsibilities that are vital to your operation, which of the following choices is the best statement of the problem(s) you face?

    A. How can I get John to change his mind about quitting the job he has held?
    B. How shall I fill the position that John held?
    C. How can I reassign the duties and responsibilities that John had?
    D. How can I get John to stay with our organization even if he doesn't go back to the position he held?
    E. _____
       _____
       _____

What you decide in a particular situation depends on the definition you give to the problem you face. The trap that many managers fall into is in stating a solution in the definition of the problem. On this basis, the choices *A, B,* and *C* in Figure 24-1 are poor statements of the problem you face. Choice *D* defines a problem—assuming John would be a valuable employee in some other capacity—but overlooks your need to solve the problem of handling the duties and responsibilities that John has had. I believe you face a two-part problem that I would state as follows: (1) How shall I see that the duties and responsibilities that John had are carried out? and (2) How can I convince John to stay with our organization?

Once you have defined your problem, you may still be in deep water unless you know the real cause of your problem. Otherwise, you may decide on wrong solutions. In checking with John, for example, you may find that the real cause of your problem is his wife's attitude toward his job.

Through the above example, I have tried to illustrate some of the method that is involved in sound decision making. In this respect, Louis A. Allen, author and management authority, says:

Many managers find it difficult to look upon decision making as conscious work, subject to principles and rules. The professional manager knows that a sound decision results from the systematic application of mental effort. He recognizes that decision making is a skill which is made up of separate elements and which can be learned as can any other skill.[1]

Let's analyze decision making further.

KINDS OF DECISIONS

Some decisions are much more important than others; yet some managers spend more time deciding on what dictating equipment to buy than they do in deciding on their annual objectives. Such managers often have a penchant for details or perfection and they have difficulty distinguishing what is really important in their operations.

The decisions that you have to make can be classified as very important, important, and unimportant. These decisions can have a very significant, significant, or insignificant impact upon the success or failure of your operation. Very important decisions are those that you make to develop major policies, set primary objectives, develop organization structure, and staff for key positions. Important decisions are those that you make to set secondary objectives, develop minor policies, develop noncritical procedures, and staff for minor positions. Unimportant decisions are those that you make to purchase inexpensive equipment, control the usage of inexpensive supplies, handle the business of accounts with small sales potential, and enforce minor rules for housekeeping. Obviously, you should try to delegate any insignificant decisions that you now make.

DECISION-MAKING TOOLS

Some decisions are unbelievably complicated. The trend toward managers having to make these kinds of decisions has been described by John E. Swearingen, president of Standard Oil Company (Indiana). In an address on executive decision making, he said:

> One of the challenging by-products of our nation's history of growth is the multiplication in the volume and complexity of decisions to be made, particularly at the upper levels of management.
>
> The very scope of decisions has tended to escalate. Instead of four or five major competitors, they must take dozens into account; instead of hundreds of employees, they can affect thousands; instead of tens of millions of dollars in assets, they often involved hundreds of millions.
>
> Compounding the problem has been a mounting need to make longer-range decisions at a time when exploding technology has made the job of

prediction increasingly hazardous. As if this were not quite enough, we have seen accelerating demands to make decisions more quickly, under the pressures of competition and instantaneous communication.[2],*

To assist him in making very complicated decisions, today's manager often relies upon decision-making tools. Examples of these tools are listed in Figure 24-2.

FIGURE 24-2   Examples of Decision-making Tools[3]

1. Operations research

2. Probability and statistics

3. Monte Carlo and waiting-line techniques

4. Linear programming

5. PERT, CPM, and other network techniques

6. Computer simulation

All these tools are used to quantify and evaluate the effects of many variables for decisions such as

Where to locate plants
How to schedule major construction projects
Where to locate points of distribution and warehousing
Evaluating capital investment alternatives
Selecting research and development projects
Pricing
Inventory management
Production planning and control
Economic and sales forecasting
Investment portfolio selection

Many managers are afraid to learn how to use the decision-making tools that are available to them, and, for example, they gloat childishly when a computer goes awry. Little do they realize that they may someday be replaced—not by computers but by managers who understand how to use computers and other decision-making tools.

HOW TO DECIDE

I know a president who recently filled a key position with someone whose knowledge and experience were quite different from his own.

* Reprinted with permission of *News Front,* Management's News Magazine, copyright 1969.

He did so deliberately because he wanted someone who was number-oriented and could provide him with engineering perspective when he had to make important management decisions. He considered the ability to deal with people to be less of a required qualification because he felt he was already strong in this area and could provide any necessary help and direction when the occasion demanded.

This president illustrated one way to implement this chapter's key point: *Tailor your decision-making methods to your personal strengths and weaknesses.* As is everyone, you are a unique individual with certain innate characteristics and with a combination of knowledge and experience that no one else has. You have certain strengths and you have certain weaknesses. There is very little you can do, for example, to change your basic intelligence or to change yourself from an introvert to an extrovert; but you can develop decision-making methods that are best for you—providing you make a deliberate decision to do so.

Dr. Howard K. Holland, professor of education at the College of William and Mary, has studied decision making as related to personality. He says:

> Intelligent persons can think their own thoughts. Moreover, a measure of critical introspection is imperative in any well-lived life. They must recognize outward signs of anxiety: depressions, peculiar habits and mechanisms and view these as symptoms of causes which lie in repressed drives or counter-drives. Most highly civilized people are shocked when they recognize powerful negative emotions in themselves. Yet we all have hostilities and fears and we can learn to discharge these without damage. Administrators can admit primitive, egotistical drives for power and omnipotence and deal with these wisely, with a sense of amusement at themselves. Or recognize irrational, perfectionistic compulsions as signs of their over-developed conscience. They can get their centers of gravity back in their own hands and away from the primitive impulses and counteracting inhibitions.[4]

What you can do, for example, if you have a tendency to be much more depressed than most people is to commit yourself to making important decisions by certain deadlines; in this way, you can avoid damaging procrastination. If you have a tendency to take retaliatory action when you get angry, you can train yourself to get the counsel of someone inside or outside of your organization before you act—or at least delay any decision to act until the following day. If you have "irrational, perfectionistic compulsions," you can train yourself to be more concerned with the results that your people achieve than with the precise methods that they use to achieve the results.

On the positive side, you should develop decision-making methods that enable you to take advantage of what you and each of your people can do uncommonly well. Peter Drucker advises:

> To look for one area of strength and to attempt to put it to work is dictated by the nature of man. In fact, all the talk of "the whole man" or the "mature personality" hides a profound contempt for man's most specific gift: his ability to put all his resources behind one activity, one field of endeavor, one area of accomplishment. It is, in other words, contempt for excellence. Human excellence can only be achieved in one area, or at the most in very few.[5]

This quotation helps to explain why a genius in one field may be a complete flop in another. Henry Ford, for example, was an engineering genius, but his management methods almost ruined his company.

Here are four other guidelines that will help you make sound decisions.

1. *Make sure your decision is needed.*   If your decision will not have a significant impact upon the success or failure of your operation, you should try to delegate it. If you find that you are making many unimportant day-to-day decisions, consider whether you should revise your organization structure, policies, or procedures. If you are in relatively good shape in those areas, consider whether you should improve your staffing or the training that you give your people.

2. *Identify the right problems(s).*   As discussed earlier in this chapter, try to make sure that you do not include in your problem definition an alternative solution. In addition, try to make sure that you are dealing with the real cause of your problem. A shortage of cash may be due to too much inventory; too much inventory may be due to poor sales forecasting; and poor sales forecasting may be due to the overly optimistic judgments of your salesmen.

3. *Use a decision-making method that fits your problem.*   Don't swat a fly with a sledge hammer; by the same token, don't use a fly swatter when you require a sledge hammer. If you have a very important decision to make, perhaps you should use one of the decision-making tools such as linear programming or computer simulation. Or perhaps you can get by with a less sophisticated method such as a decision tree. A simplified example of one is shown in Figure 24-3.

Here your decision is whether to make or buy a certain product. If you have a 10 percent sales increase, you will realize a $350,000 profit contribution if you make the product, but only a $300,000 profit contribution if you buy the product. If you have a 10 percent sales decrease, you will realize a $280,000 profit contribution if you buy the product but only a $230,000 profit contribution if you make the product. If you decide there is a 70 percent probability that sales will increase 10 percent and a 30 percent probability that sales will decrease 10 percent, you have the basis

FIGURE 24-3 Sample Decision Tree

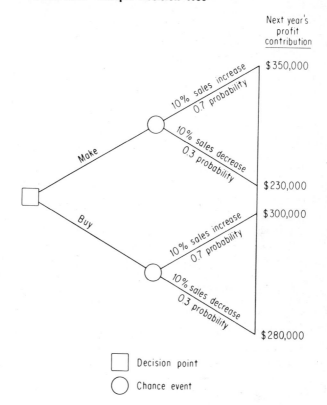

Next year's profit contribution

10% sales increase
0.7 probability
$350,000

Make

10% sales decrease
0.3 probability
$230,000

Buy

10% sales increase
0.7 probability
$300,000

10% sales decrease
0.3 probability
$280,000

▢ Decision point

◯ Chance event

for deciding whether to make or buy. By multiplying the probability by the respective profit contribution, and by adding the totals for the make decision and for the buy decision, you will find that your profit contribution will be $314,000 if you make the product and $294,000 if you buy the product. On this basis, you would decide to make the product.

Another method for solving problems and making decisions has been developed by Charles H. Kepner, a social psychologist, and Benjamin B. Tregoe, a sociologist. Making the best decision, they say, will involve a sequence of procedures based on seven concepts:

1. The objectives of a decision must be established first.
2. The objectives are classified as to importance.
3. Alternative actions are developed.
4. The alternatives are evaluated against the established objectives.
5. The choice of the alternative best able to achieve all the objectives represents the tentative decision.

6. The tentative decision is explored for future possible adverse consequences.
7. The effects of the final decision are controlled by taking other actions to prevent possible adverse consequences from becoming problems, and by making sure the actions decided on are carried out.[6]

Another method for solving problems and making decisions is shown in Figure 24-4.

FIGURE 24-4   Example of Defined Problem-solving Method [7]

1. *State the Problem*

   - What has happened where and when that can have a negative effect on what you are trying to accomplish through your people?
   - Who is affected?
   - What is likely to happen if problem is not solved?
   - How soon is solution required?
   - What are possible causes?

2. *Get Facts and Opinions*

   - Are there policies, procedures, or precedents which apply?
   - Are there reports, records, or manuals that you should review?
   - Who has solved a similar problem in the past?
   - What are possible causes and solutions as suggested by those affected?
   - Does problem need to be redefined into one or more problems?

3. *Select the Best Solution*

   - What is the simplest solution?
   - What are likely reactions to solution?
   - What could go wrong?
   - Should there be both short- and long-range solutions?
   - Can solution be tested?

4. *Sell the Solution*

   - What acceptance do you need within and outside of your department?
   - Is management approval required?
   - Should you sell key people individually?
   - What should be put in writing?
   - When will timing be best for selling your solution?

5. *Implement Solution and Follow Up*

   - What are immediate reactions and results?
   - Are there unforeseen problems?
   - Does solution need revision?
   - What reporting of results is required?
   - Did solution solve the problem?

One of the advantages of this particular checklist is that it includes items that you should consider to sell your solution—i.e., to sell the decision that you believe is best.

No one can tell you what decision-making method you should use to solve a particular problem or to take advantage of a certain opportunity. But you should be aware of the various methods that you can utilize yourself or through others to make your decisions. Chances are the more methodical you are in your decision making, the better your decisions will be.

4. *Face up to bad decisions.*   Many managers stick to their decisions come hell or high water. This is admirable when the decisions are right but foolhardy and self-defeating when the decisions are bad. Right now, for example, there are thousands of unnecessary staff positions that are continued simply because responsible managers can't believe that they made bad organization planning decisions.

You are less likely to stick with bad decisions if you are aware of a psychological phenomenon known as "cognitive dissonance." In describing this phenomenon, psychologist Mortimer R. Feinberg credits psychologist Leon Festinger and says:

> Festinger's theory centers around the idea that when confronted with two sets of facts that create an uncomfortable psychological imbalance, the mind adjusts those facts to make them more harmonious and thus reduces "dissonance."
>
> . . . The mind "processes" what it is forced to accept and makes it more palatable. It also processes many things that it can't have and makes them more undesirable.[1,*]

Managers are also affected by "cognitive dissonance" when they criticize, or refuse to consider rehiring, capable employees who have resigned and gone with other organizations.

The time to ask yourself whether you are sticking too long with a bad decision is when you are not achieving the results you expected. You may also find it valuable to get the ideas of individuals who will level with you and are not beholden to you.

Ultimately all decisions boil down to a yes or a no—even those that are made by the passage of time when, for example, you neglect to take advantage of a temporary opportunity. The care with which you make such decisions, however, will determine your success as a manager and as an important contributor to your organization both now and in the future.

HOW TO DECIDE

1. Make sure your decision is needed.
2. Identify the right problem(s).
3. Use a decision-making method that fits your problem.
4. Face up to bad decisions.

KEY POINT: *Tailor your decision-making methods to your personal strengths and weaknesses.*

REFERENCES

1. Louis A. Allen, *The Management Profession*, McGraw-Hill Book Company, New York, 1964, p. 247.
2. "Executive Decision-making," *News Front*, October, 1964, p. 56.
3. H. B. Maynard (ed.), *Handbook of Business Administration*, McGraw-Hill Book Company, New York, 1967, p. xxiv.
4. Howard K. Holland, "Decision-making and Personality," *Personnel Administration*, May-June, 1968, pp. 28–29.
5. Peter F. Drucker, *The Effective Executive*, Harper & Row, Publishers, Incorporated, New York, 1966, p. 74.
6. Charles H. Kepner and Benjamin B. Tregoe, *The Rational Manager*, McGraw-Hill Book Company, New York, 1965, pp. 48–50.
7. "Solving Supervisory Problems," a workbook from *Supervising by Objectives Program*, Loen-Brandt Inc., Palo Alto, Calif., 1968, p. 25.
8. Mortimer R. Feinberg, "Getting Personal," *Business Management*, January, 1969, p. 10.

25

COMMUNICATING

COMMUNICATING *Exchanging information with
subordinates, associates, superiors, and others
about plans, progress, and problems.*

"Do you know what our big problem is around here? Communications!"

I suppose I've heard this kind of complaint a thousand times. Managers everywhere seem to feel that they have communications problems in their organizations. However, each manager defines "communications" differently and it's hard to know what he means without considerable discussion. One manager feels he doesn't know what's going on; another feels that the people in his organization don't know how to write clearly; another feels that his organization has too many meetings; another doesn't believe his boss knows how to listen; another believes that the assignment of duties and responsibilities is fuzzy; and so on. When I ask a manager what he's doing about the communications problem he sees, often he is taken aback; he tends to feel that the problem should be solved by someone else.

If you feel your organization has communications problems, I hope you have assumed the responsibility for doing something about them. In any event, as a manager, you must communicate in connection with each managing element. The more effective you are at communicating, the more effective you will be in all your planning, directing, and controlling activities.

YOUR BIGGEST PROBLEM IN COMMUNICATING: ASSUMPTIONS

You cannot communicate with anyone unless you make certain assumptions. But you can get into trouble if you are unaware of your assumptions. To what extent do you make the kinds of assumptions shown in Figure 25-1?

FIGURE 25-1 Do You Make Any of These Assumptions When You Communicate?

(✔)

_____   1. Your people understand when they say they do.
_____   2. You do a good job of listening to your people.
_____   3. You run a good meeting.
_____   4. Those to whom you write read and understand what you write.
_____   5. What you do is consistent with what you say.
_____   6. Persons inside and outside of your organization will recognize that you are acting in the best interests of all concerned.
_____   7. You have adequate communications skills for present and potential responsibility.

In making such assumptions, you may be right; on the other hand, if you are wrong, you may be causing some of the communications problems in your organization. Furthermore, you may be disappointed—and even dismayed—when your people and others do not perform according to your expectations.

WAYS TO COMMUNICATE

No doubt you rely mostly upon the communications media with which you are most experienced and with which you are most comfortable. There is nothing wrong in your doing so unless you rely upon such media to the point where you overlook communications opportunities simply because you are a creature of habit. Communications media with which you should be familiar are listed in Figure 25-2.

FIGURE 25-2   Communications Media for Managers

1. Discussion meetings with individuals

2. Discussion meetings with groups

3. Written media such as memos, letters, reports, proposals, policies, and procedures

4. Talks or presentation to groups

5. Electric, electronic, or mechanical media such as telephone, wire, tape, radio, television, video tape, slides, and movies

6. Printed media such as forms, newsletters, house organs, brochures, cards, newspapers, and magazines

7. Visual, touch, taste, or smell media such as charts, photographs, drawings, color coding, models, and samples

8. Design of physical environment—e.g., relative to office construction, furnishings, color, heat, light, noise, traffic flow, and efficiency

9. Personal example

If, for example, you have avoided public speaking opportunities, you may not have developed your ability to make a group presentation that will give you the support you want for a new marketing program. If you have avoided writing opportunities, you may not have developed the ability you need to prepare a written proposal that will get board of directors' approval for expenditures that you want to make. In general, you will have to communicate with larger numbers of people in a more structured environment as your responsibility increases and as your organization grows. Because you cannot contact enough individuals personally and often enough, you must use communications media that require much more formal preparation than may have been necessary earlier in your career.

Among all the communications media, personal example is the most important. The way to introduce a cost-reduction program, for example, is to reduce the costs in your own operation. Over a period of months or years, you communicate much more by what you do than what you say in policies, procedures, directives, and meetings. Ralph Waldo Emerson reminds us: "What you *are* stands over you the while, and thunders so that I cannot hear what you say to the contrary."

HOW TO COMMUNICATE

If you have ever taken a course or done reading on the subject of semantics, you have probably been exposed to the idea, "Words don't mean; people mean." This is a short way of saying that communicating is complicated by the particular people involved and the way they happen to think and feel at any given point in time. Therefore, you can never be sure what you are communicating; but there are certain actions that you can take to help ensure that you will communicate effectively.

1. *Think through what you wish to accomplish.*   The board chairman of a major corporation recently fired the firm's president, whereupon the deposed executive called a news conference and explained that he didn't know why he was fired. The implication was that the chairman was arbitrary and unfair. I doubt whether the chairman enjoyed this kind of public relations, but he may have found himself in this position because he had not thought through what he wanted to accomplish beyond the actual firing of the executive.

Because of the human dynamics involved, it is always well for you to try to think through what you are trying to accomplish before you communicate—whether for the purpose of selling an idea, getting information, laying the groundwork for future action, or whatever. But it is especially important that you have your objective clearly in mind when what you communicate can have critical effects on the success or failure of your operation—when, for example, many employees or others will be affected.

Bad news is often the most difficult to communicate, especially if you must give the bad news to your boss. In this respect, Joseph A. Robinson, a consultant in management communication, says:

> . . . we hesitate to bring bad news to the boss because, justifiably or not, he may react against us personally. However, if we do not keep him well informed, he may make bad decisions based on incomplete data—which he then holds against us.[1]

In other words, when you have bad news that should be communicated to your boss or to others, it may be better to take your lumps now rather than to delay the information.

2. *Determine the ways you will communicate.*   Before you decide whether to call someone on the phone, write him a memo, have a meeting with him, or communicate with him in some other way, consider his temperament or his emotional makeup. Charles H. Vervalin, a management and personnel editor, observes:

> Much of the effort to improve communications seems to be directed at a "typical" man who doesn't exist—someone who is expected to check his emotions at the timeclock in the morning and pick them up again on the way home. Comparatively little attention is paid to the point—confirmed by everyday experience—that communications is also an emotional process ("He was so angry he didn't even listen . . ."), which involves man at his most fundamental—as an individual with all his prejudices and quirks.[2]

Groups also have emotional makeups. In determining how you will communicate to a group, consider whether it is likely to be friendly, enthusiastic, skeptical, or hostile. You may not want to make a personal appearance before a group that is likely to throw rotten eggs at you.

3. *Appeal to the interests of those affected.* Most people are more concerned about how they will be affected personally than they are about how you or your organization will be affected. For example, your news about the big contract your firm just received may be met with something less than joy if your people feel that they are already overworked. If you want to make such an announcement, you might communicate better by explaining that you have an extended delivery schedule or that you are going to take some other action to help solve the problems your people currently face. Likewise, in communicating with an individual, appeal to his particular interest—especially if he will face any special problems in connection with your request or proposal.

I am not suggesting that you use salesmanship methods (by appealing to the interests of those affected) every time you communicate, but you should do so for your more important communications. There are times when you can rely upon the authority of your position to request that something be done or to get some other message across; however, you will generally be more effective by using a little salesmanship.

4. *Give playback on what others communicate to you.* If you have ever had an attitude study conducted in your organization, you may have been surprised to find that your people had different viewpoints than you expected. For example, I once found that a group of production employees were more concerned about their lack of training than about the hazardous working conditions that their managers assumed was the main problem. Either the managers did not ask the right questions to find out what their people really thought or they did not listen carefully to what their people said.

The point I'm making is this: Communication should be a two-way process. There should be an exchange of information between the parties involved. Generally the best way to prove that you understand the other person is to give him playback—i.e., repeat to him the essence of what he said. Give him your understanding of the problems he sees or the reactions you believe he has.

If you are to give playback, you must know how to listen. Suggestions for listening are given in Figure 25-3.

Among the five suggestions, perhaps the second is most important. Many people are not able to express themselves well even when they want to; others may not express what they are really thinking. For example, I know of one instance where a manager threatened to quit

---

FIGURE 25-3   Guide for Listening

---

1. With your *head,* listen to what is said.
2. With your *"heart,"* listen to what isn't said.
3. With your *hands,* listen by taking notes—when important to remember.
4. With your *body,* listen by reacting physically—with posture, gestures, nods.
5. With your *voice,* listen by asking questions and by responding with playback, words, or silence.

SUMMARY: *Listen with your WHOLE SELF.*

---

if he did not get a promotion. What he was really saying, however, was that his department was losing money and he did not want to stick around long enough to get the blame.

Just as you may not want to communicate bad news to your boss or others, you may find it difficult to receive bad news. By listening well enough to give playback about bad news, you are more likely to understand what you should know and you encourage others to give you bad news in time to take corrective action.

5. *Get playback on what you are communicating.*   Asking the other person if he understands what you said is a poor way to find out whether he really understands. He is likely to say yes so he can get back to doing something else, or so he can avoid appearing stupid. You will do better to ask him for his understanding of what you want him to do—providing he knows that the burden is on you to make clear what you are trying to communicate.

You can also get playback when you communicate in writing. You can do so by asking your receivers to confirm their understanding to you in writing, by telephone, or by some other means. Many managers make the assumption that what they write is crystal clear, but they are often disappointed when they find that they do not get the compliance or action they expected.

Getting playback may not be important for your routine communications, but it may be very important when you want the assurance that new assignments are understood, special deadlines will be met, and so on.

6. *Test the effectiveness of important communications before relying upon them.*   Many managers are so busy that they don't take time to get sample reactions to what they want to communicate in an important meeting, presentation, written communiqué, or the like. Then they spend days or weeks putting out the fires that they didn't mean to start. For example, I know of one sales manager who made a sales meeting presentation that ruined the morale of his sales force for several weeks. He gave the impression that his salesmen were to blame for factors over

which they had no control. He could have avoided this unfortunate result if he had gotten reactions to his talk from one or two of his people before he made it.

In summary, here is what I believe to be the key point in communicating: *Give and get playback to ensure understanding.* This is the best single way to ensure that you understand and are understood. In addition, it enables you to take into account the differences in individuals and in groups.

The application of this key point, as well as the other communications actions discussed above, is indicated in Figures 25-4, 25-5, and 25-6. Shown are guides for giving instructions, holding group discussion meetings, and writing business letters.

FIGURE 25-4   Guide for Giving Instructions[3]

1. PLAN

   - Decide what specific action is required by whom.
   - Decide whether to use oral and/or written instructions.
   - Decide proper timing to get desired reactions.
   - Review the problem with doer if problem is not apparent; make sure he understands why he is involved.
   - Get suggestions of doer if practical.
   - Show that you support the need for action versus relying on other authority.

2. GIVE

   - Give instructions in the form of requests — to get voluntary cooperation.
   - Use direct orders only when requests fail or when quick action is required.
   - Keep language simple.
   - Give only as much detail as individual doer needs.
   - Set appropriate deadlines for reporting progress and for completion.
   - Answer any questions which doer has.
   - Have doer repeat or confirm important instructions.

3. FOLLOW-UP

   - Let doer carry out instructions.
   - Check doer's progress before any serious damage is done.
   - Evaluate whether instructions accomplished desired results.
   - Determine how future instructions can be made more effective.

FIGURE 25-5   Guide for Holding Group Discussion Meetings

1. Make sure a meeting is necessary.
   - a. Use a meeting to evaluate a solution to a group problem, but not to develop the solution. Never accomplish in a group meeting what one or two individuals can accomplish outside of the meeting.

b. Use a meeting to inform only when attendees need the information as a basis for action.
2. Set meeting objectives. Ask yourself: What do I want attendees to *do* as a result of the meeting?
3. Decide who should attend, and make meeting arrangements.
4. Conduct meeting.
   a. Begin on time.
   b. Review and follow agenda.
   c. Allot time in relation to importance of each subject.
   d. Encourage participation from everyone; limit the participation of those with tendencies to dominate.
   e. Get playback—to check understanding of what was presented.
   f. Give playback—by repeating the essence of important contributions.
   g. Keep meeting on subjects of interest to entire group.
   h. Decide who will do what by when; try to arrive at unanimous decisions when group support is necessary.
   i. End on time; schedule additional meetings(s) with one or more attendees if major problems still exist.
5. Follow up to see that planned action is taken and is effective.

FIGURE 25-6 Guide for Writing Business Letters

1. Have only one objective or purpose per letter. Ask yourself: What do I want reader(s) to *do* as a result of this letter?
2. State what you want done—or the essence of your letter—in the first sentence; give your reasons later.
3. Write as you talk: use active verbs, avoid trite and formal expressions.
4. Use people references—personal pronouns and names.
5. Use one-syllable words about three-fourths of the time.
6. Limit length of average sentence to about seventeen words.
7. Limit length to one page whenever possible.
8. Have a strong ending—e.g., deadline, appeal for action, or request for confirmation if message is especially important.
9. Get eye appeal—e.g., through margins, indentations, captions, short paragraphs, type style, and quality paper.
10. Weigh carefully who gets copies; don't send copy to recipient's superior unless it's a letter of praise.

You are affected personally by what and how you communicate. For example, I know a certain manager who is disappointed in the progress he has made with his organization; he seems to have reached a plateau. He has many fine qualities. Those around him feel that he is knowledgeable, intelligent, ambitious, hard-working, loyal, and so on. However, there are some differences in the way he sees himself compared to the way others see him.

He assumes he is honest with others — yet his people feel he is destructively critical. He assumes he is profit-oriented — yet his people feel he is niggardly in making legitimate expenditures. He assumes he is creative — yet his boss feels that his ideas are incomplete rehashes of what he read someplace. He assumes he thinks young — yet his clothing is noticeably out of style. In short, he is a good man but he has some problems obvious to others that he doesn't seem to realize.

Perhaps someone will get through to him what he needs to do to change his image, for he *is* what he communicates. In any event, it is his responsibility to change if he wants to progress further up the managerial ladder. Perhaps he will change, but I doubt if he will until he learns to give and get playback about what he is communicating to others about himself. What do you think?

HOW TO COMMUNICATE

1. Think through what you wish to accomplish.
2. Determine the ways you will communicate.
3. Appeal to the interests of those affected.
4. Give playback on what others communicate to you.
5. Get playback on what you are communicating.
6. Test the effectiveness of important communications before relying upon them.

KEY POINT: *Give and get playback to ensure understanding.*

REFERENCES

1. Joseph A. Robinson, "How Engineers Can Communicate More Effectively with Managers," *IEEE Spectrum,* 5(6):49, June, 1968.
2. Charles A. Vervalin, "The 'Untalk' of Communication," *Hydrocarbon Processing,* 44(7):160, July, 1965.
3. "Giving Instructions," a workbook from *Supervising by Objectives Program,* Loen-Brandt Inc., Palo Alto, Calif., 1968, p. 29.

26

IMPROVING

IMPROVING   *Developing more effective and/or
economical methods of managing.*

Many managers suffer from personal obsolescence.

Theodore Levitt, professor of business administration at the Harvard
Business School, puts it this way:

> The management of a large organization is far more difficult than most men
> who manage are themselves aware. Few in fact are managers. They are
> custodians. Somehow the enterprise keeps on going at an acceptable rate,
> but usually only because its competitors are no better. Most managers
> unfortunately do very little thinking in the course of their work. They are
> entirely unaware of how much they manage by formula, by dogma, by
> principles, textbook maxims, and resounding cliches; and of how much, in
> the process, they are forfeiting the one distinction by which we tell man from
> animal. Their resort to easy generalization is explained by the heavy burdens
> of their job. But to explain it is not to condone it.
>
> When you reach some stage of your maturity, you want to look into the
> mirror and be sure *you* are there. You want to know that it is you and not
> the ventriloquist for some ancient soothsayer who is really running things.

There comes a time in the life of every business when you have to abandon old formulas and do what's right for new times.[1]

One man's opinion? No. Consider this:

A three-year study of one thousand executives in the $8,000–$20,000 bracket revealed that the majority of these men, all of whom work for multi-million dollar companies in such capacities as executive vice president, comptroller, chief engineer, planning director, were virtually ignorant of the latest management techniques. They had little or no knowledge of such subjects as linear programming, turnover ratios, product-moment correlation and material audit. These men had stopped learning when they left the campus, and were operating with outmoded techniques passed on by their superiors in on-the-job training.[2,*]

These quotations are thought-provoking as applicable to managers in general, but are they applicable to one manager in particular: you?

HOW UP TO DATE ARE YOU?

If it is your intention to progress in the field of management, it is logical to assume that you are knowledgeable about emerging concepts for getting results through your people. Seven such concepts are listed in Figure 26-1. To what extent are you knowledgeable about each of them?

FIGURE 26-1   Are You Up to Date with These Managing Concepts?[3]

Yes	No	
____	____	Managing by Communication
____	____	Management by System
____	____	Management by Results
____	____	Management by Objectives
____	____	Management by Exception
____	____	Management by Participation
____	____	Management by Motivation

The seven concepts aren't just sets of buzz words, for there is a recent book published under each of the titles shown. There is in-depth knowledge to support each concept. Unless you have exposed yourself to such concepts and evaluated their application for you and your organization, you may be on shaky ground as far as your future in management is concerned. This is aside from whatever technical knowledge and skills you need in your industry and in your functional area of responsibility.

* Reprinted with permission of *News Front,* Management's News Magazine, copyright 1969.

WHY MANAGERS DON'T IMPROVE THEIR MANAGING METHODS

Often a manager who believes that he is performing well doesn't see any real need to improve his managing methods. Further, he doesn't know what he doesn't know; he can't apply new managing methods if he doesn't even know they exist. Only when someone is promoted over him or he is shoved aside by the new management of a takeover firm is he shocked to realize that something is wrong. Perhaps he wouldn't be in trouble if he had known earlier in his career that improving is as much a part of his responsibility as any other element of managing. But even knowing this, he would still face certain obstacles.

1. *Previous success.*   It is inconceivable to many persons who have achieved notable success that they should change their methods. Until something dramatic occurs, they are unaware that they suffer from a "success syndrome." For example, many a president has been stunned when his stockholders want to sell out—not because his firm is in trouble, but because his firm has achieved an enviable cash position or has other resources that an acquisitioner feels are underutilized.

2. *Defensiveness.*   "Here comes a head chopper." That's an extreme but fairly frequent defensive reaction that some managers have when a change agent (such as a staff specialist or management consultant) comes to evaluate their operations. Either they fear for their jobs or they fear that any potential improvement in managing methods will be considered a reflection on their past efforts. A more subtle form of defensiveness takes place when a manager has a comprehensive study made of his operation and then does little or nothing about the recommendations.

3. *Too much conformity.*   In any organization, managers must conform to certain managing methods. Otherwise, there will be incompatible objectives, policies, procedures, and so on. Unfortunately, however, many managers get the impression that they shouldn't rock the boat— especially if they have suffered embarrassment or rebuke when they have made or proposed changes in past managing methods.

4. *No goals.*   This is probably the biggest single reason why managers do not improve their managing methods. They have no specific objectives for improving their methods of planning, directing, and controlling —as applied to their own operations or to their organizations as a whole. A few progressive organizations have staff groups with responsibility for researching and developing improved methods of managing. However, what such groups can accomplish is limited as compared to the combined efforts of every manager in an organization.

HOW TO IMPROVE YOUR MANAGING METHODS

With all that is said and written in the field of management, you may feel overwhelmed about all there is to know. However, there is only so much that is applicable to your operation and that you can apply. Probably your most important guideline is expressed in their chapter's key point: *Base your improvements on a defined concept of managing.*

Only by having a defined concept of managing (such as shown in Figure 1-2) can you have the security of knowing how the parts relate to the whole. For example, I doubt whether you would want to develop improved reports for control purposes without considering whether you have an effective method to set meaningful objectives.

Here are four specific actions that you can take to improve your managing methods.

1. *Set improvement objectives.* Your improvement efforts will be more meaningful if you have objectives to solve specific problems. Look for problems in the way your department or your organization sets objectives, develops programs, develops its organizational structure, does staffing and training, compensates its people, measures progress toward objectives, communicates, and so on. Then pick one or two of your most pressing problems and set objectives to effect or propose solutions by specific deadlines. For example, I know a vice president who recognized a pressing need to improve his method of sales training in view of the anticipated expansion of his organization. Based upon the objectives he set, within nine months he had developed and implemented a method that spread the training effort over a large number of people—during both the development and the presentation of the training material.

2. *Get help from your people and others.* Since your people are affected by the managing methods practiced by you and other managers in your organization, they may have the best ideas about what improvements are needed. The way for you to find out is to ask. In doing so, you also lay the groundwork for later cooperation that you may want in implementing your improvement.

You can also get improvement ideas from your boss, staff specialists, and outside management consultants. Some organizations have their managing methods evaluated by a management consulting firm every year or two. In this way, there is generally more objectivity and a broader basis for comparison with the managing methods used by a variety of outside organizations.

3. *Think through and get approval for your improvements.* Some of your improvements in managing methods will involve other departments or expenditures that will require top management approval. For

example, suppose you wish to improve your forecasting method with the aid of a mathematical model that requires significant computer time. You will stand a better chance of getting top management approval if you think through and provide answers to the questions in Figure 26-2.

FIGURE 26-2.   Considerations in Selling Improvements

1. PROPOSED

   Exactly what do you suggest be done?

2. NEED

   What is the nature of the present problem relative to output, cost, waste, sales, profit, or the like? What benefits will be realized by the proposed?

3. STEPS

   What steps should be taken to carry out the complete proposal?

4. COST

   What is the proposed cost (investment)? What is the relation of cost to the minimum anticipated benefit?

5. IMPLEMENTATION

   Who is qualified and available to implement proposal? Where will money come from—existing budgets or elsewhere?

6. TIMING

   What will your organization lose if it doesn't act now? What approval or decision (easy first step) is needed now?

Some managers are more successful in selling their ideas externally than internally. Often the reason is that they don't do as much homework when they have an internal sale to make.

4. *Implement and/or follow up improvements.*   Because of the pressure of day-to-day activities, you will probably be tempted to put off actions for making improvements in your managing methods—even though you may have necessary approvals. Further, you have a psychological barrier because you know that those affected may react negatively and cause you problems on top of your present problems. This is the time to remind yourself that future crises are best prevented by what you do now—both to implement your improvement and to follow up to see that it works.

It's hard to improve something without understanding it. Thus, when you improve your managing methods, you tend to prove that you really do understand what many managers don't understand—their jobs. In addition, you tend to prove that you're not a candidate for personal obsolescence and that you're not one of those managers Theodore Levitt was talking about.

HOW TO IMPROVE YOUR MANAGING METHODS

1. Set improvement objectives.
2. Get help from your people and others.
3. Think through and get approval for your improvements.
4. Implement and/or follow up improvements.

KEY POINT: *Base your improvements on a defined concept of managing.*

REFERENCES

1. Theodore Levitt, "The New Markets: Think before You Leap," *Harvard Business Review,* May-June, 1969, p. 67.
2. "Insville, U.S.A.," *News Front,* May, 1966, p. 14.
3. William H. Bayliss, "Management by CSROEPM," *Harvard Business Review,* March-April, 1969, p. 85.

Part **6**

CONCLUSION

27

APPLYING WHAT'S IN THIS BOOK

•

I once saw a cartoon in which a secretary was observing her approaching boss. The caption was: "Good gosh! What happens now? The boss has read another book!"

I don't know how many secretaries react that way when their bosses read books, but I'm sure that most authors would be pleased to know that they had persuaded some of their readers to act. Unfortunately, many readers do little, if anything, to apply what they have read.

PROBLEMS IN APPLYING WHAT YOU HAVE READ

It is unlikely that you will apply what you have read unless you feel that you have a real need to change or improve. Before you will decide to improve your managing, you must recognize the need as evidenced by these indicators (described in Chapter 1): You have difficulty in distinguishing managing from doing; you have unsatisfactory results; you have frequent "fires"; your objectives are not defined in numbers; you have turnover of good people; you have no trained replacement; and you have little innovation in methods or services. However, you may not see yourself as others see you. You may have a managing myopia as far as your own performance is concerned.

If, for example, you are middle management, you may be interested in this *Dun's Review* quotation:

> What is wrong with the average middle-ranking executive? Ask a cross section of corporation presidents and you get a rich variety of answers. He fails to delegate responsibility, say some. He does not practice what he preaches, complain others. A third complaint is that he does not recognize the needs of other levels of the organization. But to President Allen J. Greenough of the Pennsylvania Railroad, a different problem is the most basic. "Far too many," Greenough insists, "concentrate on day-to-day details, paying little attention to the real fundamentals of setting objectives, planning for improvement, evaluating results and developing subordinates."[1,*]

If you are dissatisfied with your own progress in management, it is likely that this quotation is applicable to you; you need the emotional jolt that your superiors, associates, and even subordinates can give you to make you aware of your needs. Your boss and others around you may be reluctant to tell you what your needs are, so you may have to solicit their suggestions about what you might do for your own personal development in managing.

With an awareness of your managing needs, you may face this problem: you suffer from a common disease called "busy fever." You may be so busy that you don't have time to become a better manager.

Day-Timers, Inc., has spent many years studying the way managers spend their time. The firm has found that managers waste much of their time through the twenty-five time leaks listed in Figure 27-1.[2]

FIGURE 27-1   Which of These Time Leaks Are Applicable to You?

($\checkmark$)

____ 1. Spending too much time on problems brought to you by subordinates

____ 2. Oversupervising subordinates

____ 3. Undersupervising subordinates, with consequent crises

____ 4. Scheduling less important work before more important (and possibly more unattractive) work

____ 5. Starting a job before thinking it through

____ 6. Leaving jobs before completion

____ 7. Doing things that can be delegated to another person

____ 8. Doing things that can be delegated to modern equipment

____ 9. Doing things that actually aren't part of your real job

____ 10. Spending too much time on your previous area of interest or competence

*Reprinted by special permission from *Dun's Review*, April, 1967. Copyright, 1967, Dun & Bradstreet Publications Corporation.

_____ 11. Doing unproductive things from sheer habit
_____ 12. Keeping too many, too complicated, or overlapping records
_____ 13. Pursuing projects you probably can't achieve
_____ 14. Paying too much attention to low-yield projects
_____ 15. Failing to anticipate crises
_____ 16. Handling too wide a variety of duties
_____ 17. Shrinking from unfamiliar duties
_____ 18. Failing to build barriers against interruptions
_____ 19. Allowing conferences and discussions to wander
_____ 20. Allowing conferences and discussions to continue after their purpose is fulfilled
_____ 21. Conducting unnecessary meetings, visits, and phone calls
_____ 22. Chasing trivial data after the main facts are in
_____ 23. Engaging in personal work or conversations before starting business work
_____ 24. Socializing at great length between tasks
_____ 25. Reading trade journals, newspapers, and unimportant documents and reports

By plugging such time leaks, chances are you can cure yourself of "busy fever" and find the time to develop further your managing skills.

There is one more problem that may prevent you from becoming a better manager: you think you'll remember what you read. This is unlikely, however, because learning-retention studies show that a person remembers only about 10 percent of what he reads. So far in this book, for example, I have recommended 126 guidelines or actions plus 26 key points. Unless you have a relatively simple program for putting these ideas into effect, it will be difficult for you to do much about them.

HOW TO APPLY WHAT YOU HAVE READ

Do you have a personal development program? If not, you probably lack a practical means for acting upon pertinent managing ideas from among the hundreds that you read about in the course of a year. In terms of this chapter's key point: *Develop and implement annually your own personal development program in managing.*

As far as the content of this book is concerned, I believe there are four actions that are most important. You will have a first-year personal development program if you take these actions.

1. *Set one to three primary objectives for the next six to twelve months.* These are objectives for output, sales, cost-reduction profit, project com-

pletion, innovation, or improvement. Consider having at least one objective to improve the managing methods of your department or organization.

2. *Develop a one-page program of major actions for accomplishing your objectives.* If you limit your major actions to those that you can list on one page, you are more likely to get them accomplished. Make sure your actions are those that you must accomplish through your people rather than through your personal efforts.

3. *Carry out your program and make periodic progress checks.* This involves both directing and controlling actions: viz., staffing, training, supervising, delegating, motivating, counseling, coordinating, measuring, evaluating, and correcting.

4. *Keep "Guide to Help You Manage More by Doing Less" where you can refer to it often.* Advertisers know that it takes repeated exposures to get through to people. In the words of Alfred Whitehead, "Knowledge keeps no better than fish." You can remind yourself of the key points covered in this book by referring occasionally to Figure 27-2.

FIGURE 27-2   Guide to Help You Manage More by Doing Less

	Accomplish *planned* results *through* your people.
PLANNING:	*Get the participation of your people when you plan.*
Objective:	Set measurable objectives to ensure balanced results in your critical areas of responsibility.
Program:	Visualize yourself as a strategist—to get a maximum return on a minimum investment.
Schedule:	Time each major action to get maximum acceptance by those affected.
Budget:	Develop your budget to support your program.
Forecast:	Forecast with a view to what you can make happen.
Organization:	Organize around necessary activities rather than around people.
Policy:	Define your policies so your people can make most decisions.
Procedure:	Develop standard procedures or methods for your repetitive operations with significant cost-profit impact.
Standard:	Develop performance standards that are measurable.
DIRECTING:	*Tailor your leadership and human relations methods to your people and your objectives.*
Staffing:	Select each of your people on the basis of his past performance.
Training:	Have scheduled training for your people based upon what they can apply.

Supervising:	Supervise your people according to their individual differences.
Delegating:	Hold your people more accountable for results than for methods.
Motivating:	Help each of your people define and attain what he wants from his job.
Counseling:	Help each of your people solve his own problems.
Coordinating:	Help your people integrate their activities with those of others affected.

CONTROLLING: *Control through management by exception.*

Measuring:	Check regularly to determine cumulative progress toward planned results.
Evaluating:	Obtain additional facts and opinions before deciding upon corrective action.
Correcting:	Let your people take the corrective action whenever possible.

INTEGRATIVE ELEMENTS

Deciding:	Tailor your decision-making methods to your personal strengths and weaknesses.
Communicating:	Give and get playback to ensure understanding.
Improving:	Base your improvements on a defined concept of managing.

Develop and implement annually your own personal development program in managing.

You can also use this guide as a reminder to go back and review a certain chapter when you have current problems in a managing area such as organization, training, or communicating.

By applying what's in this book, you will not only manage more by doing less, but you will get a better understanding of managing as a concept. Understanding each element of managing is not enough. For example, a backyard cook may use the same ingredients that a master chef uses, but a master chef usually gets a far superior result. Likewise, it's the way you put the elements of managing together that makes the difference and that can make you a master manager.

NEED FOR BETTER MANAGING

I believe there is no higher calling than management. Managers at all levels in all fields can help to solve problems and take advantage of opportunities that may eventually determine our survival. As long as people are hungry, sick, homeless, uneducated, or afraid, none of us is secure. Further, population is growing. As population grows, problems grow. Our solutions must also grow.

Managers in government, business, labor, education, professions, and religion have the responsibility to develop and implement growing solutions to growing problems—through the efforts of tens, hundreds, thousands, and even millions of people. I hope you are doing your part, and will prepare yourself to assume the managing role that will be required of you tomorrow.

HOW TO APPLY WHAT YOU HAVE READ

1. Set one to three primary objectives for the next six to twelve months.
2. Develop a one-page program of major actions for accomplishing your objectives.
3. Carry out your program and make periodic progress checks.
4. Keep "Guide to Help You Manage More by Doing Less" where you can refer to it often.

KEY POINT: *Develop and implement annually your own*
personal development program in
managing.

REFERENCES

1. "Why Don't Executives Get Off Dead Center?" *Dun's Review,* April, 1967, p. 29.
2. "Start Accomplishing More . . . Right Now!" *Business Management,* April, 1968, p. 60.

INDEX

D

P